What They Heard

Music in America, 1852–1881

John Sullivan Dwight
From a painting dated 1883 by Caroline A. Cranch, daughter of Dwight's
friend Christopher Pearse Cranch
Courtesy of the Harvard Musical Association

What They Heard

Music in America, 1852–1881

From the Pages of
Dwight's Journal of Music

Irving Sablosky

Louisiana State University Press
Baton Rouge and London

Copyright © 1986 by Louisiana State University Press
Manufactured in the United States of America

Designer: Christopher Wilcox
Typeface: Galliard
Typesetter: G & S Typesetters
Printer: Thomson-Shore, Inc.
Binder: John Dekker & Sons, Inc.

Library of Congress Cataloging in Publication Data

Sablosky, Irving
    What they heard.

    Includes index.
    1. Music—United States—19th century—History and
criticism.   2. Dwight's journal of music.   I. Title.
II. Title: Dwight's journal of music.
ML200.4.S2   1985   780'.973   85-13016
ISBN 0-8071-1258-5

For Juliet

Contents

Illustrations

Preface

The idea of this book occurred to me some years ago when research on a more general history of American music led me to consult *Dwight's Journal of Music*. It was too bad, I thought, that Dwight's paper was now left mainly to scholars. Surely a sampling of its contents would be enjoyable and informative to a far wider readership. As I thought of making an anthology of articles from the *Journal*, I saw that the projected book could be more than a simple collection of the best of Dwight's. The selection could be made not only to represent the *Journal*, but more broadly, to picture American musical culture as Dwight and his contemporaries experienced it.

With this dual purpose in mind, I selected the sixty-odd articles that appear in the following pages. From the hundreds that tempted me, I chose those that would best stand on their own, with a minimum of comment or interpretation. My brief linking narrative, then, was designed to bring out points Dwight and his correspondents could not have known they were making, and to lend the cumulative picture a coherence they never sought. The lengthier Introduction provides historical context; the Biographical Register supplies information that might otherwise have appeared in footnotes.

I have not edited the texts from *Dwight's*, except to shorten some of them, for concision's sake, where that could be done without distorting or omitting a story's point. Cuts are indicated by ellipses (. . .). Otherwise, the writers' language and syntax are intact. I have corrected some obvious printer's errors, but have left some misspellings, particularly of names, because an informal approach to orthography seems to have been a stylistic trait of the period. I have sometimes supplied first names (in brackets) where Dwight, again as a matter of style, identified people only by surname. In a few cases, my research failed to yield even this small clue to the identity of a now-forgotten performer.

Each extract from the *Journal* is headed by the date of the issue in which it appeared. I have grouped the selections topically in five parts, following chronological order within each part. A reader will thus survey the *Journal*'s three decades five times over, from early to late, each time from a different standpoint. The period will perhaps emerge with more depth and clarity in this layered arrangement than would have been likely in a single chronological sequence.

Here let me add a note of acknowledgment of the support and help I received from the Library of Congress, specifically from the Research Facilities Office and in the Music Division Reading Room.

What They Heard

Music in America, 1852–1881

Introduction

Three quarters of a century after the Declaration of Independence, features of an American musical culture were only beginning to be discernible. John Adams had anticipated the lag. It was his duty, he wrote in a letter from Paris in 1780, to study "the arts of legislation and administration and negotiation" to the exclusion of all other arts; his sons, then, would have "liberty to study mathematics and philosophy . . . geography, natural history and naval architecture, navigation, commerce and agriculture, in order to give their children a right to study painting, poetry, music, architecture, statuary, tapestry and porcelain." So the generations had succeeded each other; institutions of government, of commerce and agriculture had been established and had begun to flourish. And the appearance of *Dwight's Journal of Music: A Paper of Art and Literature* in 1852 was a manifestation of the third generation's rising interest in those other arts.

John S. Dwight sensed that his was a crucial time for music in the United States. He saw music fast becoming "the popular art *par excellence*"; if only the best of it could be properly appreciated, he was certain, it would be "an important saving influence" in the democratic life of the rapidly expanding country. "Very confused, crude, heterogeneous is this sudden musical activity in a young, utilitarian people," Dwight wrote in his first issue. "All this requires a regular bulletin of progress; something to represent the movement, and at the same time to guide it to the true end." He published his newspaper about music, weekly or biweekly, from April 10, 1852, to September 3, 1881—1,051 issues in all—through a period that witnessed a succession of events, discoveries, and institutional beginnings that had an enduring effect on America's musical culture.

There was no doubt in Dwight's mind as to the nature of the true end. His *Journal* was to be "a severe, friendly voice to point out steadfastly the models of the True, the *ever* beautiful, the Divine"—which meant, for Dwight, music in the German classical tradition. At the same time, in the prospectus that stood at the head of Volume I, Number 1, he promised to report on current musical thought and activity in all its diversity. Dwight remained as faithful to his prospectus as the Pilgrim Fathers were to the Mayflower Compact. In the eight thousand densely set pages of *Dwight's Journal of Music*, he reported not only the progress of Boston's Handel and Haydn Society, New York's Philharmonic Society, or Philadelphia's Academy of Music, but also the Great Peace Jubilees, the conventions of amateur singing societies, the exploits of itinerant Yankee "singing masters" and German "professors."

His correspondents followed Jenny Lind and Ole Bull, Gottschalk and von Bülow and Rubinstein in their far-flung American appearances, but they also wrote of minstrel shows, musical freaks, organ-grinders and brass bands. Dwight was among the first to recognize the beauty and significance of Afro-American music. He was a tireless advocate of Beethoven, Bach, and Mozart, but he reported faithfully on the latest Verdi or Wagner to be introduced to the United States, and did his duty by *H.M.S. Pinafore* when it took the country by storm. He found it difficult to be encouraging to American composers, but conscientiously kept his readers informed of early attempts by William Henry Fry and George Frederick Bristow and later ones by John Knowles Paine and George Whitefield Chadwick, while taking note too of the music of the Moravian communities and the songs of Stephen Foster. From his seat in Boston, he searched across the continent for news of musical interest, and welcomed correspondence from San Francisco, New Orleans, Chicago, Milwaukee, Cincinnati and St. Louis, from remote towns in Texas, Mississippi, Minnesota, and from abroad: Europe, Japan, India, even the Fiji Islands.

No scholar of American music of the period has failed to turn to *Dwight's Journal* for information, thought, and flavor, and surely most have felt both rewarded and tantalized as they searched through those forty-one large-format volumes. Material is there in abundance, but frustration often awaits the scholar now trying to trace an idea or a person or an event through the welter of miscellany that crowds the *Journal*'s pages. Dwight was, after all, publishing a newspaper, not an encyclopedia, and though he did provide indexes for his annual bound volumes, they are maddeningly erratic. Nor was Dwight a disinterested chronicler. All that went into his *Journal of Music* was filtered through the lens of his personal vision. Boston, Harvard, and transcendentalist idealism were part and parcel of his way of looking at the world.

Directly descended from one of the original settlers of Dedham, Boston-born John Sullivan Dwight was nearly forty when he began publishing his *Journal of Music*. It was, he said, his "last desperate (not very confident) grand *coup d'etat* to try to get a living." In fact, anyone who knew the proverbially unworldly Dwight knew that how he would "get a living" was less important to him than what he lived *for*. Twice earlier Dwight had made what he thought were life choices: in 1836 when he graduated from Harvard's Divinity School and set out to be a Unitarian minister; and five years later, when he left the ministry to join in the associationist experiment at Brook Farm. In both cases he was following some vague inner yearning to see a new kind of society, harmonized by a universal sense of beauty. Music, more than anything else, embodied for him the possibility of harmony for humankind; in committing himself to publishing a musical journal, he was still pursuing that ideal.

Although he had little formal training in music, Dwight had been writing about it since his youth. He did not merely love music; he believed in it. His Harvard dissertation was entitled "The Proper Character of Poetry and Music for Public Worship." Published subsequently in the *Christian Examiner*, the paper was a plea for recognition of music's value not only for its own sake but "as a means of culture." Dwight would repeat that theme tirelessly over the next four decades, and no one who heard him speak or read his writings could doubt his conviction that great music was destined for a role in "leavening, refining, humanizing, our too crude and swaggering democratic culture."

Music was a preoccupation with him even in those post-Harvard years when he was trying to make his way as a minister. He was no sooner out of the university than he set about organizing alumni of the college musical club, the Pierian Sodality, into what was to become the Harvard Musical Association, with the express aim of making music a regular branch of instruction at the university. He wrote about music for various newspapers and magazines, and he spoke of it often from the pulpit.

Shy, soft-spoken, rather abstract in his utterance, Dwight was not a success as a preacher, though his gentle nature and the questing sincerity of his thought won respect and affection. Ralph Waldo Emerson, ten years Dwight's senior, found the younger minister "a good, susceptible and yearning soul"; and when Emerson quit his pulpit in East Lexington, he recommended Dwight as his successor. Dwight preached there as a guest on a number of Sundays, but the congregation decided to look further for its new leader. By the time Dwight did gain a pulpit of his own, at Northampton in 1840, he, like Emerson, had come to doubt the validity of the ministry and of formal worship itself.

From the start, fresh out of Harvard, Dwight had been one of that seminal circle of individualists and reformers around Emerson who were dubbed the transcendentalists. And when one of them, George Ripley, sought to put some of their ideas into practice at Brook Farm in 1841, Dwight left the ministry to live in the community. There he gave piano lessons and taught Latin, did his share of the manual labor, and wrote—mostly about music—for Ripley's associationist journal, the *Harbinger*. With his quiet but certain belief in the utopian ideal, and his dauntless optimism, Dwight often helped to smooth dissensions and lift morale when the experiment came upon rocky times. When it finally collapsed in 1847, he was one of the last to leave the little farm at West Roxbury to return to worldly Boston.

Friends from Brook Farm—George W. Curtis, Charles A. Dana, Ripley himself—were now making their way in New York and sought to find a place there for Dwight. But though he continued to write for the *Harbinger*, Dwight remained firmly based in Boston. Through the Harvard Musical Association he wanted to strengthen the musical life not just of the university but of all Boston. He was pressing for a new music hall for the city; he was organizing public concerts of chamber music. He drew deep pleasure from the leisurely but stimulating society of the "Transcendental Club," the Town and Country Club, the Saturday Club, those successive fraternal circles in which he shared the company and thought of Emerson, Ripley, Parker and Alcott, Lowell and Longfellow, Holmes, Agassiz, Channing, Henry James, Sr., and others of comparable eminence.

He had no steady means of support—never had such a thing; he could just cover his modest needs through his articles and occasional lectures, and by placing in newspapers and magazines some of his loving translations of poems of Goethe and Schiller. In 1851 he conceived the notion of publishing a weekly journal that would be a vehicle for his now scattered advocacy of music as a means of culture. Besides, he was thinking of marrying Mary Bullard, whose sweet singing had brightened the evening musicales he used to arrange at Brook Farm; the pending marriage must have given him added incentive to find some more orderly means of livelihood.

At last he sought the help of his friends: Would they back him in the publishing venture? Some were doubtful that Dwight should attempt the mundane tasks even a small publishing enterprise would entail; he clearly had no head for practical matters. But the faithful rallied around, and with the decisive support of the Harvard Musical Association, in February of 1852 (a year after his marriage to Mary), Dwight was able to invite the public to subscribe to a new journal that would be "an organ of what may be called the Musical *Movement* in this country, of the growing love of deep and genuine music, of the growing consciousness that music, first amid the other forms of Art, is intimately connected with Man's truest life and destiny."

The journal that appeared two months later did provide a living for Dwight, if only barely, for nearly thirty years. Always on the brink of financial failure, he and his paper were rescued more than once by his loyal friends. After six years as both editor and publisher, Dwight made a somewhat more stable financial arrangement by turning the business of production and distribution over to Oliver Ditson and Company. The music-publishing firm entered its own advertising in the *Journal* and added supplements of printed music, while Dwight retained complete editorial control. Twenty years later, when Ditson pressed him to give the *Journal* a more popular slant, Dwight indignantly took it to Houghton, Osgood and Company, publishers of, among other things, the *Atlantic Monthly*. But the paper could not pay its way, and a testimonial benefit concert arranged by Dwight's friends in 1880 only briefly postponed the end.

After he gave up the *Journal*, Dwight devoted himself mainly to the Harvard Musical Association, of which he was now president as well as librarian. (He made his spartan home in the association's rooms after Mary's death in 1860 while he was away in Europe.) He wrote occasionally for a newspaper or magazine, turned out a brief history of Boston's music, and completed the first volume of a history of the Handel and Haydn Society, begun by C. C. Perkins. He died in September, 1893, not quite four months after his staunch life-long friends had gathered in his rooms to celebrate his eightieth birthday.

In some ways, Dwight would seem to have been unsuited to the role of editor and chief critic of a powerful musical journal. Those who knew him described him as unworldly, diffident, sensitive in the extreme, bashful, even, according to George Ripley, "lacking in will." Furthermore, he lacked any deep background in musical theory or practice. He was able, nonetheless, to produce and sustain a journal that clearly spoke to its public with a voice of authority, and was accepted and respected far beyond the small circle of its subscribers (perhaps never many more than a thousand). Dwight, the gentlest of souls and a musical amateur, became through the persistent force of his idealistic conviction an arbiter of musical taste, whose views were noted, if not heeded, not only in Boston but nationally and even in Europe.

Still, in many ways, *Dwight's Journal of Music* was a true reflection of its editor, and not merely in his stubborn idealism. Although narrow in his personal tastes, Dwight was wide-ranging in his interests. Except for one extended visit to Europe (1860–1861), he never ventured far from Boston; but the intellectual and cultural outlook he shared with his remarkable circle of friends—steeped as they were in German, French, and British thought and literature—made him and his journal anything but provincial. Lofty in his standards, he was still neither a snob nor an elitist. Street music, bands and barrel organs, always delighted him. During his sixteen-month stay in Europe, no experience moved him more than attending Karl Liebig's popular concerts in Berlin, where the convivial audience could enjoy beer while listening to Beethoven.

Dwight was certain that the greatest music could and should belong to all.

A selection of articles from *Dwight's Journal of Music* made with the narrow aim of capturing a contemporary view of American musical life can hardly suggest the range and depth that characterized the *Journal* as a whole. Part of the paper's significance lies in the fact that in its pages Americans first read Forkel's biography of Bach, Schumann's advice to young musicians, Liszt's sketches of Chopin, Oulibicheff's biography of Mozart, and, despite Dwight's personal distaste for his thought and music, some of the controversial essays of Richard Wagner. The *Journal* reprinted thoughtful writing on music from British books and journals as well as in translation from German and French. It was a compendium of the period's musical writing in history, biography, theory, and philosophy—European as much as American.

At the same time, Dwight provided a running chronicle of musical activity in his America. With all respect for his motivating principles, it is possible to adopt criteria of our own, quite a different set from Dwight's, and draw from the *Journal* something Dwight had not necessarily intended to show: a picture of a period in American music, a period both formative and rich. The picture is in some ways quaint and distant, but it reveals, too, features that survive in our musical life today.

When *Dwight's Journal* first appeared, the nation was only on the verge of defining itself clearly. In music all the more, everything was in the process of being shaped. Just as Americans were finding new ways of ordering their society, so they were arriving at musical ways that would suit the social and geographic patterns of the expanding country. By mid-nineteenth century, when Dwight began his *Journal*, that peculiar chemistry, the American experience, had been working on the country's music for more than two hundred years; Dwight was on hand to watch as some American ways of doing musical things took on clearer and more lasting forms.

Concerts, for example, had been a familiar diversion of sophisticated Americans for more than a century; yet Dwight was able, in the *Journal*'s first year, to report the opening of the country's first proper concert hall—Boston's Music Hall. Till then, concerts had been given in private rooms, churches, or theaters. Even in colonial times, local devotees had often joined with newly immigrated professional musicians to give performances of the orchestral and choral music of eighteenth-century Europe. But before Dwight's time, there was hardly such a thing as a permanent organization for musical performances. Boston's Handel and Haydn Society, founded in 1815, managed to survive by publishing a commercially successful book of hymns, while striving to develop both the choral forces and an audience for English and German oratorios like *Messiah* or *The Creation*. New York's Philharmonic Society started in 1842 as a club of musicians who met in their spare time to play the symphonies of Haydn, Mozart, and Beethoven, and were content to share whatever small profit (or loss) might come through selling tickets to the public. Even in the largest cities, it was a struggle to muster the resources, either musical or financial, to sustain such an activity.

Opera was having even a harder time. In Europe it had been thriving for two centuries. Monteverdi, Rameau, and Handel had already given way to Gluck, Mozart, and Weber in the opera houses of Italy, France, Germany, and England. Audiences there were enjoying the confections of Rossini, Bellini, Donizetti, and Meyerbeer, and they were coming to know Verdi and Wagner. Grand opera was in its heyday, but not in the United States.

Manuel Garcia and his family had introduced Italian opera to New York in 1825, and after that fashionable American audiences were no longer satisfied with the ballad operas and other English fare their theaters had been offering. Yet in New York, one attempt after another at resident Italian opera met with failure. Opera houses were built, flourished for a season or two, and then were rented to acrobats, animal shows, and blackface minstrels. "Ethiopian opera" prospered while Italian opera struggled for existence.

One established opera house existed in the United States: In New Orleans, the French Opera was the pride of elegant society. But New Orleans was a French-Caribbean city, even more distant culturally than it was geographically from the seaboard cities northeast. Up there, opera was a high-risk enterprise for sharp impresarios who organized not real opera companies but barnstorming troupes of European singers tempted to undertake a season's trans-Atlantic touring by a sense of adventure and the possibility that the fashionable entertainment they offered would capture some of the new American wealth.

The wealth was real, and many of the growing number of Americans who enjoyed it were indeed attracted to the diversion offered by concerts and operas. Not only opera singers but concert artists and even small orchestras came from Europe, beginning in the 1840s, to try their fortunes in the New World. New York, Boston, and Philadelphia were the first stops before the most successful or enterprising set off westward. An international music business was beginning, and the visiting soloists, ensembles, and opera troupes boasted a glamour and, often, a level of accomplishment local musicians rarely could match.

Fortuitously, the midcentury surge of German immigration into the United States brought a sudden increase both in the number of professional musicians capable of playing and teaching concert music and in the size and extent of the public with an appetite for it. From the 1850s on, European virtuosos and opera stars would find a ready audience in America, not only in the East but in Milwaukee, Cincinnati, Chicago, St. Louis, and smaller cities scattered to the Far West. The immigrants and the visiting performers would help lay groundwork for the development of American orchestras, chamber groups, and even opera companies, and for American conservatories, performers, and composers who would begin to emerge before Dwight ceased publishing.

Beyond the eastern seaboard, music was beginning to be cultivated by growing numbers of a westward-moving people. Particularly in the midwestern cities where Germans were settling, symphonies and chamber music, opera and oratorio could claim a growing public; and even in the smaller towns, the itinerant singing teacher or resident "professor" often succeeded in winning an audience for Beethoven and Mendelssohn, even if their music could scarcely challenge the popularity of the ever-present minstrel shows or the garlanded albums of sentimental songs that adorned so many parlor pianos.

The years of *Dwight's Journal* were years of astonishing growth for those inland cities. Chicago, for example, was a town of perhaps 30,000 when *Dwight's* first appeared; at the time of the last issue, it was a city of half a million. In the same period, the population of St. Louis quadrupled (to 350,000), and that of Cincinnati more than doubled (to 255,000).

These were the cities "at the West" in Dwight's early issues, but by the end of the *Journal*'s run, "no longer of the west, but of the centre." Increasing population and wealth brought increased resources for local music-making and increased appetites for traveling virtuosos and singers, instrumental ensembles and opera troupes. Still there was no institutional base for such activities.

On one hand, a small number of professional managers promoted traveling spectacles, always built around imported performers, whether they were soloists or opera troupes. On the other, local groups of aficionados worked to establish some means for the regular enjoyment of musical performances. The local devotees were sometimes sadly at a disadvantage when competing with glamorous visitors for the attention of an inexperienced public.

Dwight's major interest was in guiding and promoting the development of resident musical organizations, like his own Harvard Musical Association, that were beginning to find strength in many parts of the United States. He watched anxiously for signs that American musical institutions were developing along the lines of those already flourishing in Europe—not only resident symphony orchestras and opera companies, but musical conservatories and music festivals that could bring together scattered local resources for performances of great oratorios.

At the same time, he did not fail to notice that there were some indigenous American musical institutions, long established and still surviving, to influence the shape of the country's musical culture. One was the "singing school"—no school at all, really, but a custom, persisting from colonial times, of classes held by itinerant singing masters in local churches and meeting houses. Originally, their aim had been to teach individualistic frontier churchgoers the proper way of singing the psalms. Now that aim was passé. By the 1850s the singing schools were more like clubs, a popular form of diversion where secular songs and even oratorios were added to the church choir's more austere Sunday fare. The clubs in turn were becoming tributaries of conventions and normal schools—training grounds for music teachers—that proved to be early stages in the development of American conservatories and music festivals.

Hardly less widespread than the singing schools, though by no means as respectable, were blackface minstrel shows, a new form of entertainment in the 1830s and 1840s, which by the 1850s had swept the country right to its westward-moving limits. Ironically, while the popular minstrel shows purported to give humorous or sentimental pictures of southern plantation life, the real music of the slaves was virtually unknown to the public at large.

Most of the musical development to which *Dwight's Journal of Music* bore witness had the appearance of slow but perceptible growth of audiences, musical resources, and institutions. The existence of an Afro-American musical culture, however, appears in Dwight's pages as a sudden discovery, almost a revelation. There had been hints of that culture for at least a century before *Dwight's Journal* was published. In the mid-eighteenth century, Protestant circuit riders in the South had sent north accounts of the extraordinary musical aptitude they found among plantation Negroes, and of the fervor with which the blacks seized on hymn singing. Some noted, too, that slaves invented their own "sings" in camp meetings or at work, music that travelers from the North or from abroad described as strangely beautiful and moving. Such reports appeared occasionally in northern magazines, but the music itself was unheard by whites, except those few travelers whose ears were caught by it, and southerners, many of whom were inclined to suppress it as disquieting.

From the early issues of his *Journal of Music*, Dwight showed sympathetic interest in the notion that the blacks were "a musical people." Deeply opposed to slavery, he saw the slaves' musical accomplishment as evidence of their humanity, cruelly violated in the South, and of their susceptibility to European "civilization." He kept a wary eye on the popular minstrel show as a threat to the musical taste he wanted to see cultivated; as to its connection with genuine black music, he was as unclear as anyone else.

The Civil War freed the music as it freed the slaves. As the authentic music of the blacks emerged from the obscurity of slave life, Dwight welcomed accounts of it. He took notice when the music of a Negro spiritual was transcribed and printed for the first time during the war. And in recording the later achievement of the Fisk Jubilee Singers, he published without blinking the claim that in their songs, at last, "the American school of music has been discovered."

Dwight's Journal of Music appeared for the last time September 3, 1881. The editor's "Valedictory" was a message of disappointment not free of bitterness. "The truth is," Dwight wrote, "we have for some time been convinced that there is not in this country now, and never has been, any adequate demand or support for a musical journal of the highest character." In his farewell paragraphs, Dwight came closest to articulating the dream he must have harbored for nearly thirty years: He would do his missionary work, seriously and well; the public would come to respond, would take his beloved music for its own; and at last his journal would win the financial support it needed, from the public or from some wealthy lover of music who would want to assure the permanence of an organ that could so build and nourish the public's taste for the art.

Dwight's deepest disappointment lay, clearly, not in the fact that the support had not come, but in what that signified to him: The musical development of the country had not taken the course he had foreseen and hoped for. The American public had not been converted en masse to classical music; its taste for the popular, the spectacular, and the novel appeared to be undiminished, and the rising music trades were only too happy to pander to it. Dwight was not lamenting just for his journal when he wrote, "The musical papers that live and flourish financially are those that serve the interests of music trade and manufacture, and which abound in endless columns of insignificant three-line items of intelligence or news; the slang term 'newsy' is a description which they covet. A journal which devotes itself to art for art's sake, and strives to serve the ends of culture, however earnestly and ably, gets praise and compliments, but not support."

A hundred years later, it is clear that America's musical development did, indeed, take a different course from that which Dwight imagined. He had conceived a lofty musical culture growing from a convergence of the old American singing school–convention tradition on one hand and the great German tradition of classical music on the other—a culture at once popular and pure, in which the people would have learned to prefer, spontaneously, the experience of "the True, the *ever* Beautiful, the Divine" to anything vulgar, ephemeral, *ad captandum*. Some such convergence did take place, but the musical culture that emerged from Dwight's time was to be characterized not by its purity but rather by a fertile interplay between popular and classical, in which many kinds of music continued to flourish, separately and together, in lively suspension.

In some aspects, the lines of that development can be projected from Dwight's accounts: The growth of American symphony orchestras and their audiences; the slower, more erratic development of American opera companies; growing opportunities for musical education and training; a thriving concert stage, peopled by artists visiting from abroad but also, increasingly, by American musicians. Another generation would have to pass before American composers would find their voice—a generation that would see the new music of jazz emerging from the experience of free blacks, and a new kind of musical theater growing out of the interplay of minstrelsy, extravaganza, Gilbert and Sullivan, and a variety of other influences, including that of jazz itself.

Dwight had chronicled three decades of vital musical growth and change. At the last, he no longer had the zest to follow trends that he saw leading away from the ideal goals he had cherished for his country's musical culture. It is our loss that there was no such paper as *Dwight's Journal of Music* to continue the record in the generation that followed.

First page of *Dwight's Journal of Music*, Volume I, Number 1, April 10, 1852 (actual size, 24 cm. x 33 cm.)
Library of Congress

Part One

In the Concert Hall

1. *Music in Boston*

In the first issue of the *Journal*, Dwight looked back over Boston's musical activity during the winter just past and judged that the season was so rich in its offerings that it "marks a period in our musical growth." Concerts were "thronged, the winter through, by eager listeners" to symphonies and oratorios, to chamber music, and to virtuosos, coming and going.

All had been "ushered in most nobly" by the last of Jenny Lind's concerts at the Melodeon. Then there was the return of "our own finished cantatrice," the Boston-born soprano Eliza Biscaccianti, one of the earliest American singers to go to Europe for training and recognition before taking up a career at home; and a farewell concert by Adelaide Phillipps, a young Boston contralto about to depart for studies in England, with Jenny Lind's encouragement (including a thousand dollar check). There were opera performances by a troupe of Italian singers traveling up from Havana, including the soprano Angiolina Bosio. And there were chamber music concerts by the Mendelssohn Quintette Club, a group of Boston musicians just making the transition from private performances to public concerts.

Two different ensembles gave orchestral concerts, and in reviewing them Dwight makes plain the difference between the homegrown and the imported in symphonic performance of the day. The Musical Fund Society was a struggling precursor of the Boston Symphony Orchestra (still thirty years in the offing), made up of local musicians who necessarily spent most of their time in other pursuits. The Germania Musical Society, on the other hand, was a well-knit band of some twenty players who had immigrated from Germany in 1848 and had since been touring the United States, taking symphonic music, or a serviceable approximation of it, for the first time to cities and towns all the way to the Mississippi. When the little orchestra disbanded in 1854, after playing concerts in most of the States, its members scattered to become influential figures in the musical life of New York, Boston, Baltimore, Chicago, and other American cities. In the winter of 1851–1852, they were still together, and Boston was their home base.

Dwight's Journal of Music, April 10, 1852

The Musical Fund Society

We place this first, because it is the largest combination of our best resident instrumentalists, united on a permanent basis, devoted mainly to the high forms of the Symphony, Concerto and classic Overture, having also in its constitution an element of charity, or rather of mutual guaranty against the often cruel fortune of musicians. . . .

Numbering some sixty instruments, with due preponderance of the string family, this orchestra possesses the means of presenting, in their full proportions, the gigantic symphonies of Beethoven and others. A band much larger would rather fall into the modern "monster" category. The string department has been excellent; but there has been continual complaint of want of unity, of precision, of true intonation, of musical quality of tone, &c. &c., in many of the wind instruments; and this, if we are rightly informed, is partly owing to the fact that some of the members, who are skilled in the use of one instrument, are here set to playing others, with which they are less perfectly familiar; and partly to the fact, that the various instruments have not been regulated primarily and exclusively to the sphere of this orchestra, but have been drawn from various minor orchestras and bands, acquiring, as it were, their local temperaments and habits. The evil, we believe is understood, and will no doubt ere long be remedied, when we shall have an orchestra that may be compared with the Philharmonic orchestra in New York.

The Fund Society have labored under two other disadvantages. First, to see a paying audience, they have been driven to the very unmusical and uninviting hall of Tremont Temple. May our new hall be ready for them in the autumn!—Secondly, owing to the multifarious private occupations of the members, they have had but one rehearsal in a week, and that a public one, in the presence of 1,500 to 1,800 auditors! In fact, an afternoon concert. Now these public rehearsals are most excellent things for the public, and we would not on any account have them discontinued. They are an invaluable stimulus and education to the higher musical taste of hundreds of young men and women, of whole families. Through them, a generation is here growing up in the love and knowledge of the noblest compositions. The general cause of music cannot dispense with them. But there is an obvious restraint upon the freedom and dry, wholesome discipline of a rehearsal, in the presence of all these witnesses. We trust that by some means the Society will contrive to secure hours both for private and for public rehearsals.

Looking over the programmes of the six subscription concerts, now completed, (together with the extra, Benefit Concert, under the direction of the Lady Associates, to which we may allude hereafter) we can feel proud of the amount of good music that has been presented. Of symphonies, we have had the *Eroica*, the C minor, and the number 7, in A, (decidedly the three grandest) of BEETHOVEN; the third in A minor (Recollections of Scotland), and the fourth (posthumous, Italian) of MENDELSSOHN; the great "Jupiter," with four-fold fugue, of MOZART; and the No. 11 of HAYDN. Of overtures: MOZART's to *Zauber-flote* and to *Clemenza di Tito*; BEETHOVEN's to *Leonora*; BERLIOZ's to "Waverly"; a concert overture, by GADE; and several of the lighter modern schools. . . .

The afternoon rehearsals have afforded a still richer *repertoire* of symphonies and overtures. We are happy to learn that the Society contemplate giving a series of very cheap afternoon concerts, through the Spring, the music to be in about equal proportions of light and solid, so as to combine both ends of instruction and amusement. . . .

The Germania Musical Society

The growing taste for pure instrumental music, at so many points in our wide country, has been greatly indebted for the last three or four years to the flying visits of this model abridgment of an orchestra. Though hardly twenty-four in number, these young artists have diffused among our people something nearer than we have before had, to a true idea of German music, both in its popular and in its classic forms. They have been to us in fact a live and genuine specimen of musical Germany, traveling about in the midst of us, and at each point again and again renewing the vibration from that vital heart and centre of the tone-sphere.

The advantages of such a band are these:

1. It is well selected in the first place. All its members are artists, men well suited to each other, men in every fibre of their being as it were acclimated and attempered to the artistic sphere of music; each endowed with a fine musical temperament, and imbued from boyhood with the spirit of the great German masters; accustomed to an orchestral atmosphere, instead of to that of mere military and dance music; several of them indeed persons of general culture, reading and society.

2. They have possessed, first in Herr [Carl] LENSCHOW, and latterly in Herr [Carl] BERGMANN, a conductor of the true stamp; one, who not only feels and understands the music, but who by a sort of natural eloquence of look and gesture expresses the force of each musical idea as it is coming, keeps *before* the music, visibly anticipating each effect, and so possessing all his orchestra with the same feeling in safe season for the attack. It helps even the musical enjoyment and understanding of the audience, to watch such a conductor's baton.

3. Having no other occupation, and pledged to one another, traveling and stopping together everywhere, they can keep in perfect practice, in ever fresh familiarity with their large and varied repertoire of music, trusting one another perfectly for a sympathetic *ensemble* in the rendering of every piece. Soon may the time come when our own local musicians may be able to do likewise!

On the other hand, their one disadvantage is, that they have not, (nor can their traveling life afford to have) the numbers and proportions of a grand symphonic orchestra. While their wind instruments are complete in number as they are choice in quality, their violins are very few. Hence we found it good policy to sit near, in order to hear them well; for to the remote auditor, the reeds and trumpets passed directly over the heads of the few violins, which in their nature could not tell so prominently; and thus in many a symphony he caught the brighter masses of coloring, while the finer outline of the musical idea, entrusted to the strings, was faintly perceptible. At the best, in *forte* passages, the violinists had to bear on with great energy to partly counterbalance the wind band, since even their admirably precise and pure outline was not always sufficient. Of course the disadvantage was greatest in the grander class of symphonies, like the "Jupiter" of Mozart, and the C minor, the *Eroica*, &c., of Beethoven. Whereas, in one so light and fairy-like as Beethoven's No. 8, and in the picturesque, romantic, delicately strong overtures of Mendelssohn, they were eminently successful.

Yet it is always a pleasure and a lesson to hear this little orchestra in any kind of music. Of great symphonies, their renderings must be regarded as fine *readings*, or outline representations. There is no confusion, no blur, or indefiniteness about them; they show you what the composer meant; they fix each theme, each musical idea and *motive* clearly in mind. We deemed it a great advantage to hear a symphony first from them, and afterwards expanded into full proportions by a larger orchestra.

In their own national waltz music (a genuine creation of the genial, rhythmic soul of Germany); in their arrangements of operatic scenes, where certain instruments take up the voice accompaniments to the singer, or the concerto-player, they are indeed a model, a charm unfailing.

Boston has been favored this time as the winter residence of the Germanians. A series of twenty subscription concerts, weekly afternoon rehearsals, and a multitude of occasional performances, have not at all blunted the appetite for their music, and they have made the rich voice and promise of Miss PHILLIPS, and the unrivalled piano-playing of ALFRED JAELL, as familiar as household words among us.

We have only room further to enumerate the important classical works, in which they have given their twenty concerts, to complete the sum of our rare opportunities the past winter in this line.

SYMPHONIES. Nos. 1, 2, 4, 5, 6, (Pastoral), and 8, of BEETHOVEN. The C major, with Fugue, ("Jupiter") and op. 58, in E flat, of MOZART. The No. 11, in D, of HAYDN. The fourth (posthumous) of MENDELSSOHN. The "Historica," illustrating four periods, of SPOHR; also, in the early season, his "Consecration of Tones." One by KALLIWODA, and one by GADE.

OVERTURES. BEETHOVEN's to *Fidelio*, to *Egmont*, to the *Men of Prometheus*, and to *Coriolanus*. MENDELSSOHN's to "Midsummer

Night's Dream," to "Fingal's Cave" (*Hebriden*), to *Heimkehr aus der Fremde* (Return from Abroad), the one called "Calm Sea and Happy Voyage" (*Meeres-Stille*), to *Ruy Blas*, to "The fair Melusina." WEBER's, to *Oberon* and *Freyschütz*.

MOZART's, to *Don Juan* and *Zauberflote*, GADE's "Echoes from Ossian," SPOHR's, to *Jessonda*. A strange one by ROBT. SCHUMANN, with Scherzo and Finale. MEYERBEER's to *Robert*, to the "Huguenots," and to *Streuen-See*. Several by ROSSINI, and other lighter kinds.

PIANO-FORTE CONCERTOS. One by BEETHOVEN and two by MENDELSSOHN, played by A. JAELL. To these add parts of the Symphony Cantata: "Song of Praise," by the latter composer; and finally the entire orchestral music (*not* the entire vocal, as was promised) of the "Midsummer Night's Dream," exquisitely accompanying the indifferent reading of Miss KIMBERLY.

Of the lighter varieties we need not speak, except to say that we thought they added rather *too much* lightness towards the end of the season. The music-lovers of our sister towns and cities also got their share of the "Germanians" during the winter, and we doubt not they will be warmly welcomed back another season. . . .

2. Jenny Lind

Dwight sensed that a growing American public was attracted to concert music. Phineas T. Barnum sensed that the attraction, skillfully exploited, could make fortunes. In 1850 he arranged for a concert tour of the United States by "the Swedish Nightingale," Jenny Lind, and proved that he was a master not merely of fakes and freaks.

Even those, like Dwight, who were skeptical about Barnum's auspices were won by Lind's artistry and by the irresistible goodness she seemed to project from the stage. Her nine-month tour under Barnum's management was so brilliantly successful that she extended her stay in the United States for another year. Altogether, she appeared in some 130 concerts in more than a dozen cities, ranging from the eastern seaboard to New Orleans, Nashville, St. Louis, Louisville, and Cincinnati before her farewell recital at New York's Castle Garden on May 24, 1852.

The program for that final concert followed the customary format of the day: The star's numbers were set off by orchestral pieces and by supporting soloists—in this case, the Italian baritone Cesare Badiali and Lind's pianist (and husband of three months) Otto Goldschmidt.

Lind's spectacular success was a powerful attraction to other European artists. Earlier, America had presented so wild an aspect that only a few had ventured to visit and tour. Now a veritable stream ensued. The German prima donna Henriette Sontag arrived in New York on the heels of Lind's departure, to be followed quickly by Italian contralto Marietta Alboni and London's operatic favorites, Giulia Grisi and Giovanni Mario. Instrumental virtuosos were not far behind.

Dwight's Journal of Music, May 29, 1852

New York, May 25

The Farewell Concert

Castle Garden, last night, presented a spectacle, the like of which we hardly hope again to witness in our mortal life. Think of *seven thou-*

sand faces, lit with sad enthusiasm, looking from every part of every circle of the vast area and gallery, so brilliantly illuminated, turned all to one focus, to greet and to enjoy, for the last time, face to face and audibly, the presence and the almost more than mortal music, of a woman who, in eighteen months, by the mere divine right of goodness and of a matchless voice conscientiously trained to perfect obedience to the highest inspirations of Art, has established a sort of moral and ideal empire in the hearts of this whole people, rude and cultivated. We believe no other human being could have drawn together all the elements of such a magnificent occasion, and blended all in such a pure enthusiasm. We doubt if it has ever had a parallel among the popular triumphs of Art. We could not help half fancying that it foreshadowed the supremacy of Woman, in the peaceful, broadly catholic and all-conciliating sphere of Art, the most human of all human occupations, whereas Man's supremacy has been in statesmanship and mere material interests. Men, to be sure, have been and are poets, painters and composers, hitherto, far more effectually than woman, but all this comes of the feminine element, which tempers even our male clay.

Well, we will not indulge in speculation, but go back to Castle Garden. The evening, after a sultry day, was wet with frequent showers, as if in sympathy with the, at once rich and melancholy, occasion. How vividly we recalled in contrast that first night of JENNY LIND in America, and all those six first nights in Castle Garden, when, through wondering crowds of a whole city, poured out for her welcome, and in the golden glow of a superb sunset, we passed in to the magical old castle of light and song, and with souls steeped with beauty again passed out, mingling with the human tide up Broadway, under the glorious moonlight, as if the whole world were keeping festival! The programme too, for this time, was in its great features, a reminiscence of that first one, making up by the charm of association for what it wanted in novelty and classical selections, as compared with the two preceding. We love Castle Garden; it is a better music hall, at all events for JENNY's voice, (and so *she* esteems it, and so did M. BENEDICT,) than Tripler Hall. And it displays an audience, in full sight of each other, and brings all eyes to a common focus, and makes the general aspect musical, as no hall, built parallelogram-wise after alleged *acoustic* laws, can do. Here then was the most fitting place, where the largest number, representing the whole population of loyal subjects could best await the last appearance of the dear and sovereign Queen of Song.

She, as if in honor of the occasion and of the land that she was leaving, (we may add, too, with a noble trust in the great public and entire disregard of the ungrateful slanders kept up through the week by certain New York papers, which outrageously charged to the designs of Mr. Goldschmidt the speculation in tickets, which, however much to be regretted, was indeed unavoidable, so long as there were plenty of people ready to buy at prices so much higher than those originally set upon them)—she, led forward amid deafening plaudits, appeared dressed in bridal magnificence, surpassing any previous occasion. She seemed as if disinterestedly merging *herself* in the full splendor of the popular heart's ideal of her. It was no *personal* end which she had before her to accomplish, but the high representative mission of a royal priestess of the Beautiful and True. Call this enthusiasm,—we should sadly suspect ourselves if we were *not* enthusiastic, and we should grossly insult that vast audience that sat around us, did we not take it at its word.

How *Casta Diva* was sung we cannot undertake to tell in words. It was a piece dignified enough to open the occasion (after Cherubini's overture to *Les deux Journées*, and BADIALI's air from *I Puritani*,) and quite in character with her and her serious tuneful office that night. It was identified with the first impression of her voice in this country; and it was the test piece with the French and Italian-opera-spoiled critics, who then carped at her interpretation of it, but which has since vindicated *her* Italian method above them all. Like the breeze in the pine woods, the first low, full tones crept sweetly, solemnly over the hearts of the listening multitude, rising and swelling into fuller, and heavenlier power, and taking deeper and deeper possession of the audience, holding them spell-bound in *perfect* attentiveness and perfect unity of feeling, as if it were the "spirit of God moving over the face of the waters." *Casta Diva* was a new music, fraught with more beauty and more meaning to us than we had ever credited to the concert-hacknied aria before. In the elaborate, rapid melody of the outburst of human passion, which succeeded, her voice rioted in a new profusion of brilliant, and sometimes extempore embellishment, triumph upon triumph of execution, a perpetual surprise to the delighted ear, yet always true to the essential spirit of the music, as it is her instinct always to elude mere hacknied figures and cadenzas. . . .

Why shall we speak—for the tenth time at least—of Madame GOLDSCHMIDT's remaining pieces; of her exquisite archness in the Rossini duett, *Per piacere*, from the "Turk in Italy," in which BADIALI's ponderosity labored in comparison with the refined *buffo* elasticity of BELLETTI; of the Trio with flutes from the "Camp of Silesia," a charming *genre* piece of musical poetry, say what you will—of her "Comin' thro' the Rye," the most sunshiny, flashing frolic of melodious gayety and archness, ever improvised upon an old theme even by *her*; or of the Swedish "Echo Song," from which we did not find one particle of charm worn off? We turn back for a moment to give credit to Sig. BADIALI for *Largo al factotum* (though the misfortune with this grave and excellent baritone is, that he is *no* factotum,) and to regret that the programme was disfigured by one specimen of the most commonplace and clap-trap sort of overtures, namely the overture to *Zampa*. . . .

But there must be an end to all good things! So felt that brilliant audience, more and more soberly, as the swift hours passed. And so felt the great singer, and she must simply utter it and end it gracefully and feelingly, in a fitting strain to fitting words. In the same spot, where, standing eighteen months ago, she sang her "Greeting" to America, she now sang her "Farewell." The poem, which we give below, was as beautiful as could well be in the limitations of the case; and the music by MR. GOLDSCHMIDT, though not of the most popular and *taking* character, was truly beautiful and worthy to embalm the farewell of the noble Muse and benefactress, whom he takes away from us to be his wife. It was sung with feeling and received with feeling, with tearful eyes and silence, rather than with tumultuous farewell plaudits. Long lingered many eyes where she departed, and long stayed many, talking over in groups their pleasure and their loss, and the great hall slowly emptied and this great ideal episode in our young national existence,—the maiden greeting of JENNY LIND, the triumphal career of the unrivalled artist, and the artistic farewell of Jenny and Otto Goldschmidt—was ended and of the past, save as it has sown seeds of beauty in our souls!

Farewell to America.
By C. P. Cranch.

Young land of hope—fair Western Star!
Whose light I hailed from climes afar—
I leave thee now—but twine for thee
One parting wreath of melody.
O take this offering of the heart
From one who feels 'tis sad to part.

And if it be that strains of mine
Have glided from my heart to thine,
My voice was but the breeze that swept
The spirit chords that in thee slept.
The music was not all my own—
Thou gavest back the answering tone.

Farewell—when parted from thy shore,
Long absent scenes return once more;
Where'er the wanderer's home may be,
Still, still with memory turn to thee!
Bright Freedom's clime—I feel thy spell,
But I must say Farewell—Farewell!

. . . J.S.D.

3. *Ole Bull*

The Norwegian violinist Ole Bull first came to play for American audiences in 1843 and returned several times, not only to perform but also to undertake such ventures as establishing a Norwegian colony in Pennsylvania and managing a season of opera at the New York Academy of Music—both failures.

As a performer, he was a popular favorite who entertained his audiences with showpieces of his own invention, playing on all four strings of the violin at once (actually, a peculiar feature of Norwegian folk fiddling) and stomping the floor to his patented version of "The Arkansas Traveller." Bull was said to have been disappointed that American audiences would not take to more serious music. Dwight's review of a Boston concert in 1852 suggests that the Norwegian's playing had qualities of spirit and imagination that sometimes transcended the format of the showy "fantasias" on familiar tunes which were the fashion of the day.

Dwight's Journal of Music, June 12, 1852

OLE BULL'S SECOND CONCERT, last Saturday evening, though not quite so fully attended, was more enthusiastic than the first. Indeed in these times an audience of nine hundred or a thousand, at the dollar price, for a purely instrumental concert, and out of the season, may be considered great success in Boston. The day is past, as we have said before, when solo-playing, even of the most extraordinary and the best appointed in the way of orchestral surroundings, can charm crowds as it once charmed.

Each part was opened by the GERMANIANS with an exquisite fairy overture, exquisitely played: the first, that to "Oberon"—*Oberon's Wunder-horn*—by Weber, and the second, that to the "Midsummer Night's Dream," by Mendelssohn,—a music, which has now become a quite familiar and delightful part of our existence; we could no more afford not to know it, than we could not to know our Shakespeare.

Ole Bull's pieces, with one exception, were to our taste of the most interesting in his *repertoire*. Especially so the first piece: *Cantabile Doloroso* and *Rondo Giocoso*, in which there was more form and unity of spirit, and a less fatiguing length of restless, shifting, zig-zag wanderings and surprises, than in many of his singularly moody and fantastic compositions. The themes were beautiful and developed with all the beauty of execution and warmth of feeling, which he knows how to throw into whatsoever musical idea he would illustrate. His second piece: "To the Memory of Washington" was much less to our taste, setting out on a false tack, which always has proved fatal to the artist in every department of Art,—namely, with the design of giving an imitative representation, through tones, of a historical period, of a great national struggle,—and forced, in order to get along with it, to resort to mere association, by introducing hacknied patriotic tunes, as *Yankee Doodle*, piped and screamed alternately with strains of "God save the King," amid discordant tremolos and battle storms of the whole orchestra. Really these seemed very cheap and melodramatic effects. But there was one saving point in it, and that was the magnificent manner in which "Hail Columbia" was harmonized for the orchestra; it made us feel that we have *one* old national tune with music in it; and we are indebted to Ole Bull for so grandly bringing out its majesty and beauty. Almost equally did we admire his own self-accompanied eloquent version of the same on his violin, preluding to the fuller illustration of the orchestra.

His third piece was as strange in music as in title: "Sounds from Old Norway: Tunes from the Old Mountains, infused through the mighty War Skaldes, in the Independent Spirits or the Young Mountains." We confess to having enjoyed it not a little; it was full of wild, poetic, northern imagination; and though vague as the misty shapes of Ossian, it had the magnetic fascination of genius. In this Ole Bull seemed altogether himself; we are sure, no other violinist could have made anything of his notes; but in his hands it became a natural language of a strong, deep, earnest soul—a kind of wild wind-harp of his intensely feeling, ardent, liberty-loving nature. His *Polacca Guerriera* is a piece of as decided character as any that he has been in the habit of performing, and still in a great measure justifies some slight notes we made of it eight years ago, to which we now refer from curiosity:

> It has a unity and a theme which is easily traced through. The orchestral parts are rich and grand. As they open with the drumbeat and prompt answering chords, he seems a hero at the head of his army, on the eve of a glorious moral conflict, inspired and inspiring all with his great purpose. Then in a thoughtful Andante the violin discourses to itself, as if the hero were reviewing his purpose, communing with his soul to see if it were strong, and committing himself to the great Source of strength; suddenly he awakes from his meditation and with a sweep of the bow, launches the whole orchestra again into the wild battle march; after which follows the animated movement called "*Polacca*," whose long labyrinth of variations we will not be so idle as to follow with the pen.

In nothing however did he give us so much unalloyed pleasure, on Saturday evening, as in his self-accompanied playing of the "Last Rose of Summer," in answer to an encore. It was exquisitely, feelingly beautiful. And this is one of his greatest arts, which he possesses, so far as we know, beyond all other violinists,—this of "double-stopping" so as to give a full quartet effect; he makes each of the four parts firm and individual, and the middle parts move about like the "figural harmony" in good organ music. His prelude to the melody, too, was full of character. . . .

Why do we turn away in sadness from one of Ole Bull's concerts! We have had our imagination excited, at least by fits; gleams of real, deeply expressive beauty have ever and anon arrested us; the unmistakeable evidences of genius were there:—yet we have missed more than we found; yet the permanent impression is of disappointment. Shall so much genius, so much feeling, so much masterly executive skill and energy, never be embodied in artistic forms of beauty, that shall *last*! The more he repeats the charm of these fantastic, wild improvisations, the more do we call on him to realize the promise of his nature by becoming a creator, a composer. Or do we ask too much! Are we demanding a Bach's fugue of the wind-harp!

4. *Jullien and His Orchestra*

Americans heard a real symphony orchestra—one hundred professional musicians under a professional conductor—for the first time on August 27, 1853, in New York's Castle Garden. The conductor was Louis Antoine Jullien, called "the Napoleon of Music" in Paris, where fashionable crowds attended his concerts in the 1830s. Deep in debt despite his success, Jullien had fled to London, and there again, with his flamboyant mannerisms, knack for publicity, and, evidently, genuine musical skill, became all the rage in "society concerts," summer concerts, winter concerts, and when funds were running short, "monster concerts."

For his American appearances Jullien brought the nucleus of an orchestra from Europe, including some of the leading players of the day; he filled out the numbers with musicians skillfully recruited in New York. Among those he spotted was seventeen-year-old Theodore Thomas, who gained his first sense of what orchestral music might be as a violinist in Jullien's concerts.

Jullien conducted with a jeweled baton, wearing white gloves presented to him on a silver salver; and at the end of a piece he would sink exhausted into a velvet-covered throne as the audience applauded. Still, he was only part charlatan. In England as in America he was credited with educating the public's taste for the music of Mozart and Beethoven, which he sometimes played, along with numerous waltzes, polkas, and quadrilles full of crowd-pleasing effects—in a "Fireman's Quadrille" a real fire was heroically extinguished by the local brigade. Amid such goings-on, scant attention was paid to the remarkable fact that Jullien also presented serious music by two American composers: George F. Bristow of New York and William Henry Fry of Philadelphia.

Skeptical John S. Dwight took his time about going to New York to hear Jullien, but when he did go, he too was caught up in the excitement of hearing a full orchestra performing with precision and polish. When Jullien later brought a reduced orchestra to Boston, Dwight had become, with just a few reservations, an advocate.

Dwight's Journal of Music, October 15, 1853

Jullien and his Orchestra
New York, October 8, 1853

Last evening we heard for the first time the great orchestra of Jullien. It was his "eleventh concert at Metropolitan Hall, and *thirty-fifth* in New York," and the crowd and the enthusiasm showed that the charm still worked. The programme was characteristic, but not one of Jullien's best, not like that of the night before, when he gave one of his "Beethoven nights," which we should prefer to hear before undertaking to fathom the depths of the great Jullien's musicianship as an appreciator and conductor and interpreter of the greatest kind of music. . . .

But such an orchestra and such conductorship, with such solo-playing on all sorts of instruments, is certain to delight one the first time, even if there be nothing great or classic in the programme; and after all, it did contain some fine and many clever things. It was undoubtedly a fair specimen of Jullien in his speciality. There was something imposing in the mere assemblage of an orchestra of a hundred persons, embracing so many celebrated virtuosos, the best on their several instruments that Europe could afford, on a stage brilliantly decorated and in that brilliant hall; and when the magician (whose outward man has been abundantly described) rose from his throne, and carefully surveying all his forces, raised his wand, it was plain that the best understanding and best feeling existed between him and all his artists.

The overture was *Semiramide*, one of Rossini's best, and rather seldom heard among us. What a rich and pure sonority in the full, loud chords! The power and blended quality of tone of that great orchestra exceeded all that we had ever heard. There were no uncertain, characterless, or noisily obtrusive sounds; it was one rich, vital tone, a harmony in the best sense of many pure, effective, justly related individual tones. The ear and mind rejoiced throughout the evening in this satisfactory and vital fulness of the *tutti*. The quartet of the horns was played deliciously sweet and crisp. The witching little theme of the violins, starting with those light and quick reiterations of the first note, was given with elastic delicacy and precision by the broad mass of strings, and the *crescendos* and *diminuendos* and *retardandos*, and other points of expression were caught with sympathetic unity and certainty from the expressive baton and gesture of the conductor. We never heard an overture made so brilliantly effective; every point of melody, of rhythm, of harmony, of instrumental coloring, of light and shade, was boldly, delicately, happily brought out. We recognized the truth of what is often said of the expressive indications of Jullien's baton, it seems spontaneously to trace the outline of each melodic figure in the air; were it a lighted stick and moving in the dark, we might almost *see* the music. Nor was it possible to doubt that there had been consummate judgment and tact in the selecting, combining, training and tempering the instruments that made up that orchestra. Every instrument seemed a distinct and living individuality, whether emerging into the foreground with a solo passage, or kept back in the humbler function of mere common chord accompaniment; there was no mere unindividualized mass of sounds in any portion of the band.

There was one brief specimen from Beethoven, the graceful Allegretto from the eighth symphony, which we have enjoyed quite as well at the hands of the "Germanians," since it does not depend for its effect on a great orchestra; but it was genially, tastefully and lovingly, as well as accurately rendered.

As for the dance pieces, in which lie Jullien's forte and popularity, we could not but enjoy them also, for some time, because of the wonderful mastery of instrumental *effects* displayed in them; although there is little in such music that survives apart from these effects of varied and contrasted instrumentation. . . . Yet as Jullien gives them, with all his orchestral resources, they are among the most brilliant and individual novelties in music. It is in these too that he displays the character and as it were draws the peculiar soul out of each solo instrument. His famous "American" Yankee-Doodle battle quadrille is certainly a wonderful exhibition of instrumental *effects*, both solo and combined. Its twenty solos, by such artists as Koenig, whose cornet is truly said to *sing*, Hughes on the ophiclide, the hard, round, solid tones of which, such as we never heard before, are grandly expressive in their way, Lavigne and Wuille, with their exquisite oboe and clarinet, were a new revelation of the best modern skill in instruments. . . .

Dwight's Journal of Music, October 29, 1853

Jullien's Concerts

So far (for three nights) the "Monster Concerts" have been on a greater scale in all respects than in that of great audiences. The Boston Music Hall, even on Jullien's "Beethoven Night," has not been two-thirds full. The terrific storm of course put a great audience for anything out of the question on the first night. This is not as it should be, nor can we believe that it will so continue. The dollar price is really cheap for such an unparalleled combination of talent as Jullien has had the enterprise and tact to muster and train together to complete unity for our entertainment. Ordinarily a dollar would be cheap for hearing any one of his five and twenty solo-players, each the very best in his speciality afforded by all Europe. Think of an orchestra in which every instrumental part is manned or led off by such artists! Add to this that all in the rank and file are good, that the orchestra is complete and in the full sense of the term a *grand* orchestra: that they play with most perfect unity and precision; that their truth of intonation is refreshingly infallible; that the *ensemble* of tone, or collective sonority of the orchestra, considered as one complex instrument, is exceedingly bright and beautiful; and that they play so much of the best, as well as so much merely *effective* music,— and the wonder is, how can the public keep away at any price! True, Jullien had a hundred in New York, and has only sixty here:—but we assure our readers that in our Boston Music Hall these sixty tell with at least twice the power the hundred did in Metropolitan Hall. . . .

Again, such education of the ear as is afforded by these concerts it would be shiftless on the part of any music-lover to forego. Never have we had such a chance to learn what a great orchestra can be and is. One evening at Jullien's is as good as a year's lessons about the peculiar characters and powers of instruments, the effects producible by various combinations, the means and possibilities of instrumental *effect*, and in impressing on the mind indelible types of *crescendos, diminuendos, staccatos,* and other dynamic and rhythmic arts. . . .

Several distinct points of interest stand out in one's recollection of a Jullien concert. First and most prominent is:

The Orchestra itself, in its *ensemble,* considered as a great organic, complex mechanism of musical effect, and without reference to the kind of music played by it. . . . The brilliancy, precision, point, expression, &c. with which this great organism performs its functions we have sufficiently indicated. The perfect symmetry and swiftness with which it rolls up a *crescendo,* from the faintest murmur to its forty drum power maximum of sound, is one of the tricks in which Jullien has trained it to infallible success. But we cannot say that we have yet heard a genuine *pianissimo* among its other remarkable virtues; it can play lightly as well as play loudly, it can drop out voices and contract its tens to units; but we do not observe that wonderfully beautiful and ideal effect of an entire tone-mass subdued to the distinctest whisper. Bright, gorgeous sunshine or gas-light, and no soft twilight, seems Jullien's peculiar sphere. His day is all noon, his house all blazing ball-room. As his art lies chiefly in effects, and grand surprises, and the nursing up of great furores in the audience, there is naturally a tendency to make the most of ponderous ophicleids and shivering trumpets and trombones. There is always something like a sonorous battle and a siege laid to your poor private castle of dullness. Your nerves are kept upon the strain, and finally the mind is fatigued with the reiterated thunder crash and lightning glare of his intense *fortissimo.* . . .

The dance music—the music in which M. Jullien is peculiarly himself. His quadrille, waltz and polka compilations are all set in most brilliant frame-work, and treated with a consummate mastery of brilliant instrumentation, which make them absolutely exciting. Here you may study the effects of all kinds of instruments. Thus his famous "American Quadrille" owes its astonishing effect to the skill with which homely, humdrum melodies are brightened up, and set off against each other with all sorts of novel and grotesque instrumental coloring; especially to the brilliancy with which he invests Yankee Doodle (thus verifying Emerson's saying: "the meanest object is beautiful if placed in a strong enough light.")—There are some happy touches here: thus his simply isolating the first note of the strain all the time by a strong accent, makes almost a new thing of the Yankee Doodle; then the manner in which it is first boyishly whistled in the flageolet and flute, then grotesquely tooted on the bassoon, then droned out, bag-pipe—like, by two oboes, &c. And finally, and chiefly, to the crescendo progress in the entire arrangement, Yankee Doodle at last coming in fortissimo by all the instruments in swifter and swifter *tempo*, and then the battle and drum cannonading, and Yankee Doodle stronger still in sign of triumph, and the shout of voices too, thrown in; the inevitable uproarious applause of the many; the preconcerted rising of the musicians, as Jullien turns with air of solemn invitation to the audience, who involuntarily rise also, as "Hail Columbia" peals forth in large chords!—This is, to be sure, making a colossal toy of the orchestra, as we have before said! but the effect is most ingeniously and most triumphantly managed. . . .

The *Classical Music*. To hear the great works of the masters brought out in the full proportions of so large an orchestra, where all the parts are played by perfect masters of their instruments, is a great privilege and great lesson. So we must think, in spite of any criticisms to which M. Jullien's conductorship in symphonies may be open. Where everything is so distinctly rendered, and all on so large and bold a scale, it cannot but open many ears and souls to the grandeur of a Beethoven's conceptions to hear one of his masterpieces from this orchestra. To take our examples from the "Beethoven Night" (Wednesday): was it not something to hear that scrambling bass passage in the Scherzo of the C minor symphony, brought out into bold, broad outline by the nine double-bassos, with BOTTESINI among them! We confess it was the first time we *ever* heard that passage actually with our ears; save for a piano arrangement we scarcely knew its shape before. And how magnificent the triumphal march became with such a powerful *tutti*! But here we are constrained to make a beginning of criticism, and to own, that after all the joy we felt in such bold renderings, M. Jullien's leading in symphonies *is* open to criticism. Why did he *omit* a large part of that glorious finale? Why was the sweet *counter-theme*, led in by the three horn notes on the dominant of key, in the Allegro, played so heavily? Why was there never any *pianissimo*? And why was the time changed so arbitrarily, more than once in the course of the same movement, and no settled rate of movement maintained? We fear the answer to such questions must be found in the answer to another: Why does he on the programme call the Scherzo "descriptive of an advancing army?" . . .

We have our doubts whether Jullien's forte lies in classical music, although we do thank him for much enjoyment of it. . . .

We should hesitate to avow these strictures, were it not that they have such confirmation from the best musicians in Germany and here. Meanwhile, we regard Jullien and his orchestra as a great God-send; and all who have any music in their souls must go and hear him while he stays. He is no "humbug," no mere superficial parader of *clap-trap*, but a thinking and observing man, who loves and studies nature, seeks the laws of tone-effects in nature, and shows a masterly power of combination in whatever he does. . . .

5. *Louis Moreau Gottschalk*

The first American pianist to win international fame was Louis Moreau Gottschalk, who returned to the United States from Europe in 1853. A child prodigy, he had left his native New Orleans eleven years before to study in Paris, where he had grown into a musical matinee idol, capitalizing on his exotic (American) origin by basing many of his show-pieces on Creole melodies and rhythms. His return as a full-fledged virtuoso at the age of twenty-four was a major musical event, and Gottschalk stayed on to tour widely in North and South America. His sudden death in Brazil at age forty caused many a young lady to weep as she played his "The Last Hope" on the parlor piano.

Ever the skeptic, and opposed to "the false and superficial tendency of the modern virtuoso school of Art," Dwight went to Gottschalk's first Boston concert with anything but an open mind. His review, cool as it is, still conveys a strong impression of Gottschalk's brilliance.

In the same article, Dwight comments on Ole Bull's latest recital and, prophetically, on the "charming child *cantatrice*" who appeared with him: "little Adelina Patti," then ten years old. She seems to have been one of the few artists of the day who did not trill variations on "Yankee Doodle."

Dwight's Journal of Music, October 22, 1853

In noticing the concerts already past, let us begin with the one which may be considered *the* novelty of the season; namely:

Gottschalk

The extravagant fame and the peculiar kind of enthusiasm which preceded the arrival of the young New Orleans virtuoso, announced in the bills always as "the great American pianist," had forewarned us what to expect of him. We expected brilliant execution, together with perhaps some little touch of individuality enough to lend a charm to pretty but by no means deeply interesting or important compositions of his own. Some of the compositions we had heard from other players, and by their triviality were forced to feel that either these belied him, or that it was by sheer professional puffery that he had been so long proclaimed the peer of Liszt and Thalberg and even Chopin; all of whom, particularly the last, have been true tone-poets, of decided individuality, which is stamped upon their written works, with which the Gottschalk *Bananiers* and *Dances Ossianiques* bear no more comparison than the lightest magazine verses with the inspired lyrics of the great bards. Yet upon composition, it would seem, he takes his stand; for in his programme of Tuesday evening every piece performed by him was of his own composing; and the newspaper and pamphlet biographies of him, innumerable letters from abroad, and eulogistic critiques in the papers, from New York to New Orleans, harp upon this with a peculiar energy.

Well, at the concert—which, by the way, did not half fill the Boston Music Hall, owing partly we believe to the one dollar price, and partly, we *hope*, to distrust of an artist who plays wholly his own compositions—our expectation was confirmed. There was indeed most brilliant execution;—we have heard none more brilliant, but are not yet prepared to say that Jaell's was less so. Gottschalk's touch is the most clear and crisp and beautiful that we have ever known. His play is free and bold and sure and graceful in the extreme; his runs pure and liquid, his figures always clean and perfectly defined; his command of rapid octave passages prodigious; and so we might go through with all the technical points of masterly execution. It *was* great execution. But what is execution, without some thought and meaning in the combinations to be executed?

Could a more trivial and insulting string of musical rigmarole have been offered to an audience of earnest music-lovers than "American Reminiscences" to begin with! These consisted of a thin and feeble preluding, in which the right hand ran with exquisitely liquid evenness and brightness up and down the highest octaves, over and over, without any progress of ideas, as if it were mere scale-exercises, followed at last by fragmentary and odd *allusions* to "Old Folks at Home," and then by that homely tune, (which seems to be a sort of catching, melodic *itch* of the times) fully developed, and then varied in divers difficult and astounding ways. Also "O Susanna" (if we remember rightly) in the same fashion. There was an eruption of silly applause here, and an encore which he answered with—"Yankee Doodle!" We say *silly* applause; for who, that admired such execution as a power worth having, could but feel melancholy to see the power so thrown away? and who that went there eager to hail and praise a young native artist, could but be mortified to see an artist so little in earnest with his Art, and to find the dilettante public still so ready to extol as Art what properly is little more than sleight of hand!

The most imposing piece of Mr. GOTTSCHALK was called "Jerusalem, a triumphal fantasia," for two pianos, in the great difficulties of which he was ably seconded by Mr. J. PYCHOWSKY, who played at disadvantage from a hastily made manuscript copy. In portions of this there was a certain De Meyer–like pomp and breadth of harmony; but the ideas seemed commonplace and the work as a whole left but a heavy and confused impression. There was a certain grace and individuality in the *Savanna* and *Bananier*, which he styles "Poetic Caprices," though not enough to build the fame of genius on. His "Carnival of Venice" we did not hear.

Skilful, graceful, brilliant, wonderful, we own this playing was. But players less wonderful have given us far deeper satisfaction. . . .

A charming feature of the concert was the admirable harp-playing of Mr. APTOMMAS, a young Welshman, who had lived long in France and England, hearing the best masters, but forming his own school. There is a fresh glow of youth and health in his cheeks, and he has the appearance of a modest, earnest, genial artist. We have never before heard the harp so played; its clear, rich, mellow tones rang through the hall like a bell. Every ear craves new refreshment from his minstrelsy. But away with the romantic stuff about "Welsh harper;" he plays the modern, artificial, Erard double action harp, (one of the most difficult of instruments), and his music is modern and metropolitan as that of Thalberg, though he is Welshman born.

In responding to the encore of his *Dance des Fées*, he had the ill luck to suppose the audience wished to hear "Yankee Doodle," not having been present in the beginning of the evening and not knowing that Gottschalk had already selected the same rare and marvellous theme. We are sure he is too earnest a musician to repeat this experiment.

Ole Bull

The Norwegian opened the season, and has given three or four concerts in the Boston Music Hall, to large and applauding audiences. He has been playing his old pieces, mostly the same by which he first introduced himself in America, in the days of our childish hero or rather virtuoso-worship. Ole Bull's position as an artist is well enough settled to require no criticism now. We heard him but once, and for a few moments. We entered the hall and found him deep in the middle of "Yankee Doodle" unaccompanied, looking as if rapt and wrestling with the inward spasms of a Pythian frenzy under the influence of that emptiest of all tunes, which people "whistle for the want of thought." And so we have it. With Ole Bull the word is "Yankee Doodle;" and Gottschalk, also, "Yankee Doodle;" and Aptommas "keeps it up;" when Jullien comes it will be "Yankee Doodle Dandie!" It would seem as if the good report of our last year's musical season, and the purification of our temple from these evil spirits by that grand series of true classic concerts, had provoked said spirits to beleaguer our fair city in the outset of the season and endeavor to surprise us unawares, reversing our fair fame; and there is always enough of the old Adam left in all promiscuous audiences to lay us open to the enemy's insidious or bold and impudent approaches. But we fear not; the good seeds have been sown.

Ole Bull played his "Carnival of Venice" with wonderful beauty, and grotesque humor. The rich tones of his instrument seemed in that hall the richest and purest that we ever heard from the violin. He was assisted by STRAKOSCH, the pianist, whom we did not hear; and by the charming child *cantatrice*, little ADELINA PATTI, whose voice is of the rarest beauty, purity and penetrating power. Her delivery of Jenny Lind's "Herdsman's Song" was truly admirable, and bespeaks the greatest promise.

6. *Sigismond Thalberg*

Sigismond Thalberg left no legacy of compositions to match that of Chopin or Liszt; but he was ranked with them as a piano virtuoso by many of their contemporaries. Chopin apart, Liszt and Thalberg were direct and bitter rivals from their mid-twenties until they appeared together in a sensational concert of reconciliation in Paris in 1836.

Twenty years later, Chopin was dead and Liszt had virtually quit the concert stage, leaving the field to Thalberg, who toured the United States in 1856 and 1857 with unqualified success. He remained in the country for a time to perform and to join with two American impresarios, Bernard Ullmann and Maurice Strakosch, in managing, unsuccessfully, a season of opera at New York's Academy of Music before resuming his career in Europe. Dwight's review of Thalberg's second and third Boston concerts, a vivid description of the pianist's style of performance, could serve as a definition of the term *virtuoso school*.

Dwight's Journal of Music, January 17, 1857

M. Thalbergs's Concerts

. . . It seems at first a strange sight to see two or three thousand people gathered for a piano-forte concert. Celebrity and novelty still carry the day, reversing the intrinsic order; Thalberg fills the Music Hall, while orchestra and symphony shrink to the measure of the Melodeon. We do not complain, for it is worth one's while to witness for once the best of its kind. And Thalberg, if we mistake not, has given us all a new idea of possible perfection in executive art, besides enabling us to judge fairly and allow full weight to a certain brilliant, ornamental school of composition, which has occupied a large share of public attention since he called it into being, and set all the young pianists on a chase after its Jack-o'-lantern glory.

Mr. Thalberg's selections . . . were chiefly in his own peculiar form of music—the Fantasia on operatic themes—and enabled us to appreciate more closely this his speciality as a composer. Thalberg is emphatically a pianist. His music is the joint product of the piano and of Thalberg. . . . He lays his ear closely, fondly to his instrument, this cabinet of hidden tones; he woos its keys with gentle or fierce touch, and draws from it and builds out from it all that it can do towards illustrating with utmost euphony and utmost wealth and brilliancy of ornament, such musical themes—say melodies—as impress themselves most strongly on his own musical temperament and please the general ear. For so far as he has a theory, it is that the aim of music is to *please*; one scarcely fancies his young soul as big with swelling thoughts and aspirations, like a young Beethoven, which must find utterance through or in spite of the best instrument that comes to hand. To make a music which should illustrate the possibilities of the piano, in a way to strike and astonish, but above all to please the general ear of music lovers, was the end for which he wrought. To weave into a beautiful, symmetrical, extraordinary arabesque of tone all the melodic passages and figures, the Aurora Borealis flame-gauze arpeggios, the wide-spread harmonies, the almost orchestrally broad combinations, the wind-like sweeps and swells, the rushing, surging basses, and Aeolian tremolos, which he had reduced in detail to such certainty of precise manipulation; to construct all these technical feats into a pleasing and connected artistic whole, as dancers weave their *pas* into some Ballet of more or less poetic significance: this seems to have been the end and motive of the operatic Fantasias.

Now this is a very different genesis, a very different method from that whereby the masterworks of musical genius have commonly been created. . . . How different this Fantasia from a Sonata or Symphony, or even from the freer tone-poems of a Chopin! How different from all the forms that had been held classic! . . . They are essentially *virtuoso* compositions—music written for the player and his instrument. The nearest stepping-stone afforded to it in the old classical forms was in the Concerto, in which the display of the performer was made an end, as well as the expression of a thought. We shall see below how Thalberg himself has marked and signalized this stepping-stone in his performance of a Beethoven Concerto.

Enough here to point out this difference. And now let us own that, after hearing Thalberg himself play them, these Fantasias do seem to us a much more genuine thing than formerly; under his hands they justify themselves. Perhaps it would be not far from the truth to say that they are "compositions" in somewhat the same sense that we speak of ornamental compositions in the arts of pictorial design. . . . The arabesque designer chooses a figure to work up and multiply and vary through infinity of changes. So the pianist takes a well known theme, a melody, for principal figure and subject in his complex musical pattern. He preludes to it by cunning and insensible approaches, charming the ear by what seems a delicate *impromptu* of his own, in which he hints ever and anon the coming theme, catches the shine of its coming afar off, sports with the piano (as if for the satisfaction of the fingers,) and with the latent theme at the same time, or lets the fingers run awhile their own way, knowing how to recall them gracefully and aptly as the business approaches. Then comes the theme, a vocal melody perhaps from *Norma* or *Lucia*, or sometimes a concerted movement, a whole scena. The voice (or voices) sings itself firmly, clearly and connectedly in the middle of the instrument (the thumbs taking much of this duty on themselves), while the harmonic foundation is laid out broadly below, and the other fingers of the right hand are free to weave in and over all a web of delicate and flowery embellishments. Then come variations and transformations, and new forms of illustration and embellishment; perhaps also some more illustrations out of the same opera; and then one of these themes is made the ornament and covering to another, which takes turn as principal. The whole grows onward with a remarkable unity and symmetry; there are splendid climaxes of gathering force, great basses rolling up and breaking in bright treble showers of diamonds, &c., and broad harmonies spread out underneath to lift all up and make what is delicate seem all the airier, and so forth, and so forth:—why describe what is so familiar to our readers? What strikes you in these compositions of Thalberg, apart from the playing, is first a certain winning grace and delicacy in the preluding and connecting parts, in which he discloses a vein of his own, a something that is peculiarly Thalberg, an atmosphere breathed over all from his own mind, and which you recognize again in those smaller works of his which are more purely his own compositions, like his *Andante*, his *Etudes*, &c.

Secondly the distinctness and expressive personality with which the theme stands out the whole time, wearing the dress for fuller self-assertion, and not obscured or smothered in it, or made ludicrous. Thirdly, the grace and splendor of the ornamentation. Then the all-pervading taste and sense of fitness everywhere, making beauty paramount and miracle subordinate, though clearly present. And finally the symmetry, the architectural balance and completeness of the whole work. This is what it is, and what we are compelled to enjoy in it, without asking ourselves what it is not, and whether it can satisfy the passion for undying beauty that torments deep natures. Go to Beethoven for that. Accept this in its way—until you shall grow tired of it. . . .

THIRD CONCERT (Saturday evening, Jan. 10.) There was no question this time, as there was the previous Saturday, between THALBERG and BEETHOVEN; for we had them both united. The mountain came to Mahomet; Mr. ZERRAHN and all his orchestra to the great pianist, helping him to bring out one of Beethoven's Concertos, besides contributing of their best stores purely orchestral. And they seemed inspired to do their best. *All* did their best; the programme was uncommonly good, the Music Hall crowded, the audience enthusiastic (far more than at the first two concerts), and altogether there was left the impression of a most delightful concert. We must record the programme:

PART I.

1. Overture: Der Freyschütz . . . . Weber
   Orchestra of the Philharmonic Concerts.
2. Aria: Semiramis . . . . Rossini
   Mme. D'Angri.
3. Concerto in C minor . . . . Beethoven
   S. Thalberg.
4. "Batti, Batti," Don Giovanni . . . . Mozart
   Mme. D'Angri.
5. Andante of Fourth Symphony . . . . Beethoven

PART II.

6. Overture: William Tell . . . . Rossini
7. Voi che sapete, Marriage of Figaro . . . . Mozart
   Mme. D'Angri.

The orchestra sounded better in the Music Hall than in the Melodeon, the sounds being better fused and softened, without loss of resonance or freshness. And yet, as before, one felt the need of more seconds and violas to offset the powerful first violins. (Of course a much larger orchestra every way is still the desideratum with us.). . . . But the memorable feature of the concert was the Beethoven Concerto, played right under the statue of the composer, by one of the world's two first pianists, and with full orchestral accompaniments. And yet it was a cruel disappointment to be cut short with only the *first movement* of the Concerto in C minor, after the whole had been announced and after that first movement had proved so witchingly beautiful, that it was hard to tear oneself from the enjoyment of so pure a work of Art, especially as such a chance of perfect interpretation on the pianist's part might never come again. But Thalberg's execution was a miracle of perfection. The orchestra seemed to feel that it must be, and that it must not be spoiled, to judge by the unity and delicacy with which they played the long introduction, and the accompaniment throughout. And what a masterpiece the composition is! To say nothing of its ideas and spirit, worthy of Beethoven, how admirably the instruments are made to lead and blend into the sounds of the piano, what exquisite contrasts and minglings of strings and reeds! Thalberg played it not only with the utmost precision, force and clearness, but with the finest light and shade, bringing out with exquisite feeling and accent all those little melodic phrases which in Beethoven's music melt out of the tone mass, like passing smiles of a celestial meaning and beauty which ever and anon light up a grand and earnest face. The ease with which it was done, too, showed to what excellent account this new power of pianism may be turned in qualifying the player for expressive interpretation of the master compositions. But what held the audience in breathless delight for some minutes was the long and elaborate cadence introduced by Thalberg at the orchestral pause near the end. It was marvellously ingenious and beautiful, an abstract, in fact, of the entire movement as if it had caught its own image in miniature in a distant mirror. Right knowingly had the pianist seized upon this transition point between the old school and the new, between music as music, and music as illustration, and shown his best art where he had the noblest subject. *Now* one could not but ask why, interesting as it is in those Fantasias above discussed, this wonderful pianism does not see for itself a higher and more glorious calling in subordinating itself more frequently and as a chief duty to the unfolding of the beauties of inspired works like those of Beethoven. For, although the Sonatas, Concertos, &c., present comparatively fewer difficulties to the fingers than the modern music, yet there is no possible perfection of skill in execution which would be thrown away in the rendering of them. Can the simplest lines of Shakespeare find too great an actor? Certainly it was clearly settled that evening that Thalberg can appreciate and can play Beethoven. . . .

7. *Homecoming from Abroad*

It was beginning to be possible to think of music as a profession in the United States, but aspiring young Americans still found it necessary to go to Europe for the training they would need to embark on a musical career. So the flow of musicians between Europe and America in the 1850s increasingly went in both directions.

John Knowles Paine was eighteen when he set off from Portland, Maine, to study organ in Berlin in 1857. He was heard and praised in Germany and in London before he returned in 1861 to launch what was to be a distinguished career as organist, composer, and teacher. While in Berlin, young Paine helped to procure a fine Walcker organ for Boston's new Music Hall, and he was among the first to play it on its inauguration in 1863. Paine took up residence in Boston in 1862 as a church organist, and soon began the Harvard lectures that led, after another dozen years, to his appointment as the first professor of music in an American university. In his first Boston concert after returning from Europe, Paine's performance of Bach's music endeared him to Dwight, who continued to encourage him, as he did few American composers, in later numbers of the *Journal*.

Dwight's Journal of Music, February 1, 1862

Mr. J. K. Paine's Organ Concert

Not even Bach's fugues could prevail against a storm like that of Saturday last, and Mr. PAINE had to postpone his concert until Monday evening. The audience (of four or five hundred people) was quite as large as such a solid and unusual entertainment could be expected to draw, so little has our public yet been educated to the understanding of true organ music. But the company was select and intelligent, composed of persons who came to listen in the hope of learning, and whose good opinion is worth something. The modest bearing of the young artist, self-possessed at the same time, was largely in his favor. And the reputation of his earnest studies, of the pure and noble direction in which he has dedicated his powers, means, hopes to Art, and of the much that he has accomplished in a few years of real study at so young an age, ensured a respectful audience. Many, who seek the best in all things, poetry, painting, sculpture, &c., and who only felt perhaps that they had never heard music which seemed to answer to the great traditions of the Organ, but who had often been assured that they would find it in Sebastian Bach, and trusted the assurance as they would the world's opinion of Michael Angelo or Raphael, before they had ever seen anything but fifth-rate paintings, were naturally careful not to let an opportunity like this go by. We believe all who came felt themselves amply repaid. Few would profess that they had fully understood; but all are ready to confess that they enjoyed. To most it was a new revelation of the significance and graudeur of the Organ. This time they heard it speak in tones, in combinations, in marvellous developments of infinite variety out of unity, which seemed to justify the grand scale on which the instrument is built and which make it a temple of harmonies.

Mr. Paine's programme was as follows:

1.	Prelude and Fugue in A minor . . . . ⎫	
2.	Choral variations, for two manuals	
	and double pedals . . . . ⎬ Seb. Bach	
3.	Trio Sonata in E flat	
	Moderato. Adagio. Allegro. ⎭	
4.	Song, "Ave Maria"	Rob. Franz
5.	Toccata in F	Sebastian Bach
6.	Grand Concert piece in G minor	L. Thiele
7.	Andante and Allegretto from an Organ Sonata	
	. . . .	Mendelssohn
8.	Vocal, "Parting in Spring"	Esser
9.	Concert variations on the Austrian Hymn . . .	J. K. Paine

The concert-giver placed as it were his best foot foremost, in playing the most important piece first. The *Prelude and Fugue in A minor* is one of Bach's greatest organ compositions. Naturally enough it called out the least demonstration from the audience,—perhaps made the least impression on them; but it comes nearer to the mark, we think, to say that it was received with silent wonder, which implies that there *was* an impression, a pretty strong one, but one which did not understand itself and did not dare to utter a response. But it was plain to all that there was something beautiful and grand, as well as most artistically ingenious and involved. How suddenly and positively the Prelude (with the smart, penetrating, richly blended tones of the full organ) took us away from ourselves, and bore us along through the labyrinth of quaint, fantastic figures, with a sense that all was tending nearer to the heart of the true tone-world! Then the Fugue, the not disappointing answer to the promise—how curious and complicated the theme; yet how distinctly, positively answered and kept up in all the four parts, each individually alive, and full of it in its own way! The distinctness of each part in so much complication, and especially the evenness and smoothness of the pedal playing must have astonished many. And yet all this mechanism, this ingenuity in Bach is always subject to idea, to the poetic inspiration. No part in the working of this fugue is more beautiful than the middle portion, where it goes on for a long time without pedals; then how grandly they come in again!

The Variation on a Lutheran Choral was played with a softer combination of stops, and is indeed a lovely composition, full of religious tenderness and rich suggestion. It is in fact a Quartet between the two hands and two feet, with the Choral melody thrown sometimes into a solo stop besides: as if the right hand played first violin, the left hand second violin, the right foot tenor and the left foot bass in a quartet of strings, with *solo obbligato* superadded. It was a capital illustration of the utility of pedals in an organ. But the mechanical part, remarkable as it was, was nothing to the spiritual beauty of the music in itself, which all appeared to feel.

The *Trio Sonata* was another instance of the way in which Bach makes the several key-boards play individual parts in concert. . . . The *Toccata* (a name given by those old masters to a concert piece, in which the subjects are only *touched*, as it were, but not worked up—a sort of free *fantasia* in fact) was a brilliant, not unmeaning, triumph over immense difficulties; those strong bold chords, whole double handfuls, were as sharply defined in their beginnings and their endings, as crisp and emphatic, as if played on a piano.

The selections of the second part were less severely classical. The Concerto by Thiele (a talented pupil of Haupt, who died full of promise), is extremely difficult, brilliant and full of deep, passionate unrest, rather than of imaginative invention. We have heard more interesting pieces by him; but this placed the great executive ability of the young organist in a strong light. The two movements by Mendelssohn were delicate and beautiful—fair specimens too of the quality of his six Organ Sonatas, which really sound tame after Bach.

Mr. Paine showed not a little contrapuntal skill and felicitous invention in his variations on the Austrian Hymn; they were not mere mechanical variations, but developed the subject-matter with new interest, and led it to a dignified close in regular fugue form. Being warmly recalled, he surprised us by a similar, and even more successful, treatment of the "Star-Spangled Banner," which was noble and inspiring throughout. One would hardly have supposed that the leading motive of that patriotic melody could have been turned into a subject for a Fugue, as it was, without sacrificing sense to ingenuity. Mrs. KEMPTON rendered valuable assistance with her expressive singing of Robert Franz's *Ave Maria*, a touching, noble melody, which sounded particularly well with organ. The song by Esser, though pleasing, was not so well suited to an organ concert.

8. *Concert in Wartime*

In February, 1862, Union troops under General Ulysses S. Grant won their first major victory of the Civil War at Forts Henry and Donelson. Two weeks later, Bostonians filled the Music Hall for a commemorative concert by the Handel and Haydn Society. The program opened with patriotic strains, including "The Star-Spangled Banner," which was gradually becoming a de facto national anthem. Otherwise, the music was the same as might have been heard on a similar occasion in Germany or Britain: Handel and Mendelssohn. Dwight, who condemned secession as fervently as he did slavery, caught the spirit of the event in his review, but kept to his musical standards all the same.

Dwight's Journal of Music, March 8, 1862

Commemoration of Victory

The concert given by the HANDEL AND HAYDN SOCIETY, last Saturday evening, was a fit musical expression of our joy and gratitude for the series of victories which have at last turned back the tide of insolent rebellion and inspired the sacred cause of Union, Western civilization and free institutions with new hope, new life and energy. Never have the walls of the Music Hall rung with the music of so live an occasion: and never has each inspiring sound there found such thrilling, heartfelt response in audience so large and representative of the best life and culture of this patriotic and progressive people. Every seat was filled; every face glowed with sympathetic fervor; the singers and the members of the orchestra looked as if their hearts were in their work, as if what they were about to do were no task, but a spontaneous irrepressible enthusiasm; the simple decorations of the stage, too, consisting of flags culminating in a wreath encircling the motto "Te Deum," the whole forming a fine background to the noble statue of Beethoven, who is certainly in place where Victory means Freedom, were tastefully suggestive. (The decorations were by Mr. Roethe).

To make all perfect and to bring the theme directly home to us, it chanced that Col. LEE and other brave officers of the 20th, had arrived home only the evening before from their captivity in Richmond since the black affair of Ball's Bluff. Their entrance with the Governor and his staff, amid patriotic strains from the orchestra, and the repeated cheers of the whole house, made an enlivening episode to begin with; which the singing of the "Star Spangled Banner,"—the solo of each verse given out with fervor by Miss WASHBURN, and the whole choir joining in the refrain, with orchestra,—carried up to a fine climax.

Then commenced the "Dettingen Te Deum" by Handel. It was composed in 1743 (two years later than the "Messiah") to commemorate a victory gained by the English and Austrian arms over the French, and has ever since been cherished as the traditional voice of national thanksgiving in times of victory among the English. . . .

[Handel] is never amiss where all Humanity would speak; never far short of the full height of a great occasion. In such hours we unfurl his fugual folds of harmony upon the breeze as naturally as we do the glorious Stars and Stripes. If we had not his greatest work, we had at any rate his style, his voice, his "large utterance," and all appropriate and inspired by victory. . . .

The choruses were in the main well sung, and with spirit, although sometimes in some portion of the vocal forces betraying a failure of unanimous attendance in rehearsals. The solo passages were very acceptably rendered by fresh and satisfactory voices, all taken from the ranks and new to the audience, with the exception of Mr. SIMPSON, the tenor from New York. Mr. [Myron] WHITNEY has a remarkably round, sonorous, musical bass voice, with which, though slightly husky that evening, he gave good effect to the trumpet air: *Thou art the King of Glory*, and the expressive but not striking melody: *When thou tookest upon thee to deliver*. His intonation is true, his manner chaste and natural; but there is need of schooling, and some slips in time had to be covered up by the quick providence of conductor and orchestra. . . .

But if anything was wanting in the first part, it was more than made good in the second, the inspiring, glorious "Hymn of Praise" by

Mendelssohn. Here the orchestra, the full Philharmonic orchestra of CARL ZERRAHN, conductor of the whole, had full play at last, in that long introductory Symphony and those graphic accompaniments to the entire Cantata, which are among the finest triumphs of modern instrumentation. We need not enter into any description of the work, it has been so often discussed in these columns when it has been produced before. It touches every key of praise and thankfulness, from the most trumpet-tongued to the most tender, sweet and trustful, like the exquisite second movement of the Symphony, which we never heard our orchestra play better, and the Duet and Chorus: *I waited for the Lord*, which Miss Granger and Miss Washburn rendered to a charm, the choral waves rolling in richly and smoothly, so that it was imperatively encored. . . . Chorus and orchestra throughout did their work admirably well and with a will, so that the interest of the thing waxed more and more exciting as it went on.—And so ended one of the most memorable of our Music Hall occasions. Is it too much to hope that these two works may soon be heard again?

9. *American Audiences*

Visiting European performers in the 1830s and 1840s had made fun of the rude habits of their American audiences, especially in the towns of the interior and in the West. As interest in classical music grew broader, some Americans who liked to consider themselves more cultivated took pains to disassociate themselves from the provincialism they imputed to those less accustomed to attending concerts and operas.

Dwight himself was seldom condescending to any concertgoers. He was trying to educate the public to the music he valued, and he was likely to be tolerant even of those who came to concerts to be seen more than to listen. Occasionally, though, he did pick up an essay from another publication that gave a snob's-eye view of the American audience—outside of Boston, to be sure. He found the one that follows in a short-lived New York paper that called itself "an outspoken, independent journal of the day."

Dwight's Journal of Music, May 14, 1864

Concert Etiquette

One of the tribulations of our life is to go to concerts and endure the ill manners and unmusical demonstrations of the people whom we meet there. A concert for the purely musical is a very rare thing—in fact, we are inclined to doubt if the majority of those who attend any but classical chamber concerts, are musical people at all. Let us look at the various kinds of city concerts given.

First, in all respects, should come those given by the Philharmonic Society, which have become as fashionable as the Italian opera, and probably for the same reason, namely, because the performances are wholly or in a great measure entirely unintelligible to a mixed audience. We mean by this, that most people find it quite as difficult to understand a German symphony as they do an Italian libretto; consequently, the necessity of occupying one's body, the mind being bored and annoyed, becomes apparent. To be sure, such people have no right to appear at concerts, but since their money is as good as any one else's and they *do* attend, we will see how they behave.

It is not unfrequent for old gentlemen to pull out a news-paper, taking care always to crinkle it during the most pianissimo portions of the music. The dowagers of fashion of course talk scandal or fall into a doze; we will not go quite so far as to say that they add to the music by snoring. At the Brooklyn Philharmonic we have often noticed ladies with their knitting, a custom which, after all, rather pleases our fancy than otherwise, or rather would do so were it not for the distressing provincial look of the thing. Think of Beethoven or Mendelssohn composing in order to make knitting the less tiresome to old women! Yet so far as these poetic ladies are concerned, it must be a pleasanter place than any other to knit in. Longfellow says in *Hyperion*: "He did not dance, but thought to music." So with these provincial neighbors of ours, knitting to music must be pleasanter than knitting to household noises; besides, we have been assured that this species of knitting is always for the soldiers.

But old gentlemen and old ladies read news-papers, talk scandal, and go to sleep, how do the young people offend? Need any one ask who has attended city concerts? Who was it that first made the suggestion that the name of the Philharmonic Society be changed to "Flirt-Harmonic?"

Flirting is so very extensive an accomplishment and possesses such numerous ramifications in the broad extent of its artistic perfection, that it would take up a great deal too much of our space should a complete analysis of its offences against concert etiquette be attempted here. So we shall content ourselves with merely mentioning a few details of it, as generally practised to our torture at the Philharmonic—or "Philharmonics," as boarding-school young ladies have dubbed these concerts.

These are talking, laughing, fan-gyrating, and lobbying—(that is, performing the part of wall flowers staring, etc.,)—programme crumpling, and chair-shuffling. We might almost add lorgnetting, although most people do consider it very good manners to stare people out of countenance with a double-barrelled opera-glass at concerts, forgetful of the fact that theatres and operatic performances are the only proper places for them, and that they do not quicken one's acoustic faculties. . . .

But we would not have our readers imagine that bad manners at concerts are by any means confined to the listeners. There seems to be no school for artists yet started in this country by which to enlighten them a little on certain points not altogether unworthy of their notice, in order to increase the comfort of their intelligent audiences.

We will take for example some charitable concert at which all the artists are on a supposed equal footing before the public; that is, they all volunteer their services, and no special prominence is given (at least in printing-ink) to any one in particular. Now, in case of *encores* at such a performance, how foolish it is for an artist to respond and reappear on the faintest apology for a recall. Yet they often do; nor is it merely to bow acknowledgments, but oftenest to sing or play again. . . .

Then again, when a real earnest, hearty, unanimous *encore* is insisted upon by the audience, it sometimes becomes a nice question to decide what to do. . . . The worst thing, however, which an artist can do, we apprehend, is to sing or play the entire cavatina or fantasia over again from the very beginning, or if it be a ballad, to repeat every blessed verse, let there be four or five of them. We have witnessed such distressing instances of ill-breeding over and over again, and it has always seemed a wonder how any musician could possibly possess so little consideration for their fellow-beings.

It is quite beyond the limits allotted to us to speak of all the detailed annoyances inflicted upon the public at concerts, such as blunderbuss-accompanyists, and those you feel so much above their duties as to constantly make pitiful attempts at *obbligato* embellishments in the worst possible taste, singers who are too lazy to commit their parts to memory and who bring the music on to the stage—which always suggests an actor doing likewise—violinists who seem to consider the flourish of the fiddle-bow of much more importance than the correct intonation of the semi-tones, double-stoppings, etc., etc., but "*verbum sat sapienti*," and we dismiss the subject, with a devout hope for improvement in some of the above particulars, ere long, in those entertainments professing to be *first-class* metropolitan concerts.—*New Nation*.

10. *The Peace Jubilee*

For its bigness, for its brash mixture of art and commerce, education and showmanship, lofty rhetoric and ballyhoo—say, for its expansive democratic spirit—the National Peace Jubilee and Great Music Festival of 1869 was an American spectacle from start to finish. Nothing like it had been attempted before, but it was to be a much-followed precedent.

The idea came to Patrick Sarsfield Gilmore quite literally in a vision, one summer day in 1867. The Irish-born bandmaster had had visions before, but this one totally possessed and drove him until, against all likelihood, he made it a reality. Gilmore had come to the United States in 1849, by way of Canada, as an eager bandsman of twenty. For a decade, with growing popularity, he led bands in and around Boston. When the Civil War came, Gilmore's band enlisted as a unit to accompany the 24th Massachusetts Volunteer Regiment into battle. Band and leader became famous for both their music and their gallantry; and in 1864, General Banks summoned Gilmore to be his chief bandmaster in occupied New Orleans. There Gilmore staged a spectacle that foreshadowed the Jubilee: a huge music festival for which he marshaled all the bands in the area and mobilized a chorus of five thousand school children.

In New York after the war, Gilmore's thoughts turned to peace. The nation was still sorely troubled, but Gilmore sensed among the people an undercurrent of yearning for unity and brotherhood. What, if not music, could bring these feelings to the surface? And so came the vision: In a gigantic, specially constructed coliseum, fifty thousand Americans would be brought together for a great feast of music and reconciliation. Gilmore imagined an orchestra of thousands, a chorus of tens of thousands, soloists by the dozen, cannons firing in time to "The Star-Spangled Banner," the president in attendance. Maybe it was a wild notion, but Gilmore's sense of the moment was uncannily right, and he was the man to seize it. It took him two years, but he realized his vision, or most of it, and with a signal success even he could hardly have anticipated.

John S. Dwight was predictably set against it from the moment, early on, when Gilmore came to him with the germ of the idea and asked for his support. All during the preparatory stages *Dwight's Journal of Music* remained aloof from the promotional flurry of reports and announcements. When the Peace Jubilee took place, however, Dwight attended and was moved, impressed as he had never expected to be. Whatever reservations he still had, and there were some, he then manfully devoted page after page of *Dwight's Journal* to accounts of the Jubilee reprinted from other newspapers and magazines. And at the request of the *New-York Tribune*, he wrote a long summary of his own views, which he reproduced for the readers of his *Journal*.

Dwight's Journal of Music, July 3, 1869

The National Peace Jubilee

To-day our columns are entirely occupied with this remarkable project, the dream, the one life purpose, for two years, of Mr. PATRICK S. GILMORE, and with its still more remarkable fulfillment in this city on the five days which an Irishman might call the next to "the top of the year," crowning the slope that leads right up to Midsummer, June 15th to 19th inclusive, making the dreamer famous, a popular hero in his way. Indeed we fear such stars as Mendelssohn just now, or Mozart, if they lived among us, would "pale their ineffectual fires" before such Calcine effulgence. The Jubilee has been the all-absorbing topic for the last month. As we have been silent about it during the preparation of the mighty work; and since, with all the extravagances of the plan, it has been pushed forward with such faith and energy that the imagination of the People, the "popular heart," perhaps we should even say the good genius of our People, fired and filled with it, has adopted it and made it its own, transforming it as it were into its own likeness; since it has been crowned with such unique success, we can do no less than gather together what we can of its history, weigh its results from our own point of view, and note the impression it has made on others. . . .

For ourselves, as our readers know, we came to it sceptically, little disposed to trust or countenance a musical project making such enormous claims, and so unblushingly heralded after the manner of things as uncongenial as possible to the whole sphere of Art. The following letters, which we transfer from the *New York Tribune* of Saturday and Monday last, describe our position candidly, before and since the feast. . . .

The Peace Jubilee Summed up

To the Editor of the Tribune

SIR:—You ask for "a careful, critical summary of the net result:"—musically, of course, you mean. But to weigh that rightly we must look at more. Your able correspondents have given you the details and impressions day by day. To see it in the right light, the whole must be put together. We must begin by going back to ask

I. *How the Plan looked at first, and how it was worked up.*

At first sight, certainly, the project was vain-glorious. The whole style of the announcement was such as to commend it more to the noisy and spread-eagle class of patriots than to still, thoughtful lovers of their country and of peace; while, in respect to music, its enormous promise, its ambition to achieve "the greatest," to "thrust" greatness upon us by sheer force of numbers, and so eclipse the musical triumphs of the world by saying: "Go to now, let us do ten times the *biggest* thing that ever yet was done"—this, and the extra-musical *effects*, the clap trap novelties, grotesquely mingled in its programmes, chilled the sympathies of the real, the enlightened, the disinterested music-lovers, who, feeling for the honor and the modesty of Art, two qualities as inseparable in the artistic character as they are in woman, inevitably shrank from such grandiloquent pretension, as much as they inflamed the imagination of the ignorant or only sentimentally and vaguely musical. . . .

The idea and the authorship presented the same aspect. That the projector, master-spirit, brain, and central organizing force of the "greatest musical festival in all the ages" should be, not a Mendelssohn, a Handel, or great musical man of any sort, or hardly one who fellowshipped with artists, but a Gilmore, a clever leader of a local band, an Irishman by birth, but zealous for the land of his adoption zealous for freedom in a truer than an Irish sense; a man of common education, singularly good natured and, we doubt not, generous; an enthusiast of rather a sentimental type; chiefly known as caterer in music to the popular street taste, dispenser of military and of patriotic airs, exceedingly fond of demonstrations, restless getter up of "monster concerts," in which classical works of genius were pressed into damaging promiscuity with musical *mix pickel* for the million; bountiful in advertising patronage (sure road to favor with the press); one of the glibbest, most sonorous and voluminous in all the wordy ways of "stunning" and sensational announcement:—that such a man should be the breather of the breath of life into the great feast of song to which "all that have life and breath" are summoned; that the grandest conceivable of all musical demonstrations should be in its spirit like unto his spirit; that our whole musical world, with all the musical resources of the nation, should be set revolving round a musician of that stamp, and that at such a bugle's blast all the makers of sweet sounds in all the land should rally to a Jubilee of Peace with him, in his way, was something too much for the common, unsophisticated intellect, musical or not, to take in at once, unless one took it in the nature of a colossal joke. How any sound mind at that time could conceive it possible for a thing so started to succeed as this has done, is inconceivable to this day, after the great success. . . .

But Gilmore was in earnest. His "fixed idea" had vital marrow in it, and he knew how to magnetize other efficient people to like earnestness. His great devotion to that fixed idea saw only the shining end, pressed onward gazing steadily into the sun, using for means whatever came most readily to hand—chiefly that cardinal lever of all modern business enterprise, unscrupulous advertising, meant innocently in this case, no doubt, though questionable to squeamish folk like you and me, dear Tribune! And had he not the example of the whole business world to tempt him? And here, too, the swell mob style, the returned Californian digger garb and heavy watch-chain air, with which the thing presented itself, was not particularly inviting to sincere music-lovers, jealous, as we have said, for both the honor and the modesty of art. The finer instincts are the more suspicious of whatever is most loudly advertised. The quiet gentleman we trust, but from the loud-mouthed quack we turn away. Not so, however, with the simple masses; high-spiced advertisement does its perfect work with them. To draw an audience of

50,000, a whole community must by some means or other first become infatuated. Never was such advertising, in editorial even more than business columns, as this same Jubilee has had. Shrewd dodges, too! Innocent Bostonian, calm and unsuspecting, opens his daily paper one fine morning, and is coolly informed that he—that all musical Boston—is in a great state of excitement about something of which he never heard a hint before! Our neighbor, in *his* (Democratic) newspaper, has read the same; and so through all the party shades of journalism—all agreed for once! Day by day, beginning with mysterious hints, do they the tale unfold foreshadowing the great event. Day by day, in ceaseless round, all vieing with each other, all the newspapers keep lifting corner after corner of the curtain that conceals the miracle too bright for mortal eyes; kindly provide us with smoked glasses too that we may bear the revelation when the great day comes. Count Cagliostro never conjured more adroitly. Biggest, best-drilled orchestra in all creation? That surely was the Press, which unseen fingers played upon, ever one theme with endless variations, as upon the keys of a piano. . . . And with a *tutti crescendo* of amazing confidence, new wonder upon wonder was proclaimed, not as a thing suggested, but as *fait accompli.* . . .

Meanwhile there had been skillful procuring of indorsements of the project; letters from influential citizens who, not musical themselves, were readily persuaded to a festival of Peace, and not unwilling to have Boston beat the world in the grand scale of its music; letters, too, from prominent musicians who would naturally be the ones to take the lead in practical performance. There was shrewd calculation shown in the order in which individuals were approached, and their adhesion won and published; the prime mover knew his men. Indeed, the thing was worked up with consummate tact; and here lay, probably, the "genius" which has been so freely ascribed to the Projector; for surely the conception, the idea itself, did not require creative imagination, nor invention, until it came to the details of execution, and here, with money, business talent was the one thing needful. And at the critical moment Business stepped in to the rescue; Business, with the money guaranty, with organizing skill, with ready way of rushing its big enterprises through. The application of Dry Goods and Railroad methods saved the whole. The work was well laid out among responsible committees.

The word went forth that now the enterprise was on its feet. Conversions became numerous; subscriptions, too; whole business streets were canvassed, and it demanded courage in the unbeliever to say no. The huge Coliseum went up as by magic. The invitation flew abroad to all the singers; 10,000 wanted; New England—Massachusetts, even—was good for nearly the amount, could honor the draft at sight. By choral societies, clubs, choirs, groups who had sung in Conventions, they poured in. Many new societies sprang up for the occasion; musical instruction in the public schools had silently been feeding all these fountains. They came together with enthusiasm; it waxed warmer and brighter with rehearsals; the sense of participating, and feeling like singing particles in the live fragments of the great whole soon to be fused into *one* conscious life, the mutual magnetism the sense of pride, of progress, of cooperation, while the grand culmination loomed beyond— this was inspiring and uplifting, was a great good in itself, almost enough to offset the brag, the claptrap and the humbug of the earlier stages, even should the consummation fail. As for the grand orchestra (1,000 instruments), it was simply a matter of business and money to bring the elements of that together.

The success of the Jubilee in some shape having become a forgone conclusion, those who now took it in hand to draw the actual working plans soon found it necessary to reduce its scale somewhat to bring it within practicable dimensions. Instead of 20,000 singers, the limit was set at 10,000; the Coliseum, instead of 50,000, was to hold less than 30,000 hearers—say 37,000, counting stage and auditorium together. Large enough, in all conscience. With every such reduction the plan gained in the opinion of really musical persons. One by one many of these gave in, accepted part in the management or in the performance, saying: Since its success is certain, let us try to make it worthy of success; let us mould its character, as far as possible, to some consistency of true artistic end and outline—make it musical in the best sense we can, eliminate some nonsense wholly, keep guns and anvils within reasonable bounds, and give the highest music a fair chance. Hence a considerable modification of the programmes. The 20,000 school children, reduced to 7,000, were to have their own day, sweet and peaceful, set apart, and not be huddled in with the general medley of noisy cannonading choruses and all the boisterous excitement sure to go therewith. The Ninth Symphony was wisely voted quite impracticable. The duration of the Festival, having been increased from three to five days, gave room for two programmes almost exclusively of classical selections. . . .

II. *A Few Notes on the Progammes & Performance*

The first day's programme was ceremonial, inaugural, sensational, patriotic. Prayer and addresses, were unheard, while that vast multitude, 12,000 facing 11,000, gazed in wonder on itself, and felt the inspiration of a scene the grandeur and beauty of which were unimaginable before. That spectacle needed no speech, no music even, to make its eloquence sublime and irresistible. That was the secret of the *great* impression throughout all the days: so many beings met and held together there in full sight of each other, and in perfect order. What but music could secure such order? Prayer and speech were brief; but, even could they have been heard, they were superfluous. What fitter prayer than that religious Luther Choral: "*Ein feste Burg*," which followed? Full, rich, solemn, grand, the chords rolled forth from 10,000 voices, supported by the great orchestra, but even more by that most powerful organ (small, but built for power), which really seemed the backbone of the chorus. We could wish it had been harmonized by Bach, instead of Nicolai, if only that Bach might have had some recognition among the other mighty masters. Two things were proved at once: that there was no increase of loudness at all proportioned to the number of voices; and that, even if the farthest voices reached the ear a fragment of a second later than the nearest, the ear was not aware of it, while many individual imperfections, even false notes, possibly, were swallowed up in the great volume and momentum of the mass. The same held good of the other pieces of plain choral harmony: Keller's "American Hymn," and the concluding "God Save the Queen" (which one of our Psalm Kings, Psalmanazar I, we dare say, has nicknamed "America") sung to "My Country," with all the spread-eagle accompaniments of drums, guns, bells, &c. The Mozart "Gloria" was a good selection for a day of Peace, and, though it moved unsteadily, yet by its animation and its clear intention made most hearers deaf to faults. Wagner's *Tannhäuser* Overture did not prove a fortunate selection for that great orchestra, nor had it any special fitness for the occasion, except as a piece of stirring effect music. In few parts of the vast space could much of it be heard; the violins and brass told well; the reeds, intrusted with the theme at times, were lost. The Overture to "Tell" fared somewhat better, at least in the spirited finale, though the opening, so beautiful with violoncellos (60 of them,) was dumb show to all but the nearest. One envied the singers their places round the rim of the great seething instrumental maelstrom, looking down into it as well as hearing. The "Ave Maria" solo, built by Gounod upon a prelude of Bach, was notable for the rich *obligato* unison of the 200 violins (though all there was of Bach about it, the arpeggio modulation, complete in itself, and used by Gounod for accompaniment, was covered up so as to be imperceptible), and for the clearness with which Mme. [Euphrosyne Parepa] Rosa's voice penetrated the whole space, although it sounded far off and in miniature, as if heard through the wrong end of an opera glass. In the *Inflammatus* her triumph was more signal, while the great choral climaxes look like the grander summits in the memory of mountain scenery. The rest was sensational: "Star-Spangled Banner," glorified by such broad treatment, with artillery and bells beside—a signal, as it were, to all the world outside that Jubilee had reached its highest moment—and with the melody so divided between deeper and higher voices as to overcome the difficulty for average singers of its great compass. That indeed was thrilling! March from "The Prophet," by full band of one thousand—business enough for all their throats of brass. And Verdi's "Anvil Chorus," causing wildest excitement—not precisely a legitimate effect of music, not the kind of excitement or emotion which musical people seek; fatal to that mood and temper of an audience in which music as such can be felt. Such effects are *extra* musical; the spectacle, the hundred scarlet firemen, &c., had much to do with it. Besides, the hundred anvils had a queer and toy-like sound, jingle of sleigh bells rather than the honest Vulcan *ring*. This was Mr. Gilmore's day, and he conducted all the patriotic pieces, including the opening Choral, in which he realized a good *pianissimo*, one of the finest effects of a vast multitude of voices. Mr. [Julius] Eichberg conducted in the Tannhäuser overture, and "Coronation March;" Mr. Zerrahn in the solos and the *Gloria*.

The second was a great day of excitement. Added to the *eclat* of the Festival, now in full tide of success, was the visit of the President, rather disturbing the conditions precedent for the "Grand Classical Programme," which had been much relied on for the conversion or conviction of the musically cultivated. The crowd was enormous—double that of the day before; curiosity, hero-worship, swelling heart of patriotism, doubtless drew more than music did. Of course not the best sort of audience either to hear or let hear. Well, the selections were all excellent; though we would except, perhaps, the opening Festival Overture by Nicolai on Luther's Choral. The plain Choral, to our mind, was grander, than with that orchestral counterpoint and trivial episodical theme between the stanzas; not being great work in that kind, like Bach's, it weakens the impression. Of three Handel Choruses, "See the conquering hero" was the most effective; "And the Glory of the Lord," was taken so slow as to make it hard to sing—a necessity, real or fancied, in conducting so vast a multitude through any labyrinthine movement. We were surprised that we could hear Miss Phillipps's voice so well: there is a weight in her rich tones that carries far and quietly pervades. The piece, one of the best for her, and one of her best efforts, Mozart's "*Non piu di fiori,*" was too good for the crowd, not heard by some on account of restless noise, and not appreciated by the majority. Such a crowd contributes nothing on its own part to music, does not truly listen, but waits to be smitten and carried away. "He watching over Israel," the gentle, softly swelling chorus from *Elijah*, strange to say, proved one of the most successful of all the choruses that week; like a broad Amazon the stream moved steadily and evenly within bounds, and the round, full, smooth quality of the collective tone is something memorable. "Let the bright Seraphim" was just the perfect selection for Parepa-Rosa in that place, and was the chiefest triumph of her voice. With [Matthew] Arbuckle's [cornet] obligato (one longs for the real crackling old-fashioned *trumpet* though) it made great effect, by no means so great as it would be in a smaller hall; but the half-musical, which is by far the larger part of any such great audience, always need the *personal element* to interest them in music, and go the full half-way to meet a solo. The intermission was of course filled with the Hero-President. Then came Part II, the great Schubert Symphony in C, Mr. Zerrahn's capital selection for his grand orchestra; great hopes had been placed on that, for what symphonic work can bear such magnified presentment, if not that work? Alas! the Tantalus cup was rudely snatched away. The Symphony was to be sacrificed; the other element, fasting from native noise and anvils and free swing of hurrah boys, had grown irrepressible. To the brave President all music is alike, they say, and how easy for some one of the irrepressibles to prompt him to express a wish for good Spread-Eagle Scream with anvils! So into the programme, unannounced, and right before the Symphony, were thrust bodily "Star Spangled Banner" and "Anvil Chorus," once and again, until the building shook with thunder of applause; all mood for finer music was destroyed, all fine conditions broken up, Prospero Schubert's wand tossed under feet. The Symphony was killed! knocked on the head by anvils! The wand, however, was picked up and waved for form's sake. But it had grown late; people were weary, restless, moving about, or starting homeward, talking aloud, in no mood to listen or let others hear; so the first movement and the Scherzo were omitted; the beautiful Andante (of the "heavenly length") was scarcely heard, and never did the impetuous sublime finale, with the thunder thumps of double basses (think of 70 or 80 of them!) sound so feebly. . . . Poor chance after this for Haydn choruses: "The Marvelous Work," and "The Heavens are telling;" for, sing as they might to an audience preoccupied, it still went: "The *anvils* are telling." . . .

It was on Saturday morning, the School Children's day, that we were touched and made to *feel* for once. The charming scene, the innocent, pure spirit of the whole, the fresh, sweet, silvery voices of the 7,000 children, admirably true and blended in three-part song and unison, their own expressions of delight, their waving of handkerchiefs, and silvery shouts of applause, the kaleidoscopic unity of movement in their physical and vocal gymnastic exercises, all combined to make an exquisite impression. It was good to be there. It meant much for the future and for culture. It was not an art occasion, to be sure, and did not pretend to be. It was unique, a side of the Festival entirely by itself; the most genuine and sincere of all, and, in many respects, the most interesting. The beauty of it was that it did not pretend or strive to be anything but just what it was. But when the exercises came to measured breathing, then to the first utterance of a pure tone, swelling and dying away with the most beautiful *crescendo* and *diminuendo* that we ever heard, and finally to the blended tones of the Trichord, purity itself, like the white ray of "holy light" divided by the prism, we were fain to call that just the most exquisite moment of the whole week's Festival. Simple, but divine; impersonal but alive; without conscious meaning, but implying all! And, after such an illustration as the whole Jubilee had given of the musical resources of our people, was it not worth the while to see the nursery where the seeds thereof are sown?

III. *The Net Results*

As an *occasion*, of a new kind, of unexampled magnitude (unless in semi-barbarous times or Oriental countries)—whatever may have been musically—the Jubilee was a success. All acknowledge it, not without joy. . . .

It seems as if—the ball once set in motion, or, rather, the vigorous first twist once given at the heart and centre of the revolving and soon formidably expanding maelstrom—as the dream and the intense will of one, magnetizing a few, then many, passed by degrees into a popular movement, assuming almost national dimensions, until the very air was full of it—soon every particle and feature of it, as it were, underwent "a sea change" in the tempering, transforming, vitalizing, and idealizing element of the new, best life and genius of a great, free People; having adopted it almost before they knew it, and hardly knowing what it was, they meant that it should be American in some sense which they could be proud of, and that the biggest gathering and musical array in human history, in spite of its extravagances, should still denote us truly, and be an earnest to the world of what an ambition for the true glory of a great nation, what a sleepless ideal of an ever higher type of Citizenship and of Society, what an energy and wealth of means, what a zeal for culture, what a principle of order and deep love of harmony are in us, spite of our diversities and the wide space over which we spread. And so it came to pass. And New England, Boston was the place for it. We need not attempt to show what has been so universally acknowledged, that such a feast could have succeeded nowhere else but here. . . .

Acoustically, or aesthetically, with regard to space and power of numbers, the Festival was welcome for its opportunities to test some problems. The vast hall had been pronounced good for sound, because a single voice, a violin, could be heard in its furthest corners. But the walls, built around the utmost limits of the range of a strong voice, were far outside that of many voices—two voices go *no further* than one, ten thousand no further than an ordinary chorus. . . . Vast volumes of tone were swallowed up in those great spaces, smothered by flags and awnings, or leaked away through crevices, before they reached the ear. . . . And, *a fortiori*, the out-and-out spread-eagle things, the popular airs with guns and anvils and all extra-musical accessories, made by far the most effect. And their effect made *peace* impossible in 40,000 people, most of whom could not be musical, nor capable of keeping very still at any time, and who, having once had the appetite for boisterous enthusiasm stimulated, could neither hear nor let hear when the real music came. . . .

Now looking to the *execution* of the music, there was very much to praise. In the great chorus there was far more unity, precision, light, and shade in rendering, than almost any one of musical experience could have believed possible. And it grew better as the thing went on. It gave one a proud joy to know that so many thousands of singers, with only one rehearsal of the whole, could sing so well together. It told of musical enthusiasm, of *esprit du corps*, of good native average of voices and of talent, good instruction, thorough and inspiring drill in separate bodies. No wonder that they all watched for each appearance of their leaders, of Mr. Zerrahn, and Mr. Eichberg, and Mr. [Eben] Tourjee, as well as of Mr. Gilmore himself, to overwhelm them with the heartiest applause. . . .

But I must hasten to a close. Whether the Festival considered musically, were very good or not, it musically *did* good. At any rate to all those singers and performers. It was a great experience for them. It has given them a new impulse, a new consciousness of strength, a new taste of the joy of unity of effort, a new love of cooperation, and a deeper sense of the divine significance and power of music than they ever had. It has caused hundreds of choral societies to spring into existence for the time being, many of which will certainly prove permanent; and their first bond of union has been the practice of *good* music, of master-works of Handel, Haydn, Mozart, Mendelssohn, which, having tasted once in such deep draughts, they will not readily abandon for weak trash. Education must come out of it. It has *planted*, well and widely, for the future.

Was it not good to be there, too, as listener, as looker-on, as sympathetic part and parcel of it? Who would willingly have been left out of such a grand occasion? The greatest assemblage of human beings under one roof ever known! A scene so overwhelming, so sublime, so beautiful from every point of view! An almost boundless sea of live humanity; and all so cheerful, all so happy, full of kindness, rejoicing in the sense of Country and of Brotherhood! Tens on tens of thousands, yet such admirable *Order*! Could any object, any influence but Music, hold such countless restless atoms in such order?

Finally, in a still wider way it has done good. It has given to tens of thousands of all classes (save, unfortunately, the poorest), who were there to hear, and, through them, to thousands more, to whole communities, a new belief in Music; a new conviction of its social worth; above all, of its importance as a pervading, educational and fusing element in our whole democratic life; a heavenly influence which shall go far to correct the crudities, tone down, subdue and harmonize the loud, self-asserting individualities, relieve the glaring and forthputting egotism of our too boisterous and boastful nationality. Thousands now have faith in Music, who never did have much before; thousands for the first time respect it as a high and holy influence, who very likely looked upon it as at the best an innocent, if not a dissipating, idle pleasure. Public opinion, henceforth, will count it among the essentials of that "liberal education," which is the birthright of a free American, and no longer as a superfluous refinement of an over-delicate and fashionable few. . . . So far as the Jubilee has wrought this conversion among unbelieving or indifferent thousands, it has done incalculable good; and if, for this alone, we cannot be too grateful to the men who (whatever our mistrust of motives and of methods once) have given us a great experience.

J. S. D.

Boston, June 25, 1869.

11. *Theodore Thomas*

Not merely the first American conductor, Theodore Thomas was without doubt the most important pioneer of the symphony orchestra in the United States. Older conductors, like Carl Zerrahn in Boston or Carl Bergmann in New York, both from the old Germania Orchestra, were Old World *Kapellmeister*, schooled but not inspiring. Thomas was a dynamo, a born leader, and when he decided in 1862 "to form an orchestra for concert purposes," the history of the American symphony orchestra began.

Thomas came to New York from Germany at age ten, and in his teens, largely self-taught, was already earning his way as a violinist. He played in Jullien's orchestra in 1853, gained membership in the New York Philharmonic Society, played in the opera orchestra at the Academy of Music, and joined the young pianist William Mason in a landmark series of chamber music concerts. Impatient with the Philharmonic Society's narrow scope, Thomas determined, at twenty-seven, to organize an orchestra of his own and to devote his energies "to the cultivation of the public taste for orchestral music." He imagined that if his orchestra was as good as he expected it to be, it would soon win the support of one of that new breed of American industrialists who were drawn to the arts as a social good. His orchestra, then, would not be a club nor an adjunct to some larger institution, an opera house or a princely court, as in Europe. It would be an institution in itself, permanent and independent.

Accounts leave no question as to the quality of Thomas' orchestra; his concerts were an immediate and unqualified success. But the hoped-for benefactor did not soon appear. For nearly thirty years Thomas strove to realize his goal of the permanent, independent orchestra; it was a heroic struggle that culminated in the founding of the Chicago Symphony Orchestra in 1891, under Thomas' leadership and according to his plan. But Chicago was not the sole beneficiary of Thomas' vision and work. He left his stamp as conductor on the philharmonic societies of both New York and Brooklyn; he lent the force of his leadership and organizing skill to begin the Cincinnati Music Festivals and the Cincinnati College of Music. And though his primary goal (the permanent orchestra) long eluded him, he succeeded memorably in two other aims still broader: He set standards of performance that have held for American symphony orchestras ever since; and more than any other, he helped to cultivate the public taste for orchestral music, mostly through his orchestra's tours. Over a period of twenty-one years, beginning in 1869, the full Thomas Orchestra traveled to every section of the increasingly far-flung country in an extended sequel to the pioneering ventures of the little German orchestras twenty years before.

John S. Dwight welcomed the Theodore Thomas Orchestra in its first visit to Boston, and though he had some reservations about Thomas' program making, he was clearly impressed with the quality of his music making. In another review, years later, Dwight indulged in some special pleading for the local orchestra (under the Harvard Musical Association aegis) whose concerts were so close to his heart. Thomas' orchestra could be an inspiration to Boston's, but it could also be a threat, Dwight warns, if the visitors should spoil the public's taste for the residents' efforts. In making his case, Dwight illuminates some of the problems then faced by local orchestral organizations.

Dwight's Journal of Music, November 6, 1869

Theodore Thomas and his Orchestra

The visit of this famous New York Orchestra has given our music lovers quite a new and quick sensation. Boston had not heard such orchestral performances before; and Boston, in the frankest humor, gave itself up to the complete enjoyment and unstinted praise of what it heard. The promise of the three concerts of last Friday, Saturday and Sunday evenings was kept to the letter. It was truly and exclusively THOMAS's New York Orchestra,—fifty-four instruments, picked men, most of them young, all of them artists, all looking as if thoroughly engaged in their work, eager above all things to make the music altogether sound as well as possible. And it was evident, from first to last, that they had perfect understanding with their leader and each other; that they were in admirable discipline, had played together very often and for years; and that they had been selected, with a determined eye to superiority in every part, in a community where good musicians are so numerous that a crude or lifeless member can always be easily replaced by a better; no holding on to places after faculty is gone, no dead wood in the tree. There was nothing which our people, our musicians needed so much as to hear just such an orchestra. They came most opportunely: for our musicians, teaching by example; for our public (and there is no better public in the world for music of the highest character than that which fills the Music Hall at all good Symphony Concerts), to show us that, with all our pride in our own orchestra, we are yet very far this side of perfection, and must take a lesson from what is better done elsewhere. . . . We have an audience that deserves the best; we have at last a quickening example of what, in point of execution at least, comes very near the best thus far; it will be our own fault if we do not improve the lesson, and take a new start in orchestral music, finding it impossible now to shut out of sight the new and higher standard which has so vividly impressed itself on every mind.

But we are anticipating; we must report, and briefly try to weigh and estimate. In candor, what we have to set down as the "net result" artistically of the Thomas concerts, is not all in praise; and we anticipate a little further, just enough to give it as our calm and clear conviction, that, while his Orchestra play vastly better than our own, still ours remain the better Concerts. Does this seem paradoxical? Let us see. Here are the three programmes, which we quote together, that we may discuss the several elements in groups of like with like:

(Friday Evening, Oct. 29)

Overture, "Tannhäuser"	Wagner.
Adagio, "Prometheus"	Beethoven.
L'Invitation a la Danse	Weber.
(Instrumentation by Hector Berlioz)	
Symphonic Poem, Preludes	Liszt.

Overture, "William Tell"	Rossini.
Träumerei	Schumann.

Waltz. "On the beautiful blue Danube" .... Strauss.
Solo for Trombone. "The Tear" .... Stigelli.
    Mr. F. Leetsch.
Polka Mazurka. "Lob der Frauen" ....⎫
Polka Schnell. "Jocus" .... ⎬ Strauss.
Fackeltanz, in B, No. 1 .... ⎭Meyerbeer.

(Saturday Evening)

Suite No. 3, in D .... Bach.
Introduction to Act III of Medea .... Cherubini.
Concerto for Piano, G minor .... Mendelssohn.
    Mr. C. Petersilea.
Overture. "Leonora" No. 3 .... Beethoven.

——————

Fackeltanz, No. 3. C minor .... Meyerbeer.
Nachtgesang .... Vogt.
Waltz. "Wiener Bonbons" .... Strauss.
Grand March for Piano. "Puritani" .... Liszt.
    Mr. C. Petersilea.
Reverie .... Vieuxtemps.
Polka Mazurka. "Libelle" ....⎫
Polka Francaise. "Kreuzfidel" .... ⎬ Strauss.

(Sunday Evening)

Symphony No. 7. A .... Beethoven.
Trio for Two Horns and Trombone .... Bergmann.
    Messrs. Schmitz, Lotze and Leetsch.
Cosatachogue, Fantasie sur une danse
    Cosaque .... Dargomijsky.

——————

Overture. "Rienzi" .... Wagner.
Träumerei .... Schumann.
Ballet. "Faust" (New) .... Gounod.
    Composed expressly for the performances
    at the Imperial Grand Opera, Paris.
Fantasie. "Ave Maria" .... Schubert.
March. "Mazeppa" .... Liszt.

Plainly, in all this, the object was to show what a modern orchestra can do, and how well this particular orchestra can do it, rather than to convey any poetic unity of impression; to startle and delight for the moment, rather than to lift into a pure, ideal atmosphere. . . . First, we note, as the most prominent ingredient, those loud and ponderous *effect* pieces of the Liszt, Wagner, Meyerbeer school. Think of the *Tannhäuser* Overture, the Lisztian "Preludes," the "Tell" Overture (which, by itself considered, of course, is good), and the flaring, blazing, crashing *Fackeltanz* (midnight orgies by torchlight) of Meyerbeer, all in one concert! The *Tannhäuser* led off, as if to smite with the first blow, that easy victory might follow. Never did we hear it so well played (unless at the Opera in Vienna); never did we enjoy the work so little. It was Wagner exposed; robbed of his glamour, if he ever had any, by setting him in so strong a light, so mercilessly truthful. But whatever it did for Wagner, the orchestra itself showed, in its own strong light, to excellent advantage. The band was all alive in the first place, vital at every point; every instrument told; every part in the Quartet was substantial, unmistakable (nowhere did the superiority of this orchestra to our own assert itself so clearly as in the middle strings, where Boston has been always weak). The fine precision and pungent quality of the violins; the warmth and richness of those five 'cellos, massed in the front, and moving with one soul; the five double basses too; the excellence of all the brass; Ella's delicious oboe; indeed everything, to tympani and tambourine, won in turn its special share of admiration. Only in bassoons and clarinet have we as good to show. Choice materials admirably blended! In the matter of *tempo*, however, there was some room for criticism; the solemn, slow part of the overture was uncomfortably slow. There was some dragging also in *Les Preludes*, which, finely executed as it was, so beautifully on the part of the strings, and with all the coloring of which Liszt is a master made so palpable, still failed to give us the impression of great music.

The "Tell" overture was played superbly; we will only specify the rare perfection of the opening passage by the 'cellos, the singularly rich tone, and searching, true expression of the leading one (Bergner) particularly; and the fine oboe again, so rich in the lower tones here commonly given by the English Horn. The trumpets, first and second, told triumphantly in this; but more so in the two *Fackeltanz*, where they have such florid *obligato* passages. There were interesting novelties to hear, full of ingenious effects and startling or pleasing fancies, yet properly belonging to the category of musical extravaganzas. Most extravagant, fantastical, grotesque of all was the Cossack dance on Sunday evening; a herd of buffaloes could not have burst in more tumultously than it did; no doubt there is plenty of the Cossack character in it. Wagner's *Rienzi* is unmitigated noise; riot set to music, one would think, and in strains coarse and commonplace.

But this served the purpose (as did one of the *fortissimo* pieces each time) of exhibiting by extremest contrast the opposite element which figured in these programmes. We mean the delicate transcription for all the strings of little piano-forte pieces like Schumann's *"Träumerei"* (Reverie) and the *"Nachtgesang"* by Vogt, which were of course so popular, that no programme could be accepted as complete without them both. The effect of such Quartet rendering (they do whole Quartets so in Paris) was indeed most beautiful; the rich full tone and perfect harmony of so many strings, the light and shade, the refining of expression and of *pianissimo* to a point where it seemed more dream than reality,—all this caused a new and exquisite sensation, which everybody wished to have repeated and prolonged. But after all, this is *effect* music, and lacks artistic justification, does not properly belong in an artistic programme. For this is not interpretation; it is simply a *Study of Pianissimo*, using for a text a simple little piano-forte piece from Schumann's *"Kinderscenen"* (Scenes from Childhood), a piece never intended to be played with such exaggeration of expression. Admirable studies these for any orchestra; but we would no more put them into a Symphony or Philharmonic programme than we would the *"Etudes de Velocité,"* in a young lady's lesson book.

The refining influence of such practice, however, appeared in all the classical interpretations of this admirable orchestra. As such we recall the beautiful Adagio, with harp, from Beethoven's "Prometheus" ballet; the *Suite* by Bach (which is down for one of our own Symphony Concerts), and the very grand and tragical introduction from *Medea*, really *great* music, which, much simpler as it is, affects the imagination almost as powerfully as the introduction to the prison scene in *Fidelio*. These were wonderfully well done, especially the *Suite*, which was applauded with a heartiness that proved there is something in Bach that appeals to general sympathy, let him once be properly presented. We thank Mr. Thomas for these choice additions to our stock of high orchestral music.

In the familiar classical selections—Seventh Symphony, *Leonora* and *Freyschütz* Overtures, Mendelssohn Concerto,—and we may add the Berlioz arrangement of Weber's "Invitation"—there was the same masterly precision in the strings, the same certainty, truth of intonation, well blended coloring, on the part of the wind band also. The rendering of the Symphony, however, was not on the whole so much superior to some of the best by our own orchestra; indeed the difference between the two was less apparent here than in most of the pieces. Yet the temper and true habit of these men tell of course in everything they do; and we must bear witness to the wonderful *staccato* of the violins in the mysterious whispered passage near the end of the slow movement; to the perfect precision of all the instruments in the Scherzo (in spite of its being taken too fast), and the superb *brio* of the finale. . . .

In a word, then, we rejoice in the coming of this orchestra. It is just the kind of thing that we for years have longed for in view of our own progress here. We sincerely thank Mr. Thomas, first, for giving us a hearing, under the best advantages, of a number of works which were new to us; some of which can hardly claim a place in a classical programme, and therefore we are the more obliged to one who gratifies our curiosity about them in another way. But more we thank him for setting palpably before us a higher ideal of orchestral execution. We shall demand better of our own in future; they will demand it of themselves; they cannot witness this example without a newly kindled desire, followed by an effort to do likewise. With the impression fresh in every mind of performances which, it is not rash to say, may (for the number of instruments) compare with those of the best orchestras in Europe, improvement is necessity.

Dwight's Journal of Music, December 14, 1872

Theodore Thomas's Concerts

Boston is glad where her turn comes to be revisited by this distinguished leader and his admirable orchestra. That it is the most perfect orchestra on this side of the Atlantic, in all respects except in numbers, is clear enough, and has been clear for several years,—indeed from the time that it began its annual circuits through the music-loving towns and cities East and West. . . .

The problem so conspicuously solved by Mr. Thomas is naturally a somewhat different one from that presented to a local organization,—say our own Symphony Concerts. With him it is to keep complete, and in prime working order at all times, a thoroughly assimilated, perfect band, equipped and ready for all instrumental tasks, omnipresent like a battery of flying artillery, and nowhere suffering the novelty to wear off; in a word to have always in training, and to carry everywhere a shining specimen of what we may call *orchestral virtuosity*. For any local organization (i.e. in this country) this, even if it were possible, as it is by no means, is not the problem, not the chief end sought. Here the point is to build up something permanent, out of our own resources, which shall be as independent as possible of outward influences, competitions, fashions, just to make sure of hearing every season at fair intervals, some programmes of the best standard instrumental music; so that Haydn, Mozart, Beethoven, Schubert, Schumann, &c., may never go too long without a hearing; to have them presented in fit combinations and in a true artistic spirit, and as to execution, why as near to the ideal as local circumstances will permit; but these can never be entirely favorable, because an orchestra made up for ten or a dozen concerts in a winter can never hope to rival an orchestra which is *always* an orchestra, whose members live by that and nothing else. Both problems are legitimate; society would be the loser if either were neglected. We need the permanent supplies at home, unfailing fountains springing in our midst; we need also the fresh surprise and stimulus of brilliant visitations from without. But the first need is vital, indispensable; as much more important than the other as is the home life more important than the fickle, changeable outside society. It is suicidal for a musical community to cease to cherish, with something like religious zeal and constancy, its own musical institutions, in which its own best artistic aspirations are embodied, even for all the brilliant novelties which all the travelling artists in the world can bring one after another, in a perpetual round of brief distracting "seasons." But so long as we keep on building for ourselves,—loyal to the true ideal of our own Orchestra, our own Oratorio Society, (would we might say, too, our own Opera!), in spite of all the drawbacks and short-comings of each given moment, so long are we in a condition rightly to profit by the bright examples and the extra holidays which men like Thomas bring to us. We think that his performances have had a quickening influence on our own Orchestra from year to year; and we shall think his mission wasted on us, if it do not help us in the long run to establish ourselves musically upon our own foundation, which shall be self-centered and enduring; so established, we can afford better to be hospitable. . . .

They came with full ranks, armor furbished bright, in perfect training, fresh and full of ardor. That is to say, the orchestra was better than ever,—if that were possible,—which we are inclined to doubt, even in spite of our own last impression. Most of the excellent members of past years were gladly recognized again, with several new and valuable accessions to their ranks. The number, of violins at least, was somewhat increased,—to 10 first violins, as in the Harvard,—the 'cellos and basses being fewer;—but the extra instruments (harp, piccolo, bass tuba, triangle, &c.) required by the new music, swelling the muster roll considerably. The very first sound was electrifying; such pure and brilliant intonation, such perfect ensemble of tone color; such sure attack and vital unity in the violins, all bowed alike. And then as the work progressed one felt the charm and individuality of each several instrument, and admired the habit or the instinct that they had of keeping themslves subordinate to the general harmonious effect. Such a crystal clear, true ring to all the brass, too! Such precision, faultless phrasing, light and shade,— in short all that pertains to perfect execution:—why need we name these qualities again, all of which have always been accredited to the Thomas orchestra, and which may now again be predicated generally of the whole week's performances, without specifying in detail how well this or that particular piece was rendered.

And *ought* it not to be a model orchestra? It is the only orchestra in this country that can be said to have a chance. For in the first place Mr. Thomas has his pick of artists; he can offer them year-round engagements, with good, sure salaries, so that they can make this their sole and constant occupation, playing always in one orchestra, under the same superior Conductor, always "up" in all the music old and new of any high pretensions, and kept aloof from damaging association with tasks less artistic. With that power, what can not a man do, if he have it in him? Whereas, in any given city, so small as our's for instance, a musician plays once a fortnight in a Symphony concert (for a few months only), and all the rest of the time perhaps must earn his bread and butter in a street band, or a theatre, or by playing all night for balls and parties, to come back jaded and sleepless to the next rehearsal of a Symphony. For local Symphony and Philharmonic orchestras there can be no sure hold upon the best musicians, because these offer them no constant and supporting occupation, but only seek their services for six or ten concerts in a winter. Thus the travelling orchestra can not only be made up of first-class material, but in the nature of the case it keeps itself in perpetual rehearsal and in practice before critical publics every day almost in the whole year,—in the hot months giving delicious garden concerts at the Central Park,—a thing which we trust our "Puritanism" will feel the need of before many summers.—Besides, preparing for this endless round of concerts, they can afford to spend time and breath upon the trial of new works, can venture into the "Zukunft" as far as they like; and here again they gain a knowledge of the new effects of instrumentation, often brilliant or otherwise interesting, and in which Liszt and Berlioz and Wagner are masters, if in nothing else; all this keeps up their virtuosity, as difficult *etudes* do with the pianist, and makes all their tasks more sure and easy.—Now we do not say that, given these advantages, it does not need a man of mark to use them. Not every one, nor one in a thousand, probably, could wield them with the power and the intelligence and subtle faculty of Mr. Thomas. He is rarely gifted for the master spirit of an orchestra; in a singularly cool and quiet way he has his forces perfectly in hand. We only marvel sometimes at his taste. And this brings us to his programmes, of which we may now speak disembarrassed from all the necessity of further allusions to their admirable execution, except now and then a question of interpretation. . . .

12. *The Nilsson Concert Company*

After Jenny Lind, no visiting soprano made quite so brilliant an impression on American audiences as Christine Nilsson, who first appeared in New York and Boston in 1870, and returned often. (She was Marguerite in the *Faust* that opened the first season of the Metropolitan Opera in 1883.)

Nilsson was held to be the only serious rival of the reigning diva of the period: Adelina Patti, who in 1861 had begun a series of European triumphs that would postpone her return to the United States for more than twenty years. Both Nilsson and Patti were part of a constellation that included some of the best singers of the time—Euphrosyne Parepa Rosa, Carlotta Patti (Adelina's older sister), Therese Tietjens, Marietta Alboni, and Pauline Lucca. Their common link was the manager of their American appearances, Max Strakosch, who, with his older brother Maurice (Adelina Patti's brother-in-law) patched together a remarkable number of the opera troupes and concert companies performing in the United States. For Nilsson's first tour, Strakosch assembled a stellar concert party including the Belgian violinist Henri Vieuxtemps, the popular Italian tenor Pasquale Brignoli, and an American contralto just beginning to come into her own, Annie Louise Cary.

Dwight's Journal of Music, November 19, 1870

Christine Nilsson

And now we come to the "musical event" of the day,—to the arrival and the triumph of the far famed, the eagerly awaited, the already, for sometime at least, established Queen of hearts, if not of Song, even in this "cold critical Athens," as silly folk elsewhere are wont to call it,— to the beautiful and fair young Swede, CHRISTINA NILSSON.

First, a word about the Nilsson *Concerts*, as such, and the musical material and *personel* which Manager Max Strakosch has brought to us.

Our readers know our dislike, as a rule, for *Miscellaneous Concerts*, in which, without artistic unity, "attractions" are huddled together in wearisome profusion in one programme, while music itself is humbled to the condition of mere tiring maid or valet for the dressing out and exhibition of My Lady or My Lord, the singing or performing person. Our musical public, too, are getting to have right notions in this matter, and sincerely to prefer the pure artistic occasion, even without "stars," to any sort of medley with stars. What we had read, therefore, of Mr. Strakosch's programmes in New York, did not prepossess us with a very strong desire to hear them. How far can the radiance of "one bright particular star" go, the mere hearing of one however real and resistless singer under such conditions,—playing central figure in a crowded, clumsy frame,—to reconcile us to a *melange* of common-place things from Italian Operas, by a superfluity of stars of lesser magnitude; her own selections, even, being hacknied arias by Verdi or Donizetti, modern French things, a few well-worn ballads, and the like? We felt this objection to the first programme here in Boston. But after hearing we must own that, for concerts of this kind, they are on the whole pretty well made up, while the selection of artists is particularly rich and choice.

In the first place we must commend a certain thoroughness with which all is done; the mere fact of an orchestra in all the Concerts,—a rather small one to be sure, and rough and boisterous too often,— under the experienced conductorship of MARETZEK, to open the bill with popular overtures like "Zampa," "Martha," "Masaniello," "Tell," "Fra Diavolo," close it with Wedding March, or march from *Le Prophéte* (to which by the way, nobody listened,—one of the marks by which you know a virtuoso concert from an artistic one), as well as to accompany the solos. And here let us add this special praise; that every piece has been given with its full orchestral accompaniment where that existed, leaving only ballads and minor encore pieces to the pianist, Sig. BOSONI, who has shown himself a good accompanist.

What can we say enough in recognition of so rare and high an artistic presence, as that of HENRI VIEUXTEMPS, one of the world's really *great* violinists? A master, sound and ripe, in every sense of the word. Sure and perfect in whatever he undertakes. That he was when he first came here twenty-five years ago, when he had finer triumph with the few than Ole Bull had with the many; and again, thirteen years ago. But then we thought the very perfection of his playing a little dry and uninspired. Now he looks older, but plays younger, i.e. with more fire and out of a deeper feeling, than before. One could listen to his pure tones, his exquisite phrasing, and watch his graceful bowing all night long. His later compositions, too, display more character and power. That "Fantaisie Appassionata" is indeed a very impressive work, dramatic, and full of interesting ideas, which he always knows how to work up like an artist, for the orchestra as well. Almost as much may be said of the "Andante and Rondo," not to mention more familiar pieces. The *Romanza*, with piano, for an encore piece, is full of true and tender feeling; while, in the frolic vein, his fantasy on "St. Patrick's Day," is full of the comic humor, and completely Irish. Nightly the veteran is recalled. What greater compliment could he have had, what better proof of an appreciative public, than on that first night, when, after the Overture, and the Duet by the two men, the vast crowd, all impatient for the Nilsson, not only listened with delight to his long and clever fantasia on Gounod's *Faust*, some twenty minutes, but even then insisted on his playing something more!

Miss ANNIE CARY, the Yankee girl, who left us four years since with the large, rich contralto voice, comes back an artist,—a genuine, good, honest singer, not perhaps of the inspired kind, but still a singer whom it is a joy to hear. And she is handsome, hearty, natural as ever; evidently well-taught, with none of the modern vocal affectations. She has proved her quality in a pretty wide range, having sung from *Semiramide*, the page's song in the *Huguenots*, *Ah! mon fils*, ballads, duets, &c. . . .

And now for the central figure. It was indeed a privilege not to be called upon for an opinion after the first night. Nor are we eager even now after six concerts, to risk the declaration of a full opinion. . . . Her individuality, so Northern in its type, yet so unique, peculiarly her own, is the great secret of her charm. It took time and acquaintance to perceive this; it will take we know not how much more to read it fully. Of most *prime donne* one knows all in a short time; you can still hear with pleasure, but you expect nothing new. In this young Swede you always are prepared for something new. It is a new kind of a nature, a fresh revelation of the genus and the genius human. It charms you at the very first, but perhaps also disappoints you. We, for one, went home from the first concert somewhat puzzled, also somehow strangely spell-bound. Next to the grace and beauty of the apparition, the sweet winning smile, and frank cordial manner, your attention is caught by strange little ways and actions, seemingly wilful and coquettish, with which she keeps you waiting for her song. Then she begins: the well-known Aria from Handel's *Theodora*: "Angels ever bright and fair." We thought she sang this, or at least began it, under some constraint, as if not quite at home with a new audience. We thought too that her singing of it seemed a little over-studied, as if she would make too much of the simple, noble melody. But there was no denying the sincere pathos of expression. It had a virginal, religious purity. One might doubt for a while whether so much delicacy of *sotto voce*, so much prolonging of a tone in *pianissimo*, were not conscious arts rather than real feeling, and whether all those tears stole into the voice unbidden; but we soon were too glad to dismiss such whispers from our mind.

The voice, as we felt partly then, as we know better now, is one of exceeding purity and beauty, not so uniformly large and great as some, but sympathetic and transparent, as it were, to such a degree that it hides itself in the expression of the song, and so eludes you as a palpable substance by itself. Her own nature, too, is so sympathetic, so dramatic in the true sense, so full of genius, that she transforms herself into her song, whatever it may be, the instant she begins to sing: and so she instantly arrests the full attention of her audience and holds it to the end. In the florid scena from *Lucia* she showed how her voice could revel in all the intricacies of such Italian bravura, and in the Cavatina from *La Traviata* she carried her audience away completely. For encores she gave a quaint old Swedish (Dalecarlian) dance tune, worked up into a witching little "Ball" scene, of changeful humor; and the homely "Minstrel" ballad of "Old Folks at Home," twice over, for the simple pathos of this was quite irresistible. Ballads by most singers make us squirm, but this was beautiful, one of Art's transfigurations. Yet has it not been given quite as many times as it will bear?

The triumph, with the many, was complete. And for the secret of it? Beauty of person, beauty of voice, the Northern nature, the rare individuality, the spell of genius still reserving far more than it shows. The voice is Northern, like herself; white (so to say) and colorless, till some emotion color it. A voice from the mountains, pure and spiritual; not sensuous and full of Southern warmth and color, as a permanent condition, but quickly flushed with color, in the play of feelings, like her own lustrous pale complexion. The harmony between her nature and her voice are perfect; voice and look and smile are one, so that you can scarce separate them; in tender, graceful passages the voice itself smiles. Moreover, she is something of a witch, an airy, tricksy Northern sprite, a sort of being one might love, admire, and yet feel a certain fear of, as of a mermaid. Even that first night one carried away the impression that there was something wierd and *eerie*, something a little preterhuman about it; the imaginative brain of the young peasant girl, who sang her songs and played her violin at village fairs, was surely cradled amid Northern Lights. There is always something unexpected to come from her. Yet how womanly, how truly human! This Undine *has* a soul. . . .

13. *Rubinstein and Wieniawski*

The nonpareil concert party of the period, perhaps of the century, was led by the Russian pianist Anton Rubinstein, whose playing moved and astonished audiences in every part of the country as he performed more than two hundred times in the single season of 1872–1873. Sharing the programs with Rubinstein was the Polish violinist Henri Wieniawski; and because American audiences were not fond of purely instrumental concerts, manager Maurice Grau brought in a soprano and a contralto.

The troupe gave five concerts in Boston early in the tour, two of them with orchestra. The conductor was Carl Bergmann, who had been conductor of the old Germania Orchestra and now led the Philharmonic Society of New York.

Dwight's Journal of Music, October 19, 1872

The Rubinstein Concerts

The first concert in our Music Hall by Mr. Grau's remarkable troupe,—presenting as it did for the first time two of the greatest artistic celebrities of Europe, ANTON RUBINSTEIN and HERR WIENIAWSKI, with a good orchestra under CARL BERGMANN's masterly direction, and a programme most exceptionally choice and rich for a travelling concert party,—of course excited eager interest in the most musical portion of our population, and was largely attended, though there was by no means a crowd.

After the performance of an Overture, which, after successive announcements of that to *Oberon* and that to the *Wasserträger*, turned out to be that to *Egmont* (either of them good enough), and in the rendering of which the small but select orchestra seemed hardly as yet warmed up to its work, the wierd, barbaric looking master and magician of the piano-forte, with his immense mass of hair and awkward movement, without a smile, or any sign of consciousness apparently of aught beside the single purpose of his music, and with a look upon his face as of one eaten up by the intensity of a life long absorption in his art, as if all the expression had struck inward, and what you saw was but the lifeless simulacrum of the man, approached his instrument, courteous to his audience if not gracious, amid applause which was but the forerunner of the outbursts that were to follow. The piece selected for his debut was the same as in New York and in many of his European concerts, his own fourth Concerto, in D minor. In considering the impression, composition and performance can not well be separated, for he is eminently a composer-virtuoso. We shall not undertake to judge or even to describe such a composition after a single hearing. It certainly did interest us greatly, hardly suffering attention to flag once or twice from the beginning to the end. . . . Passages most delicate and tender alternated with passionate crescendos waxing to stormy climaxes which made you listen with a sort of awe, wondering what might come next. Beauty, mystery and passion by turns predominated. The orchestration too was strangely beautiful, abounding in fresh and delicate traits. As for the principal interpreter of his own work, everything under the head of execution or *technique* must be conceded in the fullest perfection as a matter of course. The instrument has no difficulties for him; the mechanical is absolutely mastered and need not be considered, not standing for a moment in the way of that which it is meant to serve, the expression of musical thoughts and feelings. His tremendous force is not more remarkable than his exquisite gentleness and fineness; he *strikes* like the lightning (looking like a thunder-cloud), and he sings with the most sweet, insinuating syren melody. (Nor does he seem to know anything of you, or of the place, the audience, while he does it.) . . . In HENRI WIENIAWSKI we were listening to one of the world's *greatest* violinists. To hear Mendelssohn's perfect Concerto in E minor played by such a master was a delight without alloy, unless it came from circumstances not intrinsic to the musical experience as such; nor indeed can we compare it with anything in our memory, unless it be Joachim's playing of the Beethoven Concerto or of Bach's *Chaconne*, &c. We did not understand why Wieniawski was announced as "the only rival to the memory of Paganini," or why he should be placed in such a category. The art which he revealed to us on Monday evening is something of a far nobler, purer character than we have ever associated with the Italian "Wizard of the G string," whose gift was so sensational and so contagious, bewitching younger aspirants into a questionable devotion to the mere tricks of the violin. But here we had classical violin playing in its purity, applied to one of the worthiest and most arduous tasks. Often as we have heard that Concerto played well, we never realized the half of its full beauty until now. Such large, full tone, such infallible truth of intonation, such perfect ease and finish in all points of execution, such breadth and fair consistency of style, and such fine feeling and pervading poetry, instinct with the inmost spirit of the composition, assimilating all the grosser elements that have to enter into its outward embodiment, so that it seemed just to breathe itself upon the air, were proof enough of the consummate artist. In the second part he played a couple of his own compositions: the first a "Legend," full of poetry and a fine fairy atmosphere, which the mysterious mingling of bassoon and brass tones at the beginning, and indeed the orchestral accompaniment throughout, brought home to the imagination. Some of the purest, tenderest expression we have ever heard from strings or human voice, occurred in passages of that performance. It was followed by a fantasia upon Russian Airs, very brilliant and full of virtuosity, but never offensive to good taste. . . .

The programme of the second concert, Tuesday evening, was as follows:

Overture, "Don Juan"	Mozart.
Orchestra.	
Concerto in G, (with Cadenzas by Rubinstein) . . .	Beethoven.
Anton Rubinstein.	
Recitative and Aria. "Giunse alfin," "Deh vieni	Mozart.
non tardar,"	
Mlle. Louise Liebhart.	
Fantaisie, "Faust"	Wieniawski.
Henri Wieniawski.	
Carnaval	Schumann.

(Introduction—Pierrot—Harlequin—
Waltz-Noble—Florestan—Eusebius—Co-
quette—Reply—Sphinx—Butterflies—Dancing Letters—Chiarina—Chopin—Estrella—
Gratitude—Pantaloon and Columbine—German Waltz—Paganini—Avowal—Promenade—Intermission—March of the Davidites
against the Philistines.)
Anton Rubinstein.

Aria, "Il Giuramento"	Mercadante.
Mlle. Louise Ormeny.	
Andante, et "Carnaval de Venise"	Paganini.
Henry Wieniawski.	
a. Nocturne	Field.
b. Erl King (Schubert)	Liszt.
c. March, "Midsummer Night's Dream"	Mendelssohn.
Anton Rubinstein.	

Beethoven's G major Concerto, the loveliest of the tribe, and made familiar here by so many excellent renderings, was the piece of all others in which a Boston musical audience could fairly appreciate this wonderful pianist's power as an interpreter. It was indeed a masterly performance, showing a poetic, sympathetic insight into all the meaning of one of the most poetic compositions ever written even by a Beethoven, and such a faculty of bringing it all out in tones so pure, phrasing so perfect, accent so fine and true, rhythm so self-sustained, that there seemed to be no intervention of keys or fingers, or even of an individual playing; it was not an interpretation, (as we heard it well said), it was the music itself. . . .

Dwight's Journal of Music, November 2, 1872

Rubinstein and Wieniawski

The last three of the five concerts of that most exciting musical week (Oct. 14th to 19th) differed from the first two in being without Orchestra. No more full Concertos, therefore, either for pianoforte or for violin. In fact concerts of (mostly classical) *chamber* music given in

the great Hall of Symphony and Oratorio! And herein we note one of
the wonders of Rubinstein's phenomenal and sovereign power as a pianist: He could make the finest and the deepest music ever written for the
instrument—works by Beethoven, Schumann, Chopin—clearly heard,
felt, appreciated throughout that great hall! Never in the selectest circle of
a chamber concert have we perceived a more complete, absorbed attention than was given by that whole audience, not only to the grandiose
and fiery A flat Polonaise of Chopin, but quite as much to the "Moonlight Sonata," and (most remarkable of all, unparalleled in our experience of audiences) to one of the most profoundly spiritual and subtly
intellectual among Beethoven's Sonatas, the last of all, op. 111. . . .

Of Friday evening's concert the two great features were the exquisitely perfect rendering by the two men of the "Kreutzer Sonata,"
which seemed to unfold a new wealth of meaning and of beauty, and
Rubinstein's playing of the whole series of Schumann's *Kreisleriana*,
which, enigmatical as much of the music is to many, yet must have had a
strange charm for all. One wants to hear all these things when such an
artist comes along for once with all the power to show us what they are,
and we cannot be too grateful to this Russian man of genius, possessing
all the means and all the will, for bringing forth so freely for us out of
stores sealed to most of us. Already, of Schumann alone, the *Etudes Sym-
phoniques*, the *Carnival*, the *Kreisleriana*! . . . .

The enthusiasm reached a second climax in the final Matinee on
Saturday (19th), when the following programme was performed:

Sonata	Anton Rubinstein.
Anton Rubinstein and Henri	
Wieniawski.	
Hungarian Song, "Esa Villag."	
Mlle. Louise Ormeny.	
Chaconne, for the Violin	Bach.
Henri Wieniawski.	
"Vedrai Carino"	Mozart.
Mlle. Louise Liebhart.	
a. Nocturne	
b. Mazurka }	Chopin.
c. Polonaise, in A Flat	
Anton Rubinstein.	

{ "Robin Adair."
{ "Ruck Ruck."
    Mlle. Louise Leibhart.

Sonata, Opus 111 .... Beethoven.
    Anton Rubinstein.

"La Falletta" .... Marchesi.
    Mlle. Louise Ormeny.

{ a. Romanza in F .... Beethoven.
{ b. Airs Russes .... Wieniawski.
    Henri Wieniawski.

      { Sarabande—Passe-Pied
Suite { Courante-Gavotte .... Rubinstein.
      Anton Rubinstein.

The two memorable features of this concert were the great *Chaconne* of Bach, played, as originally written, without accompaniment, (for indeed it contains all in itself), and with by far more power and breadth, more fullness and more fineness of interpretation, than we ever heard it before by any one except Joachim (that was a dozen years ago, so that we will not venture on comparison; and it was not in the big Music Hall, but in a hotel chamber before an audience of one!); and that last of the wonderful series of Beethoven's Sonatas, in C minor, so deep and almost mystical in meaning, with its fitful and impassioned introduction and Allegro, and all the rest consisting in the marvellously subtle, seemingly exhaustless variation of that singing Adagio (*Arietta molto semplice Cantabile*, in dotted eighths, *nine-sixteen measure*). For the first time we felt that we had truly *heard* it. As we have said before, the whole great audience heard it, listened oblivious of all else, whether they understood it all or not. In this sense the achievement was almost unprecedented in a concert room. More than that, we know not when a piece of music has moved us so deeply. There was something holy in the tones which he brought out; sometimes they seemed to answer from another world, like a transfiguration of the theme or phrase once struck. Let us not despair now of any real inspiration from however deep a source, however complex and thick-set with difficulties in its development,—of any utmost reach of any Bach's or Beethoven's imagination and profoundest science, being communicable to any real music-lover. It strikes us, men like Rubinstein are sent into the world to show us that all this is possible, and prove to us, through our own feeling,—cords set thrilling in a deeper deep within us than we had before suspected,—that the last Sonatas of Beethoven are not the helpless wanderings of a brain diseased, but are divinely beautiful and full of meaning worth the searching for. . . .

The visit of these two great artists is an event in the musical history of Boston. Nothing that may occur this season, or perhaps in several seasons, will eclipse it. Our public has been electrified, and deeply moved. The power of genius, personally manifested, has been realized as not before. We have had more insight into the possibilities of music and acquired a new respect for its accomplishments. And the return of RUBINSTEIN and WIENIAWSKI,—we understand that we may look for them at Christmas time—will be hailed with genuine enthusiasm; for the more *such* artists are heard, and in such music as such artists choose, the stronger is the desire to hear them.

14. *Hans von Bülow*

Pupil and son-in-law of Liszt, intimate of Wagner (who rewarded his friendship by stealing his wife), Hans von Bülow was equally celebrated in Europe as conductor and pianist. He was perhaps the first of the modern virtuoso conductors, and both on the podium and at the piano he was one of the earliest to perform without a musical score.

Von Bülow elected to make his American debut in Boston, where John S. Dwight so welcomed his authoritative interpretations of Bach, Beethoven, and Chopin that he forgave von Bülow his identification with Liszt, Wagner, and "the Music of the Future." Dwight even managed to tolerate the "ultra-modern" music of a "young professor at the Conservatory at Moscow": Peter Tchaikovsky's Piano Concerto No. 1 in B-flat Minor, of which von Bülow's Boston performances were the first anywhere.

Dwight's Journal of Music, October 30, 1875

Hans von Buelow

Five of the seven concerts in which this great artist was to commence his American career, in our Boston Music Hall, are already, at this present writing, memories of the past; and they will not soon be forgotten. Friday evening and Saturday afternoon of this week will have completed the series. They have been rich and rare experiences; nor can any promise of the coming season be expected to surpass or hardly rival them in interest. They have been admirably managed; the programmes have put the noblest compositions of great masters foremost, if they have dealt also largely with the wild sensational productions of the modern school, which at any rate please curiosity by showing to what marvellous perfection the finger virtuosity is carried. There has been an orchestra, a small one to be sure, with the best conductor in America at its head during the first week, which besides accompanying the Concertos has played some of the very best of Overtures. And Doctor von Buelow has had instruments to play upon, expressly made for him by the Messrs. Chickering, which we believe all who have heard them will agree with us surpass anything we have ever heard anywhere in power, rich sonority, sweetness, evenness of tone and action, and which indeed have proved adequate to all requirements of such a master in such music and (strange to say) in such a Hall. For, what with the master's wonderful distinctness of touch and rare power of bringing out tone to the best advantage, and what with such an instrument to respond, everything was heard, felt and appreciated in that vast space as if it had been in a parlor, and the real wonder was that no one thought of it as wonderful.

Under these circumstances the great pianist was sure to make his full and fair impression. And sureness, certainty, is to be set down as one of the chief elements of his peculiar power. He never fails; it seems impossible for him to fail. Whatever he undertakes, he is absolutely master of it all. It does *not* (commonly at least) master him, and therein talent has its compensating advantage over genius, which has finer moments, inspirations, but is seldom sure of them.—But let us take the history in order.

1st Concert, Monday Evening, Oct. 18

Overture—Leonora. No. 3 .... Beethoven
    (Orchestra)
The Fifth Grand Concerto (Opus 73), in E Flat ..... Beethoven
    Allegro—Adagio un poco mosso—Rondo
    (Piano and Orchestra)
    HANS VON BUELOW.
Overture—Oberon .... Weber
Andante—Fifth Symphony .... Beethoven
Soli—
    (a) Nocturne .... (Opus 37), No. 2 in G
    (b) Chant Polonaise ..... (Transcription by Liszt)
    (c) Berceuse .... (Opus 57)
    (d) Valse .... (Opus 42)
                         .... Chopin
Fantaisie Hongroise—Piano and Orchestra .... Liszt
    Dedicated to HANS VON BUELOW.

Priests' March—Athalia .... Mendelssohn

No finer audience, and few larger, ever greeted any artist in that Hall. The stately programme also lent assurance. It spoke well for the interpreter, and showed an honorable desire to meet the best taste and culture of our city on its own ground, that he chose the greatest, purest music for the first manifestation of his powers, and that he saw fit to make the greatest of Overtures the prelude to the greatest of Concertos, with the most imaginative of the romantic Overtures to follow it; and again a heavenly Andante of Beethoven before his Chopin solos. It challenged recognition on high grounds when he stepped forward thus between solid pillars of the immortal temple of the divine Art. The *Fantaisie Hongroise* could at least be accepted as a pardonable letting off of fireworks when enthusiasm was at its height and sober senses getting weary; and the March from *Athalie* was certainly a good "playing out" piece, rounding the whole off classically,—ideally fit, if practically superfluous. Of all this the small orchestra, under CARL BERGMANN's baton, gave a fair outline, although, to be sure, four first violins were rather thin and feeble for the great crescendo of the "Leonora" No. 3.

Had we time to go minutely and analytically into the whole rendering of that inexhaustibly rich and glorious Concerto, it would be saying all that need be said of Doctor von Bülow's art. In conception, execution and expression, taken all together, it was in a higher degree than we have ever known before true to the whole scope and meaning of the work; while at the same time it revealed a rare peculiar faculty of his, as much a matter of the brain as of the practiced fingers, of reaching everybody. Many times as that work has been played in Boston, and well played, we doubt if it ever made its mark so signally upon a great audience. Before hearing anything more, that one performance established in us the very rare and comfortable assurance, that here was an artist on whom we could absolutely rely for a true and effective rendering of the composer's meaning for the first thing. There were no short-comings, no extravagancies; none of the wilful traits which shook one's confidence even in the midst of the electrifying moments of Rubinstein. And there was none of that sentimental trick of over-doing the *poco ritardando*, which young pianists, of the gentler sex especially, spoiled by flattering publics, are so apt to fall into. Here was the thoughtful, the self-centred master, interpreter and teacher, who *knew* what he was doing, and who only gave and did not take when hands were clapping.

Now as to all the component qualities of a consummate *technique*, as to the whole list of liquid runs, crisp staccatos, legatos, arpeggios, &c., &c., let us take it all for granted; in such an artist *cela va sans dire*; the long enumeration has been reiterated about a thousand players, in a thousand musical reports and criticisms, clothed with whatever flourish of rhetorical cleverness, and, even if we had the patience to go through it all, who would have patience to read it? The long bill may be safely passed, as they say in legislatures, after mere reading of its title. Resolved, therefore, that Dr. Von Bülow's *technique* is simply perfect. But out of all this we must specify certain traits, his in a degree that we have never seen realized before, which, while they are technical, imply a fine intellectual, spiritual force behind. First, as perhaps the most marked trait in his playing, is the power of producing *tone*, full, free, expressive, graduated to every shade of power or color; every note is heard and has its weight. The *distinctness* of his rendering is a revelation,—distinctness without the least stiffness or break of continuity. This of course implies strength and freedom of touch, exquisite shading, and mastery of the rare art of *phrasing*. It implies also sympathy with his instrument (to which he leaned so fondly and kept himself so *near*, as if to establish an electric current,) as well as an instinctive feeling of the place which the sounds were to fill, and which they did fill so successfully, as we have said before, that few seem to have said or thought how wonderful it was:—and yet we have even heard complaints that the Music Hall was too large for the fair hearing of an orchestra! Where he astonished, startled, he did not break the spell of beauty. Proportion, measure, the *repose* of Art, pervaded all. Those wide hand-full chords, how throughout their whole breadth the tones all clung at once to the keyboard and to the ear, as if fixed instantaneously and simultaneously by Sun power. And chords, where not only both hands were full, but the whole space between,—how evenly and smoothly they moved on! (Here we are anticipating; we have in mind a passage in the Hungarian Fantaisie). In the Concerto the rapid running passage in octaves was remarkably even and subdued to beautiful expression.

Now all this is remarked essentially in all his playing; it is only the difference in the music, in the author. In every case he gives you the infallible true reading. We were hearing Beethoven, as afterwards Chopin, far more than we were hearing Bülow. And that perhaps is highest praise. At the same time on reflection we feel, as so many have felt, that he plays more from the head than from the heart. The effect produced *from him* is not precisely the inspiration of genius. Yet he knows his author and his whole repertoire (which he has all by heart) as well as he knows his instrument; and there is no denying that he plays all *con amore* (we could be pleased to notice some exceptions!); that he loves the music, or takes at all events a frank delight in it; his genial smile, and half conscious looking off towards the audience, show that he feels very happy in seeking out and bringing out all the tone and all the sense that lies in every note and phrase. . . .

We feel that we have about said our say, and pass to a brief record of the other concerts, merely mentioning by the way that the fourth (Saturday) was a repetition of the first programme and more than confirmed the first impression. Here is the programme of the

Second Concert, October 20

Overture—Wasserträger	Cherubini
Grand Concerto—(Opus 16) in F Minor . .	Adolphe von
Allegro Patetico—Larghetto—	Henselt
Allegro Agitato	
HANS VON BUELOW	
Overture—Der Freischütz	C. M. Von Weber
Soli—15 Variations (Opus 35) in E Flat	
—Fugue and Finale	Beethoven
On a theme from the "Sinfonia Eroica"	
Menuet—From Symphony No. 3	Mendelssohn
Polonaise Brillante—(Opus 73) in E	C. M. Von Weber
Instrumented for Piano and	
Orchestra by F. Liszt	

. . .

Third Concert, October 22

Overture—Les Abencerages	Cherubini
Fourth Grand Concerto—(Opus 58) in G	
Major	Beethoven

With Cadences composed by
Hans Von Bülow

Concert Overture	Julius Rietz
Soli—(a) Prelude and Fugue—For the Organ, in A-Minor	Bach
(b) Prelude and Fugue—(Opus 35) No. 1	Mendelssohn
(c) Prelude and Fugue—(Opus 72) De la Suite	J. Raff
Allegretto—From the Eighth Symphony ... (Orchestra)	Beethoven
First Grand Concerto—In E Flat	Liszt

. . .

Space fails us for more now: and we are not altogether sorry, for before speaking of the new Russian Concerto, which formed the chief feature of the fifth Concert, we would gladly hear it performed again, as it will be this (Saturday) afternoon.

Dwight's Journal of Music, November 13, 1875

. . . We resume our record where we left off, in the middle of the remarkable concerts of the masterly pianist, Dr. HANS VON BUELOW. The four already reviewed were followed by three more in the last week of October. That of Monday evening, Oct. 25, had this programme:

Overture—Jessonda .... (Orchestra)	Spohr
Grand Concerto—(Opus 23) in B Flat .... Andante maestoso (introduction) ed allegro con spirito—Andantino semplice— Allegro con fuoco	Tschaikowski
HANS VON BUELOW.	
Sonata—Quasi Fantasia (Moonlight Sonata), Opus 27, No. 2 in C sharp Minor	Beethoven
Overture—Prometheus .... (Orchestra)	Beethoven

Grand Fantaisie—(Opus 15) in C Major .... Schubert
   Arranged for Piano and Orchestra by F. Liszt
   Allegro con fuoco—Adagio con variazioni
     (The Wanderer)—Presto ed allegro finale.
    HANS VON BUELOW.
Wedding March .... Mendelssohn

The Overtures went smoothly under the baton of Mr. B. J. LANG, who had been called to succeed Mr. BERGMANN, and who, being himself a pianist and an enthusiastic admirer of Von Buelow, was in better sympathy and understanding with him for the rendering of the extremely difficult, strange, wild, ultra-modern Russian Concerto. It is the composition of a young professor at the Conservatory of Moscow, a pupil of Rubinstein (indeed the work contained not a few suggestions of the master), and is dedicated to Buelow, who complimented Boston with its very first performance. A compliment well meant, and warmly responded to by the applauding audience,—twice—for this programme was repeated for the seventh concert. It opens richly and the first Allegro is full of striking passages and brilliant, but sometimes bizarre, effects of instrumentation. One peculiarity is the frequent indulgence of the pianoforte in rhapsodical cadenza-like flights of startling execution while the orchestra waits as it were outside. This lends quite a bravura character to a movement which seemed also melodramatic rather than in the classical Concerto spirit. The second movement, opening with a gentle, pastoral commingling of reeds and flutes, seemed also of the theatre; you thought of strains by Gounod, by the author of *Mignon*, and of Meyerbeer's *Dinorah*. Yet there was a certain delicacy and flavor of originality and quaintness about it. In the finale we had the wild Cossack fire and impetus without stint;—extremely brilliant and exciting, but could we ever learn to love such music? How wonderfully Von Buelow rendered it, there is no need of telling; all that a hearty sympathy, a masterly conception and an infallible technique could do for it, it had in the fullest degree; and the young author well knew that his work could not suffer in such hands. . . .

15. *American Composers*

The Centennial Exposition at Philadelphia in 1876 gave spectacular evidence of a young nation's industrial achievement, but had little to show in the way of native music. A grand concert was considered the appropriate way to open the exposition, and Theodore Thomas was chosen as music director for the occasion; but though the program included music by John Knowles Paine (the "Centennial Hymn" to verses of Whittier) and Dudley Buck (a cantata, "Centennial Meditation of Columbia," with text by Sidney Lanier), top billing went to the thoroughly undeserving "Centennial March" manufactured for the event (and five thousand dollars) by no less a figure than Richard Wagner.

After the inaugural concert, music was relegated to the fringes of the exposition. There, a series of evening symphony concerts by the Thomas Orchestra failed to attract an audience, while crowds flocked to see the French master of *opéra bouffe*, Jacques Offenbach, conduct his own music in Offenbach Gardens, expressly fitted out for his visit.

Still, before the sheriff closed the doors on Thomas' series, the intrepid conductor managed to present what must have been the first all-American program ever offered by a symphony orchestra. It began with a work by William Henry Fry, which Thomas must have remembered playing as a member of Jullien's orchestra; then there was Paine's First Symphony and a piano concerto by Alfred H. Pease; Dudley Buck was represented on the bill by an overture and a Concertstück for four horns and orchestra; and to conclude, there were light pieces by Pease ("Japanese Galop") and by Myron A. Ward ("Allemania" waltzes)—passed over by Dwight's Philadelphia correspondent as they have been by posterity.

Dwight's Journal of Music, August 5, 1876

Music in Philadelphia
THOMAS CONCERTS.—AMERICAN MUSIC

Philadelphia. July 26.—Wednesday evening, July 19, Mr. Thomas devoted entirely to the works of American composers. Of course such a programme must be meagre, and there will be many to find fault with its omissions if nothing else gave reasons for fault finding. This is in the nature of such an undertaking. Several able American composers were not represented; but where all could not appear, the names of Fry and Paine were perhaps as appropriate as any, for Fry and Paine represent the two eras of American Music—the one when it whistled as it went for "want of thought," the other after the culture of half a generation had set up the American art intellect on something like a level with that of other nations. William H. Fry, our late esteemed townsman, had many fine qualities and much ability; but as a composer he was not great. At a time when the aesthetic condition of the whole country was a feeble copy of that in other countries, he produced *Leonora*, the first opera ever written by an American. Other compositions of his will be recalled, and it was a grateful tribute to a genial man that Mr. Thomas should have opened his American programme with the little symphony: "A Day in the Country." Twenty years ago Mr. Fry delivered a racy and interesting lecture on music in this city, before the last Harmonic Society. In the course of his remarks he said: "It is the little ship which gets over the bar; the big one sticks fast in the sand." I am bound to say that Mr. Fry got over the bar—got over a great many bars in fact—of very dry, uninteresting music. But as a contribution to a chronological programme the "Day in the Country," was interesting and deserved its place.

Prof. John K. Paine, of Harvard University, born in Portland, Maine, is the most scholarly of all American composers. He earned his reputation early and has retained it; but none of his somewhat numerous and occasionally ambitious productions is at all comparable to his Symphony in C minor. The conception and the whole treatment of this work show the brain and handiwork of a master. The themes are so agreeable, the instrumentation so rich, natural and unforced, the spirit of the whole composition so healthy, and its form so symmetrical that Mr. Paine's new symphony is unquestionably the best large orchestral work yet produced by any native composer. The first movement is calm and dignified, the strings being very busily engaged. The brass is but moderately employed, and the flutes and clarinets used with rare taste and judgment. There is a slight resemblance to Mendelssohn in the graceful appropriateness of his instrumentation, although not the slightest suggestion of Mendelssohn in the subjects. The Scherzo is admirable, and contains a "trio" which is the undoubted gem of the whole symphony. This introduces the longest solo, given out first by the clarinet, then by the oboes, then the first violins take it, which then recur to the Scherzo. This theme is simply exquisite. The Adagio opens at once with a beautiful motive for the violoncellos and is handled with consummate skill and feeling.—The fourth and last movement, "Allegro vivace," is less interesting than the others, but they of themselves secure for Mr. Paine's symphony a high position among musical creations; and I entirely agree with L. B. B., in your last issue that Mr. Paine's pen should have been employed to write the March for the opening of our Centennial, and strongly urge his suggestion to the Centennial Committee to close with his new symphony if no work for the occasion can be arranged for, or produced.

"The first Concerto in E-flat," by Mr. Alfred H. Pease, was given for the second time. Its first performance was at one of the Peabody concerts in Baltimore some months since, where its success was said to be quite marked. It is a work of a very high order of merit, very effective, and is finely instrumentated. Too many octave passages abound and he too frequently makes the piano merely the accompanist, while the orchestra carries the burden of nearly all the themes. Mr. Pease performed the piano part well; he is a good player, having a firm and even touch. The success of the concerto here was quite pronounced and Mr. Pease was recalled by a storm of applause, in which the entire orchestra joined, and was taken by the hand by Mr. Thomas and congratulated on his success.

Mr. J. N. Pattison, Mr. L. E. Levassor, Mr. Fred Boscovitz, Mr. Bialla, and Mr. Courlander give pianoforte recitals at the Exposition daily. Mr. Pattison's and Levassor's recitals are better attended than any of the others. . . .

The Brass Band competition advertised by the Centennial Commission to take place this month failed to come off. Only eight bands entered, and on the day of trial only two put in an appearance, who refused to play, so that there was no playing for a prize at all. Quite a number of Band Masters were present who gave various reasons for their Bands not competing; some said the conditions did not suit them; others that it was not soon enough; and again some said it was not late enough, etc.

16. *Apthorp on Wilhelmj*

With his American appearances in 1878, the thirty-three-year-old August Wilhelmj began a four-year-long tour that took him through North and South America and then to Asia and Australia before he returned to his native Germany. A close associate of Liszt and Wagner, Wilhelmj was concertmaster of the orchestra at Bayreuth when "Der Ring des Nibelungen" had its first performances in 1876. He founded an influential school of violin playing and possibly deserves better than to be remembered, as he is, only for his corruption of the air from Bach's Third Orchestral Suite, which he played as "Air on the G String."

For a review of Wilhelmj's Boston performances, Dwight turned to young (thirty) William F. Apthorp, then writing for the *Boston Sunday Courier*. Dwight was pleased to encourage Apthorp, pupil of John Knowles Paine and son of an old Boston family, who seemed bent on a career as music critic, a profession then virtually nonexistent in the United States. Besides Dwight himself, only the eccentric composer-journalist-lecturer William H. Fry might have qualified.

Apthorp got his real start as a critic in 1872 when William Dean Howells called him to New York to be music editor for the *Atlantic*. After four years there, Apthorp returned to Boston to write for the *Courier*, the *Traveller*, and finally the *Transcript*, where over a period of twenty-two years he established a permanent reputation. He left a legacy too as program annotator for the Boston Symphony Orchestra.

Even while writing for other papers, Apthorp frequently contributed thoughtful articles to *Dwight's Journal*. In this early review of Wilhelmj, he appears knowledgeable and fluent, with a pronounced kinship to Dwight in his musical standards. Clearly, a torch is being passed.

Dwight's Journal of Music, November 9, 1878

The Wilhelmj Concerts
(From the Boston Courier)

Herr August Wilhelmj has come, seen and conquered; his conquest of our public has been complete. Yet before entering upon the consideration of his in every way marvellous playing, may I be permitted to express my astonishment at one not unimportant point in the great artist's first appearance here?

It matters nothing whether Wilhelmj is the "greatest" living violinist or not; probably no man can fairly claim the title, and in this matter the opinions of the contemporary German press can have but little weight. The contending musical parties in Germany are as acrimoniously polemical as our own political parties. Joseph Joachim is known to be a close friend and ardent admirer of Johannes Brahms; August Wilhelmj is known to be an equally warm friend and enthusiastic admirer of Richard Wagner. In view of the intensely partisan spirit which reigns over German musical criticism, it is not difficult to tell to which of the two great violinists a Brahmsite paper would give the title of "greatest," nor upon which of them a Wagnerite sheet would confer the same mark of distinction. But, as I have said, the title has no value except to advertising agents and lion-hunters. To musicians it means nothing, and Herr Wilhelmj, for one, is certainly great enough to dispense with it.

Wilhelmj is undoubtedly a very great violinist (to take the element of comparison from an otherwise fitting superlative), and by this term we understand now-a-days something more than a great executant; we take it to mean a great artist.

Now with what does this great artist make his first bow before an audience whose musical qualifications he has no sound reason for despising? With a Beethoven concerto in D, a Mendelssohn or Mozart concerto, or even with Joachim's Hungarian concerto? with anything that can be fairly ranked as belonging to the highest class of violin music? No! It was with Paganini's concerto in D, a composition which may be considered a violin classic in a certain very restricted sense, but which has little to recommend it as music, saving its, by this time, rather time-tarnished brilliancy. This was followed by an arrangement of the air from Bach's D-major suite, made by Wilhelmj himself, and arranged in a way that, if it showed the violinist's eye for the effect to be drawn from fine cantabile playing on the G string, also showed the musician's utter disregard for the integrity of Bach's work, and what is equally bad, the most crass want of appreciation of its intrinsic beauties. Ernst's *Airs hongroises* and Wilhelmj's transcription of a Chopin Nocturne are excellent things of their kind—fascinating *hors d'oeuvres* when the main dish has been satisfying, but not things one would care to judge a great artist by.

Apart from all considerations of Herr Wilhelmj's relation to his audience, what opinion must we form of his relation to art and to the glorious list of really great compositions for his instrument, when he comes before us for the first time with such a meagre—one is tempted to say such a compromising—provision of music? He stands in the very foremost rank among modern violinists, and utterly forgetful of what is meant by *noblesse oblige*, he lowers himself at the outset to the level of a mere virtuoso. On subsequent evenings he has played some really noble music, but why did he not stand forth at once as the artist every one believes him to be, and not dash our expectations in the beginning by doing a—comparatively—low thing, only to be at the trouble of redeeming his character afterwards? This must be said to approach as nearly to the immoral as anything in the range of instrumental performance well can.

But now, to take Herr Wilhelmj as we have found him, and to put a truce to wishing for the thing that is not, his remarkable qualities as a violinist are apparent on the very surface. In the first place it may be safely said that such a violin tone has never been heard here, so full and round, of such commanding volume, yet without lacking that delicate, incisive quality, which is characteristic of the violin. It has all the warm glow of Vieuxtemps, the delicacy of Wieniawski, the mellow sweetness of Ole Bull—and added to these, it has a vigor and volume which are entirely its own. No violinist has yet visited us who had at his command such variety in *timbre*. In so far as quality of tone, *per se*, is concerned, Wilhelmj can fulfil the requirements of every class of violin music. Of his executive ability, his technique, it is needless to speak—call it absolute, and you have hit upon the right word, which in all cases is as good as a whole page. In considering the higher artistic attributes of the man, the most notable point in his playing is the rare balance he shows between an intense and eagerly passionate nature and that power of self-command which can only come from a naturally stout and well-cultured intellect. He has plenty and to spare of musical powder to burn, but he never wastes it. This is the point in which he is, upon the whole, the superior of his predecessors here; in the intense quality of his nature, and in his absolute command over it.

In some other qualities some of the great violinists we have heard in Boston can over-bid him. Of the almost feminine grace of Wieniawski, of that peculiar Gallic power of fascination which Vieuxtemps possessed to such an extraordinary degree, there seems to be little in him. Grace and winsomeness are not his striking qualities. But in virile force he far surpasses his rivals. No one whom we have heard here could play the ever glorious Bach *Chaconne* as he did. That is a crucial test of the artist's mettle. It takes the highest man to do the highest work. . . .

It is easy to see that whatever Wilhelmj takes hold of, he takes hold of in grim earnest. It is uncommon to see a man take everything so seriously as he does. Hence it comes that the greater the music he plays, the better he plays it. If he have a failing, it lies in a certain want of versatility of conception. His phenomenal tone and noble breadth of phrasing make every thing he does more than enjoyable, yet at times one could wish that the earnestness and breadth of style which find proper food in a Bach chaconne or a Mendelssohn Andante, did not invade the domain of music of a less serious, often of a frivolous character.

But Herr Wilhelmj unites more and higher qualities in himself than any violinist we have heard here before. He possesses that spark of genius which compels enthusiasm, and the intellectual power of making that enthusiasm lasting. His playing is on a very high plain, and if he sometimes plays music in many ways unworthy of himself, he does his best to raise it to his own high level, and to prevent its dragging him down. Of trickery, of mannerism even, there is not a trace in his playing; all is nobly straightforward and honest. Even those little mannerisms which might be called inherent in almost all violin-playing do not taint his style. In a word he is a great artist; and such a *rara avis* is a really great artist; that, in the eyes of a musician, is a higher title than the loud-sounding, but trite, "greatest living" anything. . . .

The other artists of the company call for little comment. * * * * * *

Yet what a setting for such a jewel as Wilhelmj! What more than miserable programmes! That such concerts, with such an august name heading the programme, are—I will not say tolerated, but—possible in our community, shows that something is radically wrong somewhere.

WILLIAM F. APTHORP.

Part Two

At the Opera

17. New York

In the quarter-century after Manuel Garcia introduced Italian opera to New York, no fewer than four new theaters there were given the aspiring title "Opera House." Their curtains were as likely to rise on vaudeville, magic shows, and minstrels as on any opera, and what opera they could offer was scarcely an approximation of what was being seen in European opera houses of the day. Unfortunately, New York could claim no singers to compare with those of Milan, London, Paris, St. Petersburg, or (more to the point) of Havana, where Don Francesco Marty's Italian Opera Company regularly imported stellar casts from the great stages on the far side of the Atlantic.

In 1847 Marty brought his company to perform at Castle Garden, and the New York audience was not happy to settle again for Max Maretzek's lackluster offerings at the Astor Place Opera House. A return visit by Marty's company in 1850 brought Maretzek close to ruin; but the next year, Maretzek cleverly captured a half-dozen of Marty's best singers for his own company—and triumphed.

The triumph, alas, was brief. When Maretzek tried to reassemble the troupe, internal disputes split it down the middle. Suddenly there were two Havana companies performing concurrently in New York, and cutting prices with disastrous financial consequences: Angiolina Bosio, Cesare Badiali, and Geremia Bettini appeared at Niblo's Garden, leaving Balbina Steffanone, Lorenzo Salvi, and Ignazio Marini to head Maretzek's casts at Astor Place.

For his first issue, Dwight had a review of both companies by a correspondent who would continue to write from New York under the nom de plume of Hafiz. He was George William Curtis, whose friendship with Dwight dated from Brook Farm days. In this first review, Curtis ventures beyond the Italian opera to comment on the performance of Anna Thillon, a popular English-born singer-actress in the French style, who was giving Auber's *opéra comique* "The Crown Diamonds" on the opera's off-nights at Niblo's.

Dwight's Journal of Music, April 10, 1852

(From our New York Correspondent)

Music in New York

The golden gates of the opera are closed—golden, that is, to all but the manager. The experiment of a democratic opera has been tried, and it has succeeded. At least on the democratic nights—when the price was fifty cents—the house was overfull. "It did not pay," the manager said. But when did managers ever say anything else?

After the quarrel in the early winter the three capital *B's* withdrew to Niblo's, and we had two admirable operas. SALVI, STEFFANONE and MARINI sang at the Astor Place; BADIALI, BOSIO and BETTINI at Niblo's. The latter troupe you have heard, and have doubtless made your own notes upon theirs. They filled their house nightly, here, and among the other operas, they sang *Don Giovanni*. The orchestra was inefficient, which is a fatal fault in an opera depending so much upon it, and the whole time was taken too fast, so that Ole Bull went one evening behind the scenes, exasperated, to protest against such murder of Mozart—nor was the opera well sung, except by Bosio. Her Zerlina is by far the best of her roles. Nature fits her for it. She is arch and of a winning charm in action. She has a sparkling beauty, with extreme feminineness of voice and manner, and she has the ladylikeness that lurks in the gay Spanish peasant and attracted the Don.

Badiali, as Don Giovanni, was wooden and cumbrous, and indulged in unpardonable liberties with the music. To bring down the house—for one can hardly suppose ignorance of the score—he concluded both *La ci darem* and the *Serenade* with the most commonplace Italian phrases—nor had he the slightest trace of the irresistible *gentleman*, which imagination demands in the character. Sanquirico's Leporello is broad buffoonery, sometimes pushed quite beyond patience.

But with every defect it was still pleasant to hear. Music so sweet and rare enchants the eye and the ear. The puppets move upon the stages, but the fair and stately figures of the music throng imagination with their magical and pensive play. As if the music expressed only the sad undertone of life, it flows seriously on, while all the bubbles of evanescent gayety in the plot, break and gleam along its surface. Thus where Leporello is discovered, what is more pathetic than the musical movement? or where before was a minuet made a love-tale teeming with passion?

They sang also [Donizetti's] *Maria di Rohan* at Niblo's. In this, Bosio was good, because there were no foregone conclusions about the character, as there are in *Lucrezia* and *Lucia*. The heroine is an injured and passionate Italian woman, and that Bosio could represent. But the imperial Lucrezia or the lyrical Lucia are too distinctively attired in imagination to admit any other than a certain style of figure. It is a great defect of the Italian opera, that it persists in selecting historical images, which are already pronounced in the world of fact, and cannot be recreated, except absurdly as in Verdi's *Macbetto*, in the realm of music. . . . If you regard an opera as a scene of actual life set to music, it is unmitigatedly ludicrous. . . .

Against all this we have had *Robert le Diable* and *La Gazza Ladra* as the novelties at Astor Place, and to "interpret" them, Steffanone, Salvi, and Marini—

"Was willst Du mehr?"

Steffanone is incomparably the finest lyrical artist we have recently had in America. She is whimsical and uncertain and indolent, and she is always better than she does. There is that fine consciousness of reserved strength in the impression she makes, which is the certificate of genius. I did not see her Norma, which is so warmly described by those who did. But as Alice, in *Robert*, she was most successful. She was all the simple country girl, safe and strong in her simplicity, and in the very last scene, when she defies Bertram and waves him back, she struck a higher note of the genuine lyrical drama than I have ever seen in America, and which is rarely surpassed in Europe. Whenever Steffanone played, we were sure of our evening. . . .

In *La Gazza Ladra*, Steffanone, in her whole movement and method, constantly reminded me of [Marietta] Alboni. They have both a fair *embonpoint*—both the same easy, loitering movement upon the stage—the same careless indifference—the same exquisite ease in singing, as if the voice were perpetually melodizing in the lungs, like streams gurgling beyond hearing, which upon opening the coral gates, will leap and gush in an uncontrolled current.

One evening Steffanone had a little grudge against her old friend Marini, and seriously impaired the effect of the delicious trio. It was amusing to watch her, so like a great pouting girl, who knew she could spoil the scene, and would do it—and did do it; but sang the rest of the opera all the better for it. . . .

Salvi is past his prime. I do not mean vocally, alone, for I doubt if he ever had much more voice than he has had for the last three years, during which he has been heard in New York. But his *physique* is un-equal to the parts he has undertaken. The one drawback to his singing, is the sense of effort. The quality of voice is sweet and sympathetic, and the cultivation quite unsurpassed; but you perceive the *manner* too clearly. I say that Salvi could hardly have ever had more voice than now, for with such quality and cultivation he must needs have taken higher rank among distinguished tenors. But he secures to the listener the same pleasure in hearing that Steffanone does. You are sure that what is done will be first-rate, and not second-rate.

I am gossiping beyond all limits. But, although I cannot steal enough of your space to say what should be said of the Philharmonic concerts and [Theodore] Eisfeldt's soirees, I must squeeze in a word of ANNA THILLON, who is now singing Auber's operas at Niblo's. If you go to hear moving music, and to be touched with genius or feeling, you will be sadly disappointed. Madame Thillon's beauty and singing and general impression are as cold and unsympathetic as frost-work. It is all artificiality. . . .

But with all that, it is thoroughly French. It is an evening at the *Opera Comique* to hear her in Auber's roles. Your employment is Parisian employment. Instead of light you have sparkle, instead of bloom you have paint, instead of grace you have conventional posing. But if you go to hear Madame Thillon, you must not go as to Grisi or to Bosio or Steffanone. It is a ball at the *Chateau rouge*. Colored lamps—pretty women—spangled dresses—a musical whirl—that is all. Quarrel with it, if you please. I enjoy it.

No—I will not undertake the Philharmonic, at this point of my paper. Be assured that the concerts of this Society are the first in America, and that they are securely based now upon the appreciation of those who intelligently enjoy—of those, I mean, to whom music is not a tickling sensation, but a genuine delight, like the happily married thought and cadence of a great poem. Eisfeldt's soirees are of the same character, and attract a similar audience. In the security of the best music so perfectly performed,

> Calm as a Summer's morning, we
> Can all the Madame Thillons see,

nor fear that the meretricious French fascination (which is yet, however, fascination) will destroy either our opportunities or our satisfactions in the noblest music.

HAFIZ.

18. *Trovatopera*

Verdi's *Il Trovatore* had its first American performances in New York in 1855 and quickly became the most popular of Italian operas. *Rigoletto* had already been seen, and *La Traviata*, too, won quick acceptance from all but the most Puritanical. But for whom *Trovatore* surpassed anything else, much to the dismay of Dwight, *Don Giovanni* was the pinnacle of opera and even Donizetti preferable to the upstart Verdi.

In "Trovatopera" Dwight laments the fate of opera in Boston, where an English troupe's *Trovatore* closes only to be followed by an Italian troupe singing both *Trovatore* and *Traviata*—and where all hope of establishing a resident company seems vain.

Dwight's Journal of Music, October 2, 1858

Trovatopera

Our palmy days of Opera are passed. Grisi, and Mario, and Bosio, and Badiali, and the large companies in which they shone conspicuous, are but remembered splendors. Nothing better, nothing half as good, appears to take their place. The hope of *one* complete and all-sufficient organization, with its three centres in New York, Philadelphia, and Boston, with ample orchestra and chorus, as well as admirable principals, and, above all, with a rich repertoire of the best operas, seems as far from realization as it ever did. All the interest and all the managerial and artistic energy are frittered away in half a dozen little separate, cheap enterprises, which go about with hum-drum repertoires, waging an internecine warfare.—These little companies have pretty much for their whole stock in trade just the three or four articles which they can manufacture cheapest, and which command a tolerably sure market on the strength of some mere fashion of the day. Opera we have not; but we have *Trovatore* companies, plentiful as mosquitoes, and (literally) piping hot. *Trovatore* is almost the only opera; it stands for all. To that pitch all the opera companies are screwed up, as if they were so many barrel organs. There are just one or two modulations into closely related keys, called *Traviata* and *Rigoletto*, with cheap and common *remplissage* for the intervening or "off" night, by way of relief, or foil, of two or three of the most familiar and hacknied works of Donizetti or Bellini. This is all that is now meant when we see an Italian opera announced. At least, this is all that Boston gets of it.

We have had one Trovatore troupe for two weeks, singing in English, at the Howard Anthenaeum. Three successive nights the bill was *Trovatore*, of which we can say nothing new, except to repeat our wonder at its strange popularity. For, in the first place, its horrible baby-burning plot is disgusting and absurd,—the more glaringly so when sung in English. In the next place, there is not a real, a natural, an interesting character in it; the persons are all puppets, leaving no impression beyond the action of the moment; as impersonations of passion they are as coarse as the dullest caricatures in the cheapest wood-cuts. Then again, *sentiment*, anything that can be called such, is utterly wanting in the opera, as a whole, with only here and there a maudlin reminiscence in a strain or two. The music is accordingly; if there is an ingenious melody, it may please, but it does not speak to you, sing to you, as the native and intrinsic music of a sweet soul or character, as does the music of Mozart's Zerlina. It is music everywhere straining for effect, and sometimes producing it, externally, superficially, but not internally or deeply. It is not pathos, but a coarse imitation of its most conventional and common forms. It lacks all fine and subtle touches. It says more than it means or feels. It is not the music of fine natures; it is not refining or elevating in its tendency. The *sphere* of life or sentiment into which it strains itself so spasmodically to transport you, is fortunately a very unreal one, or it would be a bad one. It is therefore not strange that the general impression of the *Trovatore*, as a musical whole, is distracting and unedifying. This music lacks the sovereign quality of *geniality*; it is mechanical; it relies upon dynamic means, and knows not the true secret, the true key to open human hearts. Its appeal is really to something else than heart or soul; to those who seek excitement, recklessly, for mere excitement's sake, and not to those who live sincerely and in earnest. Plot and music, all together, make up a wearisomely glaring picture of a strangely monotonous, burnt-out, brick-dust hue. No, this is tragedy too fierce to be tragic; this is passion too demonstrative to be genuine; this is music too effective to be genial or expressive. And yet the *Trovatore* is popular!

As to the performance, Miss [Annie] MILNER manages her clear soprano finely and looks charmingly. Dr. [Charles] GUILMETTE gives a carefully studied, finished rendering of his music, while his voice is rich and manly. The tenor, Mr. MIRANDA, has considerable power and sweetness, but strains his voice in high passages, or takes refuge in a puny falsetto. Mr. RUDOLPHSEN uses well a fine bass in his secondary part, and bears (as a contemporary says) the principal burden of the chorus, which for the rest is miserable enough. The orchestra is better than last week, and Mr. COOPER shows admirable powers as a conductor, which are evidently taxed to their utmost in holding together so uncertain an ensemble.

Next week another Trovatore troupe, under the auspices of [Maurice] STRAKOSCH, are to sing at the Boston Theatre, for four nights only. They will begin with *Traviata* and end with *Trovatore*, the alternatives being *Lucrezia Borgia* and *Fille du Regiment*. Mme. [Pauline] COLSON, new to us, admired in New Orleans and New York, is to be the prima donna in the first and last named pieces. [Marietta] GAZZANIGA, the charming, does not come, (we would give much to hear her once more in the sparkling and genial music of *L'Elisir d'amore*); instead of her we have the muscular [Teresa] PARODI, whose Lucrezia will be bold and masculine enough. BRIGNOLI, AMODIO, &c., will of course be welcomed.

19. *Adelina Patti*

Adelina Patti was no visiting star but a local girl making a triumphant debut when she appeared for the first time as Lucia at New York's Academy of Music on Thanksgiving Day, 1859. "Almost an American by birth," the *Herald* called her, rather wistfully, as if she should by all rights have been the first great American prima donna. Indeed, though born in Madrid, she was not a year old when her family of roving Italian opera singers brought her to New York, where the father was to manage one of the Italian opera houses that rose and waned in the 1840s and 1850s.

She was the "child *cantatrice*" Dwight had heard in company with Ole Bull in 1853. Not yet in her teens, she had performed with Gottschalk in the United States and Cuba. Her sister's husband, Maurice Strakosch, then became her mentor and kept her off the stage for several years until she could make her debut as a full-fledged artist. She reappeared at age sixteen to launch one of opera's longest and most brilliant careers. In two years' time Patti would go to London, where she immediately dispelled any notions that the reports from America had been inflated by local bias. Paris was next to succumb, then Milan. Twenty years were to pass before Patti, still at her peak, returned to sing in the United States, which even then lacked an opera company to present her in full splendor.

Dwight's New York correspondent caught the flavor and significance of Patti's 1859 *Lucia*. And Dwight gave "little Patti" his personal blessing when she reached Boston's Academy of Music a month later.

Dwight's Journal of Music, December 3, 1859

New York, Nov. 28—It is enough to make one leap for joy, like a young hart upon the mountain, to think that at last we have had a truly brilliant success—an operatic sensation, the like of which has not been known since the days of Malibran; so say old opera goers, whose memory reaches back to the Woods, and the Seguins, and Garcia, and Malibran, and other events and individuals contemporaneous with the Deluge. I don't remember quite so much.

But I remember enough about opera and opera people, to know that since the days of Parodi and Astor Place Opera, we have had no sensation like the great sensation caused by "little PATTI," the girl who made her debut last week in *Lucia*, to the huge delectation of everybody in the house, from the Parquet to "Paradise."

She was born in music, and has been steeped in music all her life. When a child at the age when most children's vocal abilities are limited to
"Patty-cake, patty-cake, baker's man,"
and similar tuneful effusions, this Patti was warbling the melodies of Bellini and Donizetti, and putting her doll to sleep with opera cavatinas. Then she sang in concerts with Paul Jullien, and from her ninth year has been a constant singer. Bosio did not appear in public till she was fifteen.

They have got up a nice story,—I suppose its true, about the musical star that presided over the destinies of little Patti. Her mother, they say, was a prima donna, and in 1843 was engaged at the opera in Madrid. On the night of the 8th of April, she appeared as "Norma," one of her favorite parts, and on the 9th little Adelina was born. From that date the mother lost her voice, and always declared that it had gone to her child.

In 1844, the whole tribe of Patti emigrated from Italy to this country, and the embryo prima donna thus crossed the ocean when barely a year old. She has lived most of her life, (excepting while on a concert tour in Cuba with Gottschalk), in New York.

During this period, she has had every possible advantage for musical education. If a census could be taken of her relatives, the Barilis, Pattis, and Strakosch's, the world would be astonished at the result, but the families are too prolific even to admit of a classification. As they were all artists, of course they soon became scattered to remote quarters of the globe, and were heard of at intervals from Lima, from Venice, from Paris and from New Orleans. . . .

Adelina Patti has for a number of years lived with her brother-in-law, Maurice Strakosch, and as his house has been a rendezvous for all the operatic artists that have visited New York, the little girl has been heard and petted by all these people. Sontag and Alboni have indulged in glowing predictions as to her future career, and her own family have always believed that she is destined for a brilliant lyric life.

In conversation with the young lady last week, I inquired what she thought in regard to her approaching debut. She shrugged her shoulders, and remarked that it made little difference. She knew it must come some time, so it might as well be first as last. She did not dread it, but on the contrary anticipated the event with joy.

On the evening of Thanksgiving day, she appeared in *Lucia*. Her *entrée* was greeted with prolonged applause, and her first cavatina assured her success. In the repetition of the *cabaletta*, she introduced some surprising variations, and her execution created the liveliest enthusiasm. In the duet that closes the first act, she was less effective, but was three times called before the curtain.

In the second act, her earnest yet modest acting, as well as her exquisite singing, aided in eliciting the liveliest applause. But it was in the mad scene of the last act, that she achieved her greatest success. In execution it was a wonderful performance, while the sympathetic voice of the young singer, and her childish grace, added to the effect.

The next day the papers with one accord sang her praises. Fry, of the *Tribune*, declared she was already equal to Sontag, which is not so. No one ever did sing *Lucia* like Sontag; but then little Patti will be fully as good when she is older. One great reason for the *furore* she has created is in the fact that she is young and beautiful, has lived all her days in this city, and is known personally to quite a number of our opera-goers. With all her exquisite voice and her elegant execution, she would not have succeeded near so well had she been an awkward, gawky girl or a sedate matron *a la* Laborde.

It certainly would appear difficult to imagine a more exciting or brilliant career than is before Adelina Patti. She is young, beautiful, endowed with as wonderful and precious a musical genius as was ever given even to prodigy Mozart; her talents cultivated with care, and surrounded by a devoted and wealthy family. . . . From her cradle she has been destined for a prima donna, and for this object in addition to musical and elocutionary tuition she has had her attention directed to the languages. She speaks Italian, French, and English with perfect fluency and understands Spanish and German. Is not all this knowledge a great deal for a girl of seventeen to possess?

Then in the future to what heights of lyric success may she not attain? There is no reason why in ten years ADELINA PATTI will not be the greatest of living *prime donne*.

I wish I was as sure of ten thousand dollars as I am of this fact. . . .

TROVATOR.

Dwight's Journal of Music, January 7, 1860

Boston Academy of Music

Such is the new name under which what was the Boston Theatre, has been announced this week. This change is made, as we suppose, to bring it into line and system with the lyrical "Academies" of Philadelphia and New York—all three institutions being now under the common management of Messrs. ULLMAN & STRAKOSCH, whose troupes of singers make the circuit of the three. Just now *we* have them. The winter season was inaugurated last Monday night, by the first shining of the new and immense chandelier, of which we have already spoken, which was the central sun of admiration, beneath which the vocal stars upon the stage became for the time being secondary. . . . But brilliancy, and not repose, is the first attribute of Art, the first thing sought in all artistic pleasures, in these "fast" and intense days of Verdi-ism. A new Verdi Opera, therefore, was the fitting programme of the all-dazzling occasion. . . .

SECOND NIGHT. *Lucia di Lammermoor* was given Tuesday evening, and its hacknied strains seemed positively refreshing after *Les Vêpres Siciliennes*! Here at least was something genuine and spontaneous in music. . . .

The central and absorbing feature of the opera that night was the performance of the newly famous ADELINA PATTI—"little PATTI." A young girl, a mere child in appearance, slender, dark and beautiful, a delicate copy of her sister, Mme. Strakosch, with all the simplicity and natural enthusiasm of a child, she sang and even acted the part of Lucy with an ease, a truthfulness, and an artistic finish, that astonished and delighted every one, and suggested very high comparisons. That she sings as well as Lind and Bosio and Sontag is of course one of the extravaganzas of New York critics, proving, however, the real enthusiasm she created. Her voice is a delicate, pure, reedy, sympathetically vibrating soprano, very evenly developed, from brightest notes in *alt* to good positive low tones of passion. Throughout, its quality has native refinement, as if given her for fine, high uses, and not for cheap dramatic intensities or dazzling feats of mere skill. She really seems destined for an artist; she shows grace of nature. It must be by a superior instinct partly, although of course at the same time creditable in the highest degree to her education, that she can sing you all the music of so difficult a part as Lucia, in a manner almost as artistically satisfying, as her fresh, maidenlike, sincere devotion to her task is charming. The freshness and vitality of such a voice, of such a nature, united with such delicacy, such instincts of good taste, is reviving to one's faith. Her execution is certainly most wonderful for one so young,—so perfect that you continually forget to think it strange. There is an evenness and symmetry in all her voice achieves, which one expects only of high artists. This was strikingly apparent in her singing of *Spargi d'amor*, and indeed the whole of the crazy scene. We usually dread that scene; most prima donnas make it maudlin, and we squirm under it. But here a young girl gives it, both in song and action, in a manner that well satisfies its requirements, while there is nothing overdone, no nonsense about it, but all agreeable and not offending the artistic feeling.

In the great scene of the betrothal, the Sextet, she showed good dramatic qualities, an intensity remarkable for one so young, and her voice rose clear and effective above the whole mass of voices and instruments. Of course her acting cannot be called impassioned; it is chaste and simple, youthful as it should be; thank Heaven, she has not yet caught the trick of premature impassioned utterance! Nor can we call her action or her movement graceful; but it was all appropriate and well conceived. True to her part in all, she added nothing, and no applause could draw her out of her character to make acknowledgements; that was a good sign.

Whether she really have the heavenly gift of genius, is a question which we need not be impatient to have answered. So far all is good; may it only keep a good direction! Will the voice wear well? It is of that same reedy quality as her sister's, only finer, and one trembles lest by overworking it get ruined. Total abstinence from Verdi would seem at least a prudent maxim for her. With these hints we must congratulate the management upon the treasure they have got in little Patti.

20. *Clara Louise Kellogg*

Fifteen months after Patti's debut, another youthful soprano appeared at New York's Academy of Music, and it seemed that here at last was a real American prima donna. The debutante of February 27, 1861, was Clara Louise Kellogg, whose impeccable Connecticut family could be traced back to colonial times. A career on the opera stage was no easy choice for such a young lady. When she set off for serious study in New York, she felt obliged to tell her friends that she would understand perfectly if they chose not to speak to her next time they met.

Nor was the opera world exactly welcoming. Backstage, the neophyte found the Academy of Music virtually Italian territory. "It was not generally considered that Americans could appreciate, much less interpret opera," Kellogg later recalled, "and I, as the first American prima donna, was in the position of a foreigner in my own country."

However, the Italian monopoly was not quite complete. The company in which Kellogg made her debut also included the promising Albany-born Isabella Hinckley (who died a year later) as well as Adelaide Phillipps, by that time well-established in the major contralto roles. But if "prima donna" signifies leading soprano, Kellogg came to deserve the title. Half a dozen years after her debut, she confirmed her American successes in London, then returned to make her career primarily in the United States. In the 1870s she formed her own company to take opera around the country in English translation, and conscientiously cast herself in the role of public educator and trainer of young American singers.

Kellogg appeared in Boston a month after her Manhattan debut. Although Gilda had been her first role in New York, the manager feared that a Boston audience would consider *Rigoletto* no proper vehicle for a New England girl, and chose instead to present her in Donizetti's *Linda di Chamounix*. Kellogg later dared to sing Verdi even in Boston, but she came to be known best for her Marguerite in *Faust*: she sang the role when Gounod's opera was presented for the first time in New York in 1863 and came back to it often during her long career. Dwight received Clara Louise Kellogg cordially in her Boston *Linda*, and repeated for her some of the cautionary words he had had earlier for Patti.

Dwight's Journal of Music, March 23, 1861

Italian Opera

Since our last we have had the somewhat unusual excitement of the production of a new opera of Verdi's and the debut of a new American prima donna, whose claims are perhaps stronger in respect to nationality than those of any who have preceded her, being, as we learn, American in birth and education, having received her entire musical instruction in this country. Music, to be sure, is a universal language and the birth place of her servants is of small moment, still it is pleasant to see the result of a purely home education so satisfactory and even brilliant as in the case now under notice. . . .

UN BALLO IN MASCHERA.—To hear a new opera, hardly known yet abroad, never yet performed in London and only within a few weeks brought out in Paris, is quite an event in the operatic experience of Boston. . . .

We have had two opportunities since our last, of hearing Verdi's new work; it having been given on Friday of last week and on Monday of the present week. . . .

To be sure, the incongruities and absurdities were more than numerous, as seen by us, sitting here in Boston, in the old province of Massachusetts Bay, where the scene is laid. The scenery, the costumes, the manners and customs of the people and even the surface of Nature itself, as it was represented (to say, nothing of what was *beneath* the surface, in that wonderful witch's cave), were ludicrous in the extreme. We doubt whether the old Province House (the mansion of our royal governors) ever saw any such fantastic mummery as a masked ball, unless, in our own day, the "Minstrels" who now hold it, may have enacted one within its walls.

Setting all this aside, however, the plot is dramatic, well constructed and easily understood, and the cast was admirable. Brignoli as Ricardo, Ferri as Renato, Colson as Amelia, Adelaide Phillips as Ulrica and Miss Hinkley as Oscar, filling their respective roles in an admirable manner that left little to be desired. Nor shall we omit to notice Barili and Dubreuil in the important parts of the two conspirators, Sam and Tom.

The impression made at the first hearing by this opera, and entirely confirmed by a second, was very satisfactory and pleasing. The music is characteristic of Verdi, of course, yet free from his more marked mannerisms and tricks of composition, free from the almost stereotyped phrases, both of melody and of instrumentation to which we have become accustomed. In fact, the Ballo in Maschera seems to mark the beginning of a new style in the works of this popular composer, and we should incline to the belief that he has taken a leaf from the experience and practice of Meyerbeer. . . .

———————

Linda di Chamounix was selected for the debut of MISS CLARA LOUISE KELLOGG, on Tuesday evening. The sweet simplicity of the young Savoyard peasant girl is easily reproduced by the powers of a young girl, coming within the sphere of her experience and not forcing her to counterfeit passions of which youth and innocence can have but small conception. The opera is thus well adapted for a debutante.

We have rarely had occasion to record a more complete and genuine success than was won by Miss Kellogg on this occasion. An entire novice upon the stage, having appeared only some half dozen times in all, coming to us almost unheralded and unpuffed, indeed almost unknown, she has stepped into the position of a public favorite, at a single bound. In person she is slender and graceful, with a pleasing face, intelligent and intellectual, rather than a beautiful one, capable of the most varied expression. Her voice is a pure high soprano, of that thin and penetrating quality that cuts the air with the keen glitter of a Damascus blade, wanting now, of course, in that volume and power which age and time will give, yet sufficient for all practical purposes; of course, furthermore, not so full in the lower register as it will be in time. She reminds us much of Adelina Patti as to the quality of her voice, and indeed in her execution, which is finished and thoroughly artistic, savoring little of the novice, but worthy of the experience of a longer study and maturer age. Every thing attempted is done with admirable precision, neatness and brilliancy that leave little to be desired. In the opening cavatina, *O luce di quest' anima*, she exhibited at once these qualities, giving the air in a way that brought down the house in spontaneous applause. As she proceeded she evinced a rare dramatic talent and an apparent familiarity with the business of the stage that was truly remarkable. The grace and simplicity of manner that mark her, are, however, native and not acquired, and seem a real gift of nature. Through all the changes of the opera, she showed herself always equal to the demands of the scene, so that, as an actress, we should set her down as possessed of a rare instinct, if not, indeed, of positive *genius*. We do not remember any one in the character of Linda who has given it more acceptably than she. . . . Miss Kellogg impresses us as an artist full of the best promise. We trust that she may not be forced too fast, nor overworked, that the freshness of her voice and the life and energy of her young nature may not be prematurely injured by labors too great or by an unwise ambition. We are glad to learn that no necessity obliges her to go upon the stage, but that a true love for art is the only impulse. The studies so well begun, it must be remembered are only *begun*. There is no end to study in so high an art, for a person of so much promise, to whom such high achievements seem possible.

21. *An American Opera*

William Henry Fry's *Notre Dame of Paris* was produced in Philadelphia in 1864 as the opening event in a major festival for the benefit of the National Sanitary Commission, a Civil War parallel to the Red Cross. The patriotic framework naturally stimulated observers to comment on the operatic state of affairs in the United States.

If American singers were beginning to appear, what of American operas? Not till 1845 was one produced by a professional company, and that was *Leonora*, by the same William Henry Fry, performed by the Seguins' English opera troupe in Philadelphia. (It was revived in New York in 1858, in *Italian*!) Son of a Philadelphia newspaper publisher, Fry was a journalist by profession, long associated with the New York *Tribune* as European correspondent, editorial writer, and music critic. He was the first to write regularly about music for an American daily newspaper. He seems to have been a complicated, opinionated man with a passion for music, particularly Italian music. He was one of the first to complain vociferously about German domination of the American concert hall, and in lectures and in print he urged native composers to seek an American vein of musical expression. Unfortunately, Fry himself lacked the gift to discover it. On viewing *Notre Dame of Paris*, even the most charitable reviewer was unable to credit him with any originality or much skill as a composer.

Fry's belief in the historical supremacy of Italian music was directly opposed to Dwight's faith in German musical models. But if the two were philosophical adversaries, Dwight never failed to treat Fry with respect in the columns of his *Journal*. When *Notre Dame* was performed, Dwight chose not to review it himself but instead reprinted two contrasting newspaper accounts: the first by a correspondent of the *Tribune*; the other "a much more temperate, well-considered article" from the Philadelphia *Press*. Taken together, they convey something about the quality of Fry's work and also about the contemporary state of

American opera. The reader will note an inserted pair of exclamation points that are Dwight's comment on the claim that Fry "created" American musical criticism.

Dwight's Journal of Music, May 14, 1864

(From the Tribune's Special Correspondent)

Musical Festival in Philadelphia
MR. FRY'S NEW OPERA, "NOTRE DAME OF PARIS"

The musical festival in aid of the Sanitary Commission was on Wednesday evening inaugurated by the production of Mr. William H. Fry's new opera, "Notre Dame of Paris." It is a remarkable fact that the greatest public interest and expectation in regard to this event were exhibited not here in Philadelphia, but in other and distant cities. In New York and elsewhere it had for many days been a prominent popular topic, the importance of which was recognized by the most generous announcements that journalism could bestow. The occasion was moreover distinguished by the special pilgrimage hither of numerous representatives of metropolitan art and literature—a circumstance by no means insignificant, when the physical and spiritual agonies of a railway passage through New Jersey are considered. Why Philadelphia should have remained comparatively indifferent to an event of such peculiar import to itself, it is difficult to understand. Twenty years ago, when the first of American operas, by the same author, was produced at the Chestnut-street Theatre, there was no limit to the eagerness with which its performances were welcomed, and the brilliant success of the young composer was met by the proud congratulations of the entire community. Does the new generation account itself superior to the consideration of musical advancement and development? It was certainly a serious disappointment for visitors to discover so little domestic concern upon a matter which everywhere else was held in high anticipation. The fact probably is that Philadelphians are not generally aware of the artistic importance which belongs to the production of a work like "Notre Dame of Paris." Operas requiring equal magnitude of preparation are rarely attempted, even in Europe. Excepting Meyerbeer, no composer of the present day has power to procure the execution of similar works. . . .

That "Notre Dame" should, then, be undertaken in an American city, and undertaken in a spirit of liberal enterprise wholly consistent with its vast requirements, is a circumstance which ought to have engaged the utmost public attention and the heartiest public support. I even set aside consideration of the patriotic purpose of its performance, and of the personal claim which the composer may be supposed to have upon the citizens of Philadelphia. The production of the opera was, of itself, an event worthy to be celebrated. For the first time in America, an orchestra equal in numbers to the most massive of European opera-houses contributed its effect. (The orchestra of the Imperial Academy is not larger, and that of Covent Garden not so large.) The chorus was unquestionably superior to the average of the best foreign theatres. The *mise-en-scène* would not have been surpassed in Paris or Berlin. These are very striking facts. On the other hand, there were certain defects, such as would not be likely to occur abroad, but these were of minor importance, and due to the hurried condition of the first performance. . . .

The representation on Wednesday evening at the Academy of Music was witnessed by a large, though not an overflowing audience. The success of the opera was complete. I shall not assume to speak analytically of its qualities for many reasons—chiefly because I should feel ill at ease in offering critical views upon the work of a composer who has himself created [!!] American musical criticism in the very columns in which I am writing. Applause was constant, and the call for Mr. Fry, after the fall of the curtain, was enthusiastic and unanimous. The performance presented many valuable characteristics. I have mentioned the amplitude of the orchestra and chorus. Their execution, under the excellent direction of Mr. Theodore Thomas, was almost free from blemish. The natural irregularities of a first night were the worst faults. The different roles were conscientiously interpreted by Mrs. Borchard, Mrs. Kempton, Mr. Castle, Mr. Campbell and Mr. Seguin. (Mr. Seguin's father was one of the principal artists concerned in the production of Mr. Fry's "Leonora" in Philadelphia, some twenty years ago.) The exquisite scenic effects, the wealth of stage decoration and the vivid costumes of the multitude that represented alternately soldiers, courtiers, and peasants, heightened throughout the impressiveness of the representation.

Mr. Fry's musical reputation will be greatly augmented by this work. Many of its attributes are of an order which the most famous composers are glad to be credited with. The instrumentation is rich and sonorous to a degree which few have surpassed. The operas of Bellini and Donizetti do not generally show such closely studied orchestral writing. It is replete with resonant choral effects, and in the construction of the concerted pieces imagination and skill are alike demonstrated. No one could deny that "Notre Dame" stands well in all these respects beside the acknowledged works of modern writers of repute. And it is impossible not to deeply regret that Mr. Fry's opportunities for public testing of his capabilities have been so limited. The stride from his "Leonora" to his "Notre Dame" is prodigious. In another country, where all men's hands and hearts are not against the progress of art, that stride might have been made a score of years ago; and we need have very little hesitation in believing that Mr. Fry's name would now be an honored one far and near, wherever the art he has studied, and loved, and protected is held in esteem.

E. H. H

Dwight's Journal of Music, May 28, 1864

(From the Philadelphia Press)

American Opera—Mr. Fry's "Notre Dame"

The third performance of the new opera of "Notre Dame" has been a success quite as general as its first and second, and upon this fortunate fact we congratulate the composer and the public for which he has labored. The cordial hearing Mr. Fry's work has received is a promise, we trust, of much more extended favor. We again express our admiration of the splendid and spirited first scene of the opera, which, in point of stage effect, has never, doubtless, been excelled in America. Produced under direction of an American composer, with American artists and an American chorus, and an orchestra of the largest and best character, it deserves all praise. The grand chorus which is one of the chief attractions of the opera has been heard with great applause, and the improved energy and confidence of the principal artists is gratifying, as this part of the production has been the least satisfactory. . . .

Of course, it is very fulsome praise to rank "Notre Dame" with the works of Bellini, Donizetti, and Verdi—works of which it is not free of imitation, and with which it doubtfully compares in elaboration. An inspiration of one melody, equal to the least of Bellini's, upon whom Mr. Fry has modelled his sentimental music, would have given him a popular fame long ago. We could name many passages in "Notre Dame" which do credit to the study and fine taste of its able composer; a few, also, which breathe real strength, or very nearly so, in an atmosphere of imperfection; but we shall not do him the injustice of ranking him with his masters.

We again take occasion to praise the admirable light music which gives so much spirit and charm to the ballet scene, and can only regret that this scene is unnecessary to the work as a whole. *Quasimodo's* soliloquy in the belfry is among the best-modelled and strongest passages, but is spoiled in the rendering of Mr. Seguin, and weakened by the concluding Bell song, which is comparatively trivial, though excellent in subject. The fine song of the Royal Scotch Guard, which belongs to the hale and simple, but not uncommonplace English school, is well worked up, admirably sung, and will continue, we think, to receive the greatest share of the popular applause. "I know that I love him" is an ingenious and pretty piece of musical broidery; "Vision of Love" is excellent, if we ignore that it is an imitation of *Spirto Gentil*—and other clever and equally attractive things might be instanced with similar qualifications, but all would show, we think, meritorious imperfection, rather than, in the least instance, anything discreditable to the high reputation which Mr. Fry enjoys. . . .

It vexes us to think that, with so much industry and ability, he has shown so little tendency to absolute creation. From the nature of the case, it is very difficult or impossible for a foreign composer to surrender his musical allegiance to the young Italy of Bellini and Donizetti, and preserve the color of originality. . . . Genius is representative. Why yearn after the Italian mock Eden? Why attempt to rival Bellini's sweetness or Verdi's sonority? It would be ridiculous for an American to think of writing melodramas of intrigue against Alexander Dumas, and it would be just as absurd for him to attempt to follow Verdi. Our composer must think for himself, and not be carried away like a waif in the deluge of another's sensation. If it is right to compare our music with our literature, how would Mr. Fry stand by the side of Mr. Bryant? Our poet is a literary patriot, and as he breathes the great moral of the Wilderness in Thanatopsis, is a more loyal American than even Fennimore Cooper. . . . Our American composer has not received his naturalization.

Let us, however, be as patient as Mr. Fry has been. In his time and circumstances it has been an especially difficult matter to write an opera—much more difficult to produce one. Comparatively speaking, the composer has been without critics and without friends. We give him that sincere acknowledgment which we should give to an indomitable man, and heartily trust that his health will be spared for deeper and higher efforts. More than this, we hope that his excellent example will, in good time, lead many others to surpass him. Even if "Notre Dame" does not prove a permanent work, Mr. Fry has achieved a considerable success, which, everything considered, is honorable to himself and the musical cause in America. We trust that he has truly become the father of American opera, and higher recognition than this he need not wish. . . .

With all its defects, "Notre Dame" has sufficient attraction, from the great prestige of Hugo's immortal work, the prodigal magnificence of its production, and the merits of its composer, to draw all to its hearing who are disposed to appreciate a liberal stage, and to favor the cause of our own patriotism and art.

Germania Musical Society, with Carl Bergmann, conductor,
seated at the center
Lithograph by T. Sinclair, Philadelphia (undated)
The New-York Historical Society

Jenny Lind and her husband,
Otto Goldschmidt, probably in
1852
Library of Congress

Exterior view of the coliseum constructed for the National Peace
Jubilee at Boston in 1869
Chromolithograph, 1869
Courtesy of the Boston Athenaeum

Theodore Thomas
Photogravure from a photograph by Max Platz
(undated)
Library of Congress

Adelina Patti, circa 1861
Photograph by Fredericks
Courtesy of the National Portrait Gallery, Smithsonian Institution, Washington, D.C.

Clara Louise Kellogg, 1867
Photograph by Jeremiah Gurney and Son
Courtesy of the National Portrait Gallery, Smithsonian Institution, Washington, D.C.

Minnie Hauk, possibly costumed as Carmen
Sarony photograph (undated)
The New-York Historical Society

Scenes from the French Opera, New Orleans: *top*, "A Creole Family at the Opera"; *left*, the "Loges Grillées"; *right*, "The Negro Gallery"
From *Every Saturday*, July 15, 1871
Courtesy of the Historic New Orleans Collection, 533 Royal, Acc. No. 1953.90

Poster for Haverly's New York Juvenile *Pinafore* Company
Lithograph by Strobridge and Company, Cincinnati, 1879
Library of Congress

Euphrosyne Parepa Rosa
From a sheet-music cover, 1867
Library of Congress

Carl Zerrahn
Photograph by Case and Getchell, Boston, circa 1863
Courtesy of the Boston Athenaeum

John Knowles Paine
From the Harvard Class Album of 1869
Courtesy of the Harvard University Archives

Northern soldiers watch "contraband children dancing the break-down" in an "extempore musical and terpsichorean entertain-ment at the United States Arsenal, Baton Rouge, Louisiana," July, 1862
Wood engraving from *Leslie's Illustrated History of the Civil War*, 1895
Library of Congress

Fisk Jubilee Singers, 1871. *Left to right*: Minnie Tate, Greene Evans, Isaac Dickerson, Jennie Jackson, Maggie Porter, Ella Shep-pard, Thomas Rutling, Benjamin Holmes, and Eliza Walker.
Courtesy of the Fisk University Library (Special Collections)

22. German Opera

While German influence may have dominated American concert music, German opera lagged behind the Italian in winning an American audience. Italian opera had its financial ups and downs, but it was a fashionable entertainment from its first performances in New York in 1825. German opera appealed more narrowly to a German-speaking audience and began to engage a wider public only when the Wagnerian tide began to rise in the 1880s. In the meantime a curious interchange took place: German operas such as *Der Freischütz* or *Martha* were translated into Italian for performances at New York's Academy of Music; at the German theater, on the other hand, the bills of fare were sometimes seasoned with popular French or Italian operas sung in German translation.

The surge of immigration at midcentury inceased both the resources and the audience for German opera. One influential newcomer was Karl Anschütz, an accomplished conductor who arrived in New York in 1857 and remained to advance the cause of German opera more energetically than his easy-going predecessor, the old survivor of the Germania Orchestra, Carl Bergmann. Bergmann had led brief seasons of opera in New York's German theater, with locally recruited singers, in the 1850s; he even gave the first American performance of *Tannhäuser* in 1859. But now Anschütz decided to seek a wider public; he joined with a manager, Leonard Grover, to engage a number of leading singers from Germany for a season at the Academy of Music, where Italian opera customarily held the stage. The venture went well enough that Anschütz and Grover decided to take the company to Boston for two weeks. They received a warm welcome, at least from John S. Dwight.

Dwight's Journal of Music, May 14, 1864

German Opera

During the past fortnight we have had here what we had almost despaired of having for some years to come, a really good German Opera. Indeed the whole experience of Boston hitherto in German Opera has been limited to a single performance, we might call it a travesty, about seven years ago, of *Fidelio*, by a trumped up company that ran on here from New York, and did the thing so badly that the Italian fanaticos were only strengthened in their partiality, and could not perceive that Beethoven's music was half so good as Verdi's. Italian Opera, and no other, has been fashionable in all our cities, and it has not been common to believe in German singers, or that there can be any first-rate voices, any true, high art of singing, but the Italian, (or the Italianized-American), notwithstanding the fact, so pointedly set forth in manager Grover's announcement last week, that most of the Italian companies of late, both here and in France and England, have depended almost entirely upon Germans for their orchestra and chorus, while the names of many of their best principal singers, their "stars," have been German, with or without Italian terminations. But these have been chiefly engaged in executing the Italian music, or at least the Italian repertoire, which takes in Meyerbeer, Flotow, and such other German and French composers as have come half way to meet it, paying also a certain deference to Mozart. . . .

All our opera troupes and seasons, therefore, in spite of German elements in the performance, and in spite of Mozart, Meyerbeer and Gounod (what a conjunction of names!), have been Italian. A real German opera with German means, illustrating the German repertoire, we have not had an opportunity to know,—at least in Boston. We have heard of it, perchance have come upon it, some of us, in visits to New York and Philadelphia, these last years, as a sort of flitting nebular phenomenon, having but a half existence. . . . The amount of it is, that until now the German opera troupes in this country have been poor and fragmentary attempts, with some good elements, but by no means furnished for a fair presentation of the master works of Mozart, Beethoven and Weber. It is due to the enterprising spirit of CARL ANSCHUETZ, that so complete a company was organized last Fall, and due to his thorough musicianship, his mastery as a conductor, that a most refreshing degree of unity, animation and artistic feeling has been realized in their performances. He found it uphill work, however, through the winter. In Philadelphia there was more recognition than in New York; but generally the newspaper criticisms, which for the most part are reflexes of the fashions and "sensations" of the day in all matters of art and taste, praised very cautiously, and relapsed into convenient silence. What does not *pay* the manager, it does not pay to write about, seems to be tacitly adopted as the theory of newspaperdom. Then again, so fond are newspapers of praising everything in a certain perfunctory way, and so apt to praise most that which is least in Art, that earnest music-lovers here were habitually sceptical about what they read, as we are about the sensation bulletins of war news. We waited till we might hear with our own ears. And our hopes have been repeatedly raised during the winter, only to be disappointed, by the report that Anschütz was to bring his company to the Boston Theatre. Meanwhile we have gained by the postponements. Within a few months Mr. Anschütz has added to his force several new singers from Germany, some of his brightest stars, such as Mme. [Marie] Frederici-Himmer, the two admirable tenors, [Theodor] Habelmann and [Franz] Himmer, and other names, which certainly are not the ones we used to read of in the New York papers early in the winter. Moreover, reaping no material harvest at all commensurate with so satisfactory an artistic result, and finding it too much for one man to be both musical and business head of such an enterprise, it was his good luck to meet in Mr. GROVER, the proprietor of theatres in Philadelphia, Baltimore and Washington, a manager with insight to perceive the value and the capabilities of the thing, a man with means and will to assume the responsibility of it and place it once for all upon a sound material basis. Under his auspices the German Opera, thus set upon its feet again, has for some weeks past been triumphantly successful both in Philadelphia and Washington, almost eclipsing the Italian rival, and promising at all events to put an end to its monopoly from this time forth. . . .

All this we should have said in anticipation of their coming, if they had not come upon us by surprise. With only two or three days notice

Anschütz and his company were with us. The first real advertisement was the manner in which they performed Flotow's *Martha* on Monday evening, May 4th, before an audience which made up by its musical intelligence and by its enthusiasm for its exceeding paucity of numbers. It was felt by all present that that single hearing by those few had established the right of the German company to succeed in Boston. A little more time to talk it about, to allow people to shape their engagements, and a few more performances and they must win the day. And so it went on with increase of interest and of audience from night to night. The season was to be very brief, positively only a fortnight, with a different opera every evening, and no repetitions. We were to be impressed indeed, not only with the unity, the versatility, the excellence of their performance, but with the extent, variety and richness of their repertoire both in things familiar and things new to us. Here was the programme: for the first week, *Martha*, *La Dame Blanche*, *Faust*, *Der Freyschütz*, *Merry Wives of Windsor*, and *Alessandro Stradella*; second week, *Don Juan* and *Fidelio*, sure, and perhaps the *Zauberflöte*, *Tannhäuser*, *Robert* and *Das Nachtlager in Grenada*. The first half has been carried out to the letter.

Now *Martha* was not just the opera we should have chosen for the opening night. For these reasons. It has become almost too familiar, almost hacknied; every Italian company has played it, and shall not this short first taste of German opera consist of things we do not get from everybody else? Then *Martha* is not distinctively a *German* opera, although a German wrote it; many a German writes Italian music; this is as much Italian and French as it is German; in no sense is it a representative German work, like *Fidelio* and the operas of Mozart and of Weber. Thirdly, it is not a great work, not even a second or third rate work, not a work of genius; it is only clever, graceful, pretty, lively, popular, &c. We confess we have seldom been able to sit through the whole of *Martha*; after the two sparkling first acts, after the fun is mainly over, and the lover is in his lunes, and the sentimental "Last rose of summer" business begins, we have found it something stale and tedious. The more the triumph, therefore, of these Germans, that we did sit it out that evening, and were so carried away, all of us, by the uncommon vivacity and genial excellence of the whole performance, that we did so in spite of ourselves most willingly. All agreed that *Martha* never was so well performed in Boston. . . .

Tuesday, May 5th, the charming old opera of Boieldieu, *La Dame Blanche (Die weisse Dame.)* Audience considerably larger. This opera was written in 1825, and there has scarcely been a greater favorite on the French, the German, or the English stage. It was indifferently given in this city some 25 or 30 years ago, by an English and a French troupe, and much of the music is familiar, floating about in the general air, especially the beautiful overture. But the opera as such was new to us here and now. The work of a Frenchman, it is one of the operas which have become German by adoption and affinity. It is thoroughly *genial* music, Mozart-ish in spirit, and after the German heart. . . .

One of the most important roles is that of the crafty guardian and steward Galveston, which was splendidly done by Herr [Josef] HERMANNS, a magnificent basso, colossal in voice and person, dignified in action, and delivering his grand *profondo* tones or his rich ringing higher ones with equal clearness, truth and telling effect. We have had no such basso since the better days of [Carl] Formes; and he has resources yet to be found out in other characters. In the spoken dialogue, which replaces the Italian *parlando* in most German operas—not advantageously, to our taste—Herr Hermanns is particularly clear and of chaste accent. Everybody went away delighted with *Die Weisse Dame*, and hoping it would be repeated.

Wednesday, Third Night. Gounod's "Faust" is another of those operas which we would willingly have left to the Italians, at least until we have secured some half a score of those distinctively best German works, with which our people are so unacquainted. Were it not better that a German troupe at first should stand on its peculiarity, doing what others cannot or do not do, and showing its catholicity later? But "Faust" is now the fashion; many there be and loud that call for it, and what more sure to fill the house? Besides there is curiosity to compare the German with the Italian rendering. The house was indeed much more nearly full. The verdict we think must be for the German presentment. There was much more life and spirit in it as a whole. The choruses, especially those of the "Kirmesse," made a livelier sensation. Herr HIMMER's voice and action were very fine in Faust, and the Mephistopheles of HERMANNS was marvellously effective in its way, that of the popular tradition clown devil, and not the polished Iago-like gentleman, the 19th century devil, of Goethe. The Gretchen of FREDERICI was perfectly charming, more exquisite even than Miss Kellogg's, in that it seemed less like a study; she looked the type of modest, pious, lovely German maidenhood; her rich, soulful, sympathetic voice, and the seemingly unconscious truth of action, made it "a thing of beauty and of joy forever." . . .

Thursday. A crowded house for Weber's *Freyschütz.* Boston is alive to the fact of German Opera at last! The charm of the wonderful music is infallible, and the hope of hearing it for the first time well rendered made it the gala night of the week. Indeed it was an admirable performance. It was rare delight to listen to that orchestra and that wonderful instrumentation, the human and the mysterious expression of the high and low clarionet tones, the bassoons, the sylvan horns, etc., even were that all. Then the chorus, picturesque in appearance, sang so finely. . . .

But the memorable thing of all was the Agathe of FREDERICI. It was too beautiful to speak of; something almost holy in the truth and purity of feeling, the harmony of voice, song, look and action, which made it as near to Weber's ideal of the part as anything probably has ever come since Jenny Lind. The scena: "*Wie nahte mir der Schlummer,*" with the prayer "*Leise, leise,*" entranced the audience. All that we have said of her Gretchen was more than confirmed here. We have had greater executive vocalists, but, with the exception of Lind and Bosio, when so true a singer in the soul's sense of the word?

The week closed with a couple of light operas, new to Boston, with only moderate audiences.

On Friday, Nicolai's "Merry Wives of Windsor," full of sparkling, graceful music, of which the overture had given us a foretaste, extremely comical, and having the advantage of a cleverly constructed libretto, as close as an opera could be to Shakespeare. . . .

For a Matinee on Saturday, Flotow's *Stradella,* which to our surprise we found more enjoyable than *Martha.* As music it has generally the same traits. The more serious and sentimental parts are the weakest, but there are some fine comic bits; and there is an unaccompanied trio, quite in the old Italian vein, that was singularly beautiful. . . .

Here we must pause for the present. This second week has offered after all but two new things, *Don Juan* (strange to say, the worst of their performances) and *Fidelio*, while *Faust*, *Freyschütz* and *Martha* have been repeated, and *Faust* will be again repeated this afternoon, bringing the short, rich season to a close.

23. *Italian Opera Again—*
Minnie Hauk

The Anschütz-Grover company did not survive another season. The German singers retreated to the Stadt Theater in New York and traveled from there to neighboring cities to eke out their existence, leaving the Academy of Music to Maretzek and the Italian repertory.

When the Maretzek company paid Boston an autumn visit, the roster included a new teenaged soprano in the tradition of Patti and Kellogg: Amalia Hauck, who was to become (as Minnie Hauk) one of opera's legendary stars, famous for her Carmen. Like Patti, Hauk left the United States soon after her debut and returned only after her fame was established in Europe. Like Kellogg, she was American by birth and training.

It happened that the prime donna of this particular Maretzek company was Kellogg herself, but Dwight evidently found the young Hauk more interesting. He was, however, mistaken in putting her age at seventeen; in November, 1866, Minnie Hauk would just have turned fifteen.

Dwight's Journal of Music, November 24, 1866

Italian Opera

MAX MARETZEK and singers came in as [Italian actress Adelaide] Ristori left, and for a fortnight the great fashionable crowd which the Italian Opera of this day peculiarly addresses, the musical *demi-monde*, so to speak, (of course we do not mean in any moral sense) has been at fever heat. If a crowded theatre five nights and two afternoons in one week (with some falling off, to be sure, when very old favorites, like *Sonnambula, Lucrezia, Trovatore,* &c., are given), followed by increase of appetite the second week, be any proof, Italian Opera is still the most popular of all forms of musical entertainment. Its audiences, however, are peculiar; one wonders where so many well-dressed, even showy people, whom the oldest theatre and concert-goer never saw before, can have come from. Not only a new generation have sprung up, but new social elements seem to have flowed in on the tide of business. Not the highest culture of Boston, not those most deeply imbued with the love of art and music, give the tone, the dominant complexion to an Italian Opera audience, as in the days of Truffi and Benedetti, of Bosio and Badiali, of Mario and Grisi; but one who has just seen these elements assembled night after night to see Ristori, now looks round on a strange sea of faces in the great Boston Theatre; of course not without more or less admixture of the other class, but this time exceptionally, or occasionally, as when some particular opera or some *rara avis* of a singer is announced. Italian Opera relies for its success on getting up a feverish excitement; good-bye to all quiet, temperate, wholesome musical joys the moment you enter its charmed circle, if you stay there long enough to get familiar with it. For you must take it all at once, night after night, and matinees besides, or not at all. It is a kind of fever that burns over and exhausts the soil for the time being.

Nothing relies so much on flaming and grandiloquent advertisement, on the fulsome eulogy of youthful critics for the press, who seem to have no thought left for any other music. And then, the tendency to exaggeration which runs through all its performances, a fault which only seems to grow upon the most experienced singers, makes it at least questionable whether for artists this can be the best school. And to this the disposition of managers to run upon merely effective, showy operas, and apparently avoid as much as possible the noblest compositions, those whose music is immortal, like the operas of Mozart, (even, in the light, humorous kind systematically postponing Rossini's "Barber" for things which have not a tittle of its melody and genius—and that frequently in spite of promises, as in the present case.)

How far Italian Opera is a blessing and how far an evil to the cause of music, is too great a question to discuss here now. Of course, under its ample folds it covers many a good thing; and we prefer to assume that it does do good in the long run. We only speak of it in its present tendency, as nowadays administered; of the now dominant fashion of the thing. Could we have it on a more regular, established, quiet footing; twice a week, or so, instead of every night; or always, like the

Drama, the year round, an opportunity always open, but not demanding such absorbing attention through a feverish little "season;" and with frequent presentations of the intrinsically *best* operas, it might then take its place with Oratorio and Symphony among the highest means of musical culture. But now it is more a thing of fashion and excitement than of Art.

The Opera which Maretzek now brings us has many points of excellence. Of course, we cannot be so green as to chime in with so much newspaper talk about these weeks being an era in our musical history and this the most brilliant company we ever had. But we can truly say that its ensemble is very much above the average. In point of orchestra especially, and of chorus, and generally of *mise-en-scène* it may challenge comparison with any of the previous Italian visitations. All works, with few exceptions, smoothly and effectively together. It is something, too, to have the reins of musical direction sometimes in such a hand as Bergmann's, while Max himself and the other man are not bad.

The repertoire has been varied and much of it fresh and truly interesting. Of Verdi there has been only the *Trovatore* and *Ernani*—rare abstinence for these times—but quite enough. Of Bellini, only the *Sonnambula*, which is ever fresh and beautiful, among the best of quiet, unpretending things for wear. Donizetti's best, in the serious vein, *Lucrezia* and *Lucia*, have been given once. The rest fall under two heads: the sparkling comic pieces (*Crispino e la Comare, L'Elisir d'Amore* and *Fra Diavolo*), and great heavy, showy effect pieces (Gounod's *Faust*, and Meyerbeer's "Star of the North" and "Huguenots"). The comedy has been delightful.

Passing now to the principal singers, although the troupe combines much effective talent and accomplishment, it includes not one *great* artist, with the single exception of [Giorgio] RONCONI, for years the prince of baritones and lyric actors; of late years limited to *buffo* roles, in which his acting is consummate, full of the genius of fun, only too quiet, perhaps, to be appreciated by all. . . .

Of soprani and contralti there is, singularly, but one experienced and distinguished artist, namely Miss KELLOGG, who is applauded to the echo still in her Margaret, her Zerlina (*Fra Diavolo*), her Catherine in the "Star of the North," a part which she makes quite piquant, and where her silvery notes revel with rare grace and agility in Meyerbeer's long flute *obbligato* passage. All the rest are young debutantes. One of them, however, a prize. Miss AMALIA HAUCK, the maiden of seventeen, pretty and graceful, full of the charm of youth and naturalness, with a true soprano voice that vibrates purely and sweetly, a voice of real character and substance, although not a large one, but fresh and sympathetic, by her remarkable impersonation of the Somnambula, and of the more trying part of Lucia, created a delightful sensation. There is no resisting this charm of youth and innocence, when it has talent, tasteful instinct, good culture, and enough freedom and self-possession, as in this case. It must be admitted that she already sings artistically, beautifully, good both in simple song and in bravura. If it seem undeveloped to full power and evenness, it is chiefly in that running passage work, which can only be *learned*; the want is atoned for by nameless little graces which show themselves instinctively, unconsciously, sometimes in the most simple phrase or passing from one note to another. Her acting too is natural and graceful; good as far as it goes; the more refreshing that it is all within bounds; for it is the tendency of the whole school of Italian Opera to go too far. We were particularly pleased with this moderation in the crazy scene of Lucia, a sort of scene from which we almost always shrink, it is so painfully overdone. In the pretty part of Prascovia she fairly shared the laurels with Miss Kellogg's Catharine, in the duet almost equally matched as to singing, and with more charm of voice. We fear the trusting of so delicate and pure a flower to such a school as the Italian opera. Will *Verdism* get hold of her? Will she too have to give in to the fatal habit of exaggeration? . . .

24. *The French Opera in New Orleans*

Dating back to the first decade of the century, the French Opera in New Orleans was arguably the oldest musical institution in the country. It certainly was not unknown in the North. For six successive seasons, between 1827 and 1833, John Davis, the manager, had brought his company from the Theatre d'Orleans to New York. They visited Philadelphia as well, and in some years Boston and Baltimore, and introduced those cities to countless operas from the Italian and German as well as the French repertory, though all were sung in French. Their performance standard was far beyond anything achieved at that time in the northern capitals, and they were received as warmly as if they had come from Italy or France.

From the early years of the *Journal* Dwight took note of musical activities in New Orleans, often reprinting reports from the *Picayune*. "The musical taste of that city," he wrote in 1856, "has seemed to us, at this distance, to be quite a remarkable reflex of the taste of Paris." In 1868 a correspondent reported in some detail on the season at the French Opera House, in a city still suffering the aftereffects of war.

Dwight's Journal of Music, February 29, 1868

The French Opera in New Orleans

New Orleans, Feb. 18.—From all that one sees in the musical or other journals of this country, one would never suspect the existence of a permanent and well sustained Opera in this far away Southern metropolis; much less would one suppose that here, even in these depressing times, the "stock" Opera establishment is one that, in the judgment of any impartial but cultivated, nay, fastidious critic, would take the palm from any of the "Star" companies of the northern cities, about which so much noise is made. And yet I am convinced that this is the case, and, that the opera-goers of New York and Boston, Philadelphia and Chicago might know that this is no mere *provincial* boasting, as they will doubtless take it to be, I wish they might only be here on any of the grand-opera nights and hear and judge for themselves. If they did not come away feeling that, amid all the financial, civil, social distress of this city, amid all the breaking up and general dilapidation and positive ruin of its grand career of wealth and prosperity in times past, there is still left to New Orleans a native treasure which no other city in the Union can boast, then I am no judge.

"Art is long!" I never felt the force of this adage as I did last night, while I sat at the French Opera witnessing the production of "Le Prophète." Here in the midst of a city groaning under a financial and political depression never felt before, where care, and anxiety, and dreary forebodings cast their gloom over the out-door world—here is this temple of musical art, beautiful to the eye, and ever ready to lift the mind up to the fair, fresh and peaceful world of poesy and harmony. And here the people come; come as of old; come because they love Art, and look to it in times of outward depression as a sure and blessed means of relief and refreshment. It is not as a new sensation, or as the fashion of the hour, that the public, that is, the old musical public of New Orleans, now patronize their Opera. It is their old friend, their friend of palmy, bright days gone by, their friend now. It is their love for Art that makes their opera live in these days, when everything else is going over the board. Not that the season is a prosperous one financially; not that the house is nightly crowded; but that the demand for a high-toned, well sustained Opera is one of the popular demands here, and consequently, while there is money left the people will give it, rather than have their cherished institution go down. And what is the result? We have here for the whole season, which means here what it means in Europe, a season of months, not as in the northern handbills a "season" of "four" nights or "two weeks," a beautiful, well appointed Opera house, where a succession of operas of the highest order are brought out by a stock company, the Grand opera nights alternating with those devoted to lighter Opera, Bouffe and the like, or to the French Drama. . . .

The stock company of this establishment is certainly not a common one. It approaches more nearly the perfection of the royal establishments of the Continent than any other in America. The two tenors, DAMIANI and PICOT, have voices of great sweetness, richness and compass,—the latter of great power, and they sing with true artistic finish, and a nice appreciation of their role. They are intelligent and highly cultivated artists, and as such can interpret the works of a master. The baritone, LE CHEVALIER, besides possessing a beautiful figure and elegant bearing, has a very rich, round voice, and is graceful and eloquent in every gesture and motion. The soprani, Mlle. LAMBELE and Mme. PREVOST-SEGUIN, have sweet and pure voices, the former rather inclined to shrillness on the high notes, both capable of facile and nice execution, and sing truly and conscientiously. . . .

The bassi are good, if not superior. VAN HUFFLEN is powerful but a little harsh; DECRE, a very fair singer, and an admirable figure on the stage. Altogether, therefore, the combination is far above the ordinary, even though the company may not be possessed of one "Star" so-called. But being all true, careful, artistic performers, the merits of the company are such as we may look in vain for among the strolling troupes at the North, whose whole dependence is on one or two celebrities, and these often but indifferent artists at the best, however great their vocal attainments may be. . . . But I have spoken as if there were no "star" here. Well, if I do not apply that epithet to Mme. AUDIBERT, who sang Fides in the *Prophète* last night, then it is because I cannot associate anything of that clap trap phraseology with an artist so great and admirable as this lady. . . . Viardot sang this role, it will be remembered, at the first production of the *Prophet* at the Imperial Opera in Paris. Mme. Audibert has succeeded her in it on the same boards, and the mantle of such prestige falls worthily on her. . . .

Finally, I must say a word about the accessories. The orchestra numbers about forty musicians, under the able lead of M. CALABRESI. They play with great precision, and, like everything else about the establishment, seem "used to it." The house is not unlike the Imperial Opera in Paris in general design, although of course resembling it only in miniature. The parquette is surrounded with private closed boxes furnished with wicket screens. The balcony has two rows of open boxes and behind these a complete row of closed or partitioned boxes. Thus the whole interior has a thoroughly foreign air; especially as the gentlemen, without exception, come well-dressed, and those in the open balcony in evening dress; the ladies wearing no hats and appearing in the most brilliant evening toilette. Here we have, too, the cool and roomy *foyer* for the *entr'-acte* promenade, the *buffet* in the basement, the bell to ring the people in, the *three raps* on the curtain as the signal for commencing, so familiar to all European theatre-goers. In a word, if you at the north, wearied with the miserable fragmentary patchwork of Opera which you are put off with, wish to enjoy a few nights of an old fashioned standard *Opera Season*, then come to New Orleans and pay your two dollars a seat, and find youself at 7¼ o'clock in your place at the French Opera House. We can promise you no very grand spectacle, no very costly costuming and decorations; we are too poor for such things now-a-days; but we will insure you a well-bred, musical audience to sit among, an efficient and well trained orchestra, and a rendering of the masters in operatic art, which will inspire you with a determination to do what you can toward the establishment of as genuine an Opera at home.

VIATOR.

25. *The Mapleson Company—* Carmen

Minnie Hauk returned to New York in 1878 as one of the leading singers in a company brought directly from Her Majesty's Theatre, London, by its colorful manager, James Henry Mapleson. In the decade she was away, Hauk had enjoyed major successes not only in London but also in Paris, Berlin, Vienna, and even Moscow. Now she appeared in what was probably the strongest company Americans had seen. The prima donna was Etelka Gerster, Hauk's senior, considered by some to rival Nilsson and even Patti; Italo Campanini was the leading tenor, and Giuseppe Del Puente the star baritone.

They undertook a six-month tour that reached beyond New York, Philadelphia, and Boston to Chicago, St. Louis, Cincinnati, Baltimore, and Washington, with a total of 167 opera performances and 47 concerts. Hauk created a sensation everywhere with her portrayal of the new operatic heroine Carmen in the first American performances of Bizet's opera. Dwight reprinted a review of the New York performances of *Carmen*, in which the correspondent staunchly defends what was then a highly controversial work.

Dwight's Journal of Music, November, 23, 1878

(Correspondence of the Boston Courier)

Music in New York
"CARMEN" AND OTHER NOVELTIES
New York, Nov. 8, 1878

Carmen is the prevailing topic of conversation in New York musical circles. At the present writing four performances have been given and a fifth advertised. I cannot quite agree with those who claim that Minnie Hauck's acting, clever and artistic as it is, is the real cause of the success of the opera. Minnie Hauck *is* Carmen, to be sure, and it may well be doubted if there be another lyric artiste who can give a more vivid idea of the gypsy witch who leads a gallant soldier to his ruin, without remorse or pity, and who, as she shuffles and cuts the cards to tell her own fortune, is only disturbed for a moment as she reads there—*death*. The plot is not savory, the characters betray little acquaintance with the customs of polite society, and the spectator has his sympathies excited for no member of the *dramatis personae*. . . . But it is not the first opera with unpleasant features, which has been redeemed by good music. Let the plot go, then, for the present at least, and let us consider the music. There is hardly a critic who has not charged the author with imitation of one or several composers. There is a little of Auber in it, they say, a little of Verdi, a little of Offenbach and a great deal of Wagner. All these may be found reflected in the score, but there is a much larger quantity of Georges Bizet than of all the others put together. The score sparkles with bright thoughts. The rhythms, being it is said imitations of Spanish dance movements, are quaint. The melodies, though provokingly short, with, for the greater part, an apparent deliberate avoidance of thematic development, are very captivating and linger in the memory for days. Such, at least, has been my experience, and since my first hearing of the opera, I have been constantly haunted by phrases of the vocal parts or of the instrumentation. The orchestration is throughout extremely rich and ingenious, often symphonic; with marvellously beautiful and effective bits of imitation, and other evidences of its author's scholarly attainments, of which proof has been furnished in Boston in the *Suite Arlesienne*, played by Mr. Thomas's orchestra. The concerted movements are all finely constructed, and several grand climaxes are worked up superbly. I must confess that, since *Aida*, I have heard no new opera which has so impressed me with a sense of its composer's originality and with its own freshness. The *leit-motiv* theory has been observed to some extent—unobtrusively and with excellent judgment— and some writers, judging superficially, have taken this as a peg whereon to hang their charges of imitation of Wagner. How often must it be said that the use of a prescribed theme to signalize the entrance of a character, or to recall an incident in the drama, and a careful identification of music with the personage were in fashion long before the High Priest of Bayreuth knew his scales? Let me remind my readers, too, that Bizet was a declared opponent of the advanced German school, with decided opinions of his own on *Tannhäuser*, and that in *Carmen* his intention was to produce an opera in which no one of the ideas of the great German philosopher, poet and musician should be developed. And in *Carmen* there is no "revery," nor "ecstatic poetry," nor "pure symphony." On the other hand there is life, there is movement, there is melody—an opera, in short, which, in spite of its ungenteel personages and its unconventional plot, has such a charming setting that its long life may be safely predicted. . . .

The performance of Mr. Mapleson's company has won hearty and deserved acknowledgment for its uniform excellence from the press here, without an exception, I believe. The subordinate parts were in good hands; the chorus was, for once, something like a chorus (except that formed of boys, representatives of Castilian *gamins*, who displayed wonderful skill in singing away from the orchestral pitch and from each other). There were not sixty in the band, as had been announced, but there were fifty, and Signor [Luigi] Arditi kept them well in hand, and would have kept them even better, to my liking, had he more carefully restrained the natural impetuosity of his brass quartet. The cuts made were very few, and in no case disturbed the movement of the drama. A word about the audience: it was the most cold-blooded, indifferent and unsympathetic assemblage I have ever encountered at an opera. Its almost entire disregard of the stage, so far as any outward and visible sign was concerned, would have disgraced the most critical audience who ever sat, in Boston, under the most impracticable lecture on the most intangible topic in aesthetics. . . . Mme. Gerster's first appearance is now definitely announced for next Monday, as Amina, in *La Sonnambula*. The lady, it is reported, has been at death's door ever since her arrival in America, but has fortunately recovered. . . .

26. *The* Pinafore *Craze*

The success of Mapleson's first season led the manager to return with a similar company the following year; and he continued for more than a decade, dividing his time between London ventures and American tours, sometimes barely skirting financial disaster. Other companies too were taking opera to the American hinterland, some performing in English in hope of reaching a wider audience. The great English soprano Euphrosyne Parepa Rosa was a pioneer in this field (see Part Three), as was Clara Louise Kellogg, whose English Opera Company took to the road in the mid-1870s.

Opera remained nonetheless exotic for American audiences, as was made clear when *H.M.S. Pinafore* appeared in 1878 and met with a popular enthusiasm previously reserved for extravaganzas and minstrel shows. Even John S. Dwight found *Pinafore* irresistible, and he pondered on the significance of its broad appeal.

Dwight's Journal of Music, July 19, 1879

H. M. S. PINAFORE

Is it not about time that we should say a word or two about this all-pervading, all-prevailing, most amusing, and extremely clever little operetta? If we have not thought it necessary for us to praise what all the world was praising, it was not from any want of interest in the pretty thing. We have been to see and hear it more times than we dare to name; we have spent pretty freely of our time and our spare (in the sense of meagre) cash upon it, both for our enjoyment and that of younger people, without whom we should not have yielded to the attraction quite so often. We certainly should not have done so had we not enjoyed it. But to an editor there is a sort of luxury, which we, in this case, felt inclined to hug and make the most of, in standing for once in a wholly unofficial, unprofessional relation, either as editor or critic, toward the musico-dramatic phenomenon of the day—a very long day too! Indeed, it doth enhance the charm of music not to feel obliged to write about it; and yet in the end one feels the obligation all the more.

The first thing to remark about this joint product of the wit and genius of Messrs. Gilbert and Arthur Sullivan, is its wonderful, its perhaps unexampled popular success. The immense run it has had in England is eclipsed by its universal vogue in every theatre, both great and small, of the United States. Hundreds of companies, professional and amateur, have been acting and singing it. In the great cities Pinafore has held the stage in half a dozen theatres at once. When we first saw it at the Boston Museum, whence it started on its rounds, we enjoyed it as a pretty, unpretending, fresh, amusing, harmless little thing, easily appreciated, full of pleasant humor, and of melodies of a quite catching sort, yet not flat, commonplace, or namby-pamby,—never vulgar. Closer attention revealed fine musicianship, rich, fascinating, delicate orchestration; everything was characteristic: the mock solemnity of imitated classic recitative, the graceful solos, and the well-constructed duets, trios, choruses, and ensembles; and all felicitously close to the meaning and the rhythm of the half serious, half funny words. Then, too, the mere finding of so clever a performance where you would hardly have supposed it possible, all from the resources of the stock acting company of the little theatre, and finding it so much better than it pretended to be, apparently, lent a peculiar zest to the whole thing. Singing and orchestra were in the main more than passable, in spite of drawbacks, such as the transferring of the tenor part of the hero to a soprano; the acting, too, was good, that of Mr. Wilson, as the K.C.B. inimitable.

Then came a New York company with it to the Gaiety, with several artists for singers, particularly a tenor able to cope with the quite formidable music of the part. When it was announced that there was to be an "ideal" performance of Pinafore in the vast Boston Theatre, and that the unpretending, pretty thing was to be given on a grand scale by the most famous and accomplished of our native singers, we were at first mistrustful of the policy; it seemed like overdoing it, and running it into the ground. But even through that magnifying glass it bore the test, and it took many weeks to satisfy the eager crowds. Since then it has been served up in every theatre and hall; church choirs go about the country

singing it; every child sings or hums it; the tuneful images repeat themselves, as in a multiplying mirror, from every wall, through every street
and alley. The "craze" is general, and some begin to talk about the nui-
sance of having to hear music "on compulsion," whether you will or not.
We are as easily bored as any one, and shrink from what is commonplace and hackneyed; but when we think how many more pretentious
bores and vulgarities under the name of music haunt the air and ruth-
lessly besiege all sensitive ears, we are easily reconciled to innocent and
thoughtless snatches from the Pinafore, which have not the exasperating
quality of say "gems" from *Il Trovatore*, and many more high-sounding
operatic titles.

—But to complete the history of this march of progress, we should
speak of the most unique and beautiful of all these presentations, namely,
the Children's Pinafore, now in its tenth week at the Museum. But that
deserves to be a subject by itself. It is too full of matter for feeling and
reflection, too suggestive, say of ideal possibilities in the direction of
aesthetic, rhythmic, and harmonic social culture, which may supplement the common education of the children of the republic, realizing
perhaps the Greek idea with far greater means for it than the Greeks
possessed or knew, that it would be useless to begin to treat the subject here. . . .

Now this amazing popularity of the Pinafore is something significant. It is easily accounted for. In the first place it indicates a general
longing for some artistic entertainment which shall be at once readily
appreciable, light, and humorous, yet graceful, clean, and innocent,
combining real charms of music, witty poetry, and action. And all this
the work supplies. It is extravagant, yet not devoid of sense and meaning. It is fascinating, piquant, and exciting; yet not sensational, in the
sense of the modern French novels which appeal to the same taste that
finds fascination in a public execution; it is sensuous and highly colored,
but not sensual. It is cleverer than the French Opera Bouffe, and doubtless has done much to drive out and occupy the place of that unclean
drama of Silenus. Musically and dramatically, or even farcically, it is a
thousand times better and more entertaining than those extravaganzas
of the "Evangeline" stamp, stuffed full of flat inanities and fly-blown
with puns too poor to raise a laugh. In short, though it is but a trifle if

you will, it is an artistic, a truly humorous, a musical trifle. It took an artist, a man of some creative faculty, each in his own sphere, to compose it. The music, it is found, wears well; the last hearing is pretty sure to reveal in it some new trait of beauty and of subtlety, some nice orchestral effect, some exquisite fitness of sound to sense. And the libretto!—It is so good, so felicitous a hit of genius in its way, that one will find it in vain to try to alter or improve upon it; every phrase and every word stands once for all, like the song that sang itself. Mr. Arthur Sullivan and Mr. Gilbert are to be congratulated on such joint authorship. They are proving themselves the world's benefactors; long may they continue in the good work, and find the next effort more remunerative to themselves!

In saying all this we do not shut our eyes to a more serious side of the question about this Pinafore "craze,"—a view well presented by a writer in the *Fortnightly Review*, from whom we copy elsewhere, under the title "Homer vs. Pinafore." While we rejoice that the popular craving for light and entertaining music and scenic action should be met for once by something pure and harmless, something truly musical and truly witty, it must at the same time be admitted that, from the point of view of deep and earnest culture, this cheap idolatry betrays a rather superficial, indolent condition of the general mind. All the earnestness of life being monopolized and taxed to the utmost by life's groveling material necessities and business competitions, it follows naturally that all the reaction toward the free ideal life of art and joy should seek that entertainment which costs no thought, no effort to understand and to appreciate. As it is we must have entertainment; most people are not equal, and few people at all times, to Homer, Dante, or even Shakespeare, or to *Fidelio, Don Giovanni,* or Gluck's *Orfeo.* If they must have plays and music which are light, what a godsend is a thing so innocent, so genial, so charming, and so satisfactory in its way as "H.M.S. Pinafore!"

Part Three

In the Hinterland

27. A Tour Westward

From his desk in Boston, Dwight sought to gain a view of musical development to the west and south by welcoming reports from distant subscribers and by encouraging friends to recount their musical experiences when they traveled. An early report of this kind, signed merely "T.," probably came from Dwight's younger friend, Alexander Wheelock Thayer, who was to be the author of a biography of Beethoven that remains a monument of musical scholarship. For years, Thayer's column "From My Diary" was a regular feature of *Dwight's Journal*; in it he ranged from chatty personal anecdote to scholarly discussion, writing sometimes from the countryside, sometimes from New York, and later from Germany. In this early report, there is a trace of condescension in Thayer's view of musical efforts "out west," but also some real concern for the fertility of the soil in which the singing master had been "sowing the seed."

Dwight's Journal of Music, June 19, 1852

Notes of a Short Tour Westward.
June 10th, 1852.

Dear Journalist:—You ask me, what musical items I have gathered on the short trip, which I have just made westward? Alas, one can travel from Dan to Beersheba as in old times and find all is (nearly) barren. But the singing master is abroad, and in some of the larger places, Cincinnati, Chicago, Milwaukee, Cleveland, &c., I am told that the seed is sown and that some time or other the harvest will come. Heaven grant it!

I was amused at one little town in Western New York, which shall be nameless, at what was to me a novelty. A singing school happened to close with a public performance, on an evening when I was there. There was nothing particularly good, and nothing particularly bad in the singing of the school—a young lady played the piano quite respectably, and occasionally added the tones of a cultivated voice, to the rest—how instantly a little cultivation is felt!—but on the whole, it was just what we can hear in almost any of our country villages every winter. A few anthems were sung—some new psalm tunes, &c. The novelty consisted in the display of some brother singing masters, who lent their valuable assistance for that night only, and gave us some glees, sentimental songs, and the like. One of them struck me as extraordinary—he could—and actually did—more than once carry a tenor part straight through, without faltering or wavering, say a quarter of a note from the pitch; and at the next stanza, begin just where he left off! A Duo passage or two for tenor and bass proved very rich. The singing master is decidedly abroad.

On the evening of my arrival in Rochester, Catharine Hayes gave a concert in the really fine hall, which is an honor to the taste of the city. I did not attend, but heard that the audience was very small. This was not true of another concert the next evening at the same place, at which two hundred and fifty sweet little creatures from the girls' schools of the city, gave a selection of songs and duets. The pieces were such as usually form the staple on such occasions; popular airs adapted to children's (childish?) poetry. The "Spider and the Fly," "Marseilles Hymn," "Home, sweet Home," and such like common airs were sung, and were really sung exceedingly well, and greatly to the credit of their teacher. . . .

The large hall was crowded and a very lively interest was plainly felt in the performance of the little Linds and Hayeses. I look upon these children's classes as of high importance—whenever the teacher really teaches them to read notes.

I could not learn that a concert of really classical music had ever been given in the place—and yet Rochester is said to have a population of 40,000. Suppose Rochester were in Germany—what an Opera we should have, what a concert orchestra, what garden concerts, what music from Haydn and Mozart in the cathedral—but it *isn't* in Germany, and I do not expect to hear an opera there this year! Musical missionaries are wanted! In Buffalo an old friend gave me a sad picture of the state of music there; here and there is an individual, who can recognize the divine thought and emotion which pervade the "tone poetry" of a Mozart or Beethoven—but no such general taste as leads to any attempt at the formation of any society for the cultivation of a taste for classical works, either vocal or instrumental. In the smaller towns on the Ohio, and on the routes from Pittsburgh to Detroit, there seems to be no assortment of good pianoforte music to be found; and I was several times asked for a list of pieces, which at the same time are easy and yet worthy of the name classical. A few popular songs, waltzes, quicksteps, &c., seem to be generally the stock in trade both of music sellers and music teachers there. Still one sees at times, that there is a craving for something beyond—the very indifference of many a young lady player to her pianoforte arises not unfrequently from the want of something, which shall gratify a natural taste that spurns the namby pamby airs, with the old hacknied "tum, tum, tum" accompaniment, which she alone knows, rather than to any want of real music. Why cannot some of our music publishing periodicals sometimes give a page or two of *real* music? Why should not Graham or Godey sometimes give an Andante from Beethoven or Haydn, instead of a "Lament on our dead Pussey," by the sentimental Mr. Jones? . . .

Music seems to be getting established on a good basis in Detroit. The better class of singers there are familiar with some good music— Romberg's "Song of the Bell" for instance; and Mr. Mills has strong hopes that in course of the next autumn and winter something may be attempted of a still higher class.

Beyond Lake Michigan music is under the protection of the Germans, and though perhaps as yet one can hear little of the truly classical, still the songs and ballads of Vaterland will in the end lead to something higher and nobler. It would be a little curious if in a few years a Bostonian should hear as much of the "genuine article" in Chicago as at home—and yet it will not be so very strange.

T.

28. *From San Francisco*

In the 1850s San Francisco was a booming new town, its population less than fifty thousand, its main attractions gold, gambling, and wild women. Still, while variety shows and minstrels may have been the most common musical entertainments, there were stirrings of other musical activity as well. In early issues of the *Journal*, Dwight took note of the California ventures of the Boston-born soprano Eliza Biscaccianti, who in 1852 gave San Francisco its first "season" of opera.

By 1853 resident Germans had formed four singing clubs and by 1856, as Dwight's correspondent records, there were the beginnings of an orchestra in San Francisco: a "Germania Society," evidently modeled on the famous Germania Orchestra that had toured so widely east of the Mississippi before it disbanded in 1854.

Dwight's Journal of Music, Boston, May 3, 1856

San Francisco, Cal., April 4. Thinking it might be interesting to yourself and your readers to know what kind of a place California is in regard to music, I will tell you what I have seen and heard in the four or five weeks I have been here. I left Boston on the last of January with many regrets, feeling it would be a long time before I should enjoy the delightful music of such concerts and operas as we had there. But I am agreeably disappointed to find much good musical taste and good music here in this new country.

I have attended two concerts of a series of six given by the "Germania Society;" and when I tell you the programme consisted of the compositions of Weber, Meyerbeer, Mendelssohn, and three movements from Beethoven's Grand Symphony in C minor, one or two lighter compositions to vary the performances, you will decide with me in my estimate of musical taste.

The orchestral performances, by thirty musicians, who seemed to feel what they had to do, were excellent, and, judging from the goodly number present, I should think were well patronized. A flute solo by Mr. KOPPITZ, I think was superior to anything I ever heard upon that instrument. . . .

This is the first attempt of this kind, giving a series of concerts, and it meets with general satisfaction. One great trouble here I would were obviated; that is, the lack of good pianos. I heard, a few evenings since, a fine performer execute Mendelssohn's Concerto in D minor, upon an instrument said to be the best to be had. O how my ears ached for a sound *something* like those elicited from one of Chickering's Grands!

Mr. Atwill, formerly of New York, tells me he sells much first class music here; so all or any of your publishers and music dealers must not suppose the Californians will purchase anything Bostonians would refuse. . . .

I think an English Opera company might do well here; can you send one?

29. *The Moravians of Pennsylvania*

From time to time, Dwight received correspondence from readers in Salem, North Carolina, and Nazareth and Bethlehem, Pennsylvania, towns which still preserved in some degree the musical tradition of their original settlers, members of the Moravian church. The Moravians can trace their origin back to the Hussite movement in the fifteenth century, but the first American congregations came from Saxony in 1735 and settled in North Carolina and Pennsylvania around 1740. Music permeated the life of Moravian communities as in no other American settlements. Hymns and anthems were at the heart of the Moravians' religious practices, and they cultivated and enjoyed secular music both at home and as a social activity.

As long as the communities remained self-contained and self-sufficient, their music thrived, though it had almost no impact on the outside American world. Ironically, as the towns opened up to non-Moravians before the middle of the nineteenth century, their musical vitality declined and only partially revived in such events as the Bethlehem Bach Festivals, begun in 1900. Dwight's correspondent here is a former Bethlehem resident, writing nostalgically from Philadelphia.

Dwight's Journal of Music, July 24, 1858

Philadelphia, July 20, 1858.—Not many miles from the city of Philadelphia, ensconced amid the noble hills which surround the valley through which meanders the placid Lehigh, is found the time-honored town of Bethlehem, the mother-congregation of that zealous and devoted band of Christ's followers, yclept, *the Moravians*. Romantic to a fascinating degree in location, rich beyond measure in historical and aboriginal associations, endowed with most excellent schools, embracing within its limits a population of superior intelligence, Bethlehem has lured hundreds of summer tourists from the gay dissipations of Saratoga,

Cape May, and other kindred resorts, and has, in point of fact, especially since the completion of the North Pennsylvania Railroad, constituted, itself *the* favorite watering place of the pent-up denizens of the Quaker City. The peculiarities of the Moravian Church, its early origin in Bohemia, its fearful struggles against the persecutions which reigned rampant in the middle ages, its final overthrow and subsequent renewal, its untiringly faithful and self-sacrificing efforts in the mission cause in all parts of the globe,—these are doubtless familiar to all such of your worthy readers, as chance to take even a superficial interest in general church history, and it is not my design to touch upon these prominent features of Moravianism. My object is rather to point attention to the musical culture of this body of Christians, who foster the "divine Art" with all the inherent enthusiasm and assiduity peculiar to the Germans and their descendents. Sacred and secular music seem to be cultivated with equal zeal by them, and all of the light, flippant, modernized style of composition is scornfully spurned from both departments.

Every Moravian church lays a peremptory stress upon congregational singing, and the children are trained with a view to this from the earliest infancy. They are, if I may use the expression, *inoculated* with the rich harmonies and graceful movements of the church chorals, and these settle firmly into their systems. Apart from all this, however, there is attached to each church a regular choir, trained to the execution of difficult sacred music, and brought into active requisition upon festival days and solemn occasions. This body of vocalists usually finds its accompaniment in a fine orchestra, which, in connection with the village organ, very materially heightens the general effect, rendering this more imposing and swelling in anthems of glorification, and *per contra*, more impressively solemn in the requiem over the departed or in the holy ceremonies of the Passion Week. The choir and orchestra of Bethlehem have been very celebrated for well nigh a century past. Years ago, when, in the gradual growth of Philadelphia, amid the slow development of its internal resources, music first assumed a living shape in the formation of the Musical Fund Society, and when this now powerful corporation was in its puling infancy, it was very customary, upon concert occasions, to borrow from Bethlehem the material wherewith to fill up its orchestra to suitable dimensions. . . .

But I am digressing from my remarks upon the sacred music of the

Moravians; I shall enlarge upon their cultivation of the secular department in another letter.

The repertoire of every Moravian congregation comprises within its limits the works of the greatest masters, from Mozart to Spohr, besides numerous contributions of great merit from the pens of church-members, who, with less of retiring humility and more of worldliness, might have carved out for themselves prominent niches in the temple of Fame.—There are now in constant use and practice among this small body of Christians, anthems, motettos, &c., from the works of their own brethren (such as Beckler of former times,—Bishop Wolle and Rev. Francis Hagen of the present day,) which exhibit unmistakably that deep-searching, mathematically constructed *cultus*, that intellectual, ideal, aesthetical conception of music, which causes the rigorous German school of composition to be regarded as the broad foundation upon which the entire Temple of the Muses stands firm. . . .

Another feature of the sacred music department, among the Moravians, is the *trombone choir*, which announces from the steeple of the village church to the quiet inhabitants beneath, the deaths of individual members, as these chance to occur; and which usually precedes, with solemn chorals, the funeral cortege, as it winds its noiseless way towards the lovely, peaceful graveyard, not many paces from the church. This so-called *trombone choir* also performs upon other occasions, but its services are chiefly brought into requisition as above mentioned; in fact, when a death occurs, and the rich harmonies of the quartet float over the disturbed village in announcement of the melancholy fact, the mechanic lays aside for the moment his implements, and feels as though distant strains from another world were approaching him. By a systematic arrangement, he is furthermore enabled to distinguish accurately the sex and progress in life of the deceased, by the particular hymn-tune which comes to his ears. However, I greatly suspect myself to have wearied your patience with this subject, by spinning my story unduly. In my next letter, I propose to afford to your readers some idea of the secular music of Bethlehem, as cultivated by its Philharmonic Society, its excellent Brass Band, and in its individual private families.

MANRICO

Dwight's Journal of Music, August 7, 1858

Philadelphia, July 27. . . . The Moravians cultivate secular music practically and perseveringly; but although many of their prominent musicians, deeply skilled in the theoretical, ideal, and aesthetical phases of the divine art, have produced, (as I remarked in my last,) works, which, under certain circumstances, would command unqualified admiration in any part of the world, I am not aware that any of these men have ever essayed or produced secular effusions of special note. The gladsome piety which pervades the ranks of this little band of Christians has prompted these religious worshippers of the Muses to direct their talents exclusively to the praise and glory of that higher power which has blessed them with gifts so precious.

The cultivation of secular music in Bethlehem is fostered by a Philharmonic Society of many years' standing, a brass band, a sextet of saxhorns, and by the judicious efforts of excellent teachers in private families, as well as in its very justly celebrated female seminary.

The Philharmonic Society has, at almost every period of its existence, been regarded as the best organization of the kind, outside of the three great cities of Boston, Philadelphia, and New York. It finds its support in a regular number of subscribers, who, for an annual contribution, receive the enjoyment of four concerts during the winter season. Formerly a grand daylight concert on Whitsuntide was added to the subscribers' *quid pro quo*. Indeed, this Whitmonday entertainment was *the* concert, *par excellence*, of the season, as each successive year rolled onward; for the exercises almost invariably comprised a great oratorio or cantata, well rehearsed, and exceedingly well given. The "Creation," the "Messiah," the "Seven Sleepers," "Alexander's Feast," and other distinguished works, have all been frequently and satisfactorily performed at their Whitsuntide *fêtes*. . . .

The rehearsals of this society were faithfully held twice per week, for many years. These "practisings" also rest vividly in my memory; how, before the appointed hour, as each member dropped in, the older portion were wont to gather around a patriarchal old stove, and pass the news of the village from mouth to mouth, while the young sprouts ogled the girls in the main body of the old Concert Hall; but I must onward.

Some few years since, the Philharmonic Society of Bethlehem, from various causes, disbanded *in toto*. It has, however, been vigorously revived; and the names of many of its former active and honorary members stand side by side with young men who now make their first attempts in the renewed orchestra. Its present leader, Mr. Charles F. Beckel, is an admirable musician, theoretically and practically, and enjoys to a well-merited degree the confidence of his *confrères*.

The Bethlehem Brass Band, as at present constituted, has attracted much deserved commendation wherever it has been heard. Its repertoire consists of a most admirable assortment of arrangements for various occasions, all of which are executed with a precision and general excellence in detail, which leaves very little to be wished for, and which ensures for it more engagements than the individual members find time or inclination to accept. The very men who now compose this excellent *corps*, were, some years since, known as the *Juvenile Band of Bethlehem*, a clarionet band of the old style, sustained by young boys whose leader had numbered scarcely his fifteenth summer.

Another noticeable feature of the secular music of the Bethlehem Moravians, is its Sextet of Saxhorns. It is an offshoot from the Brass Band above mentioned; and the young gentlemen who comprise it really deserve much credit at the hands of a public which has time and again been delighted with its performances. I can scarcely imagine a more delightful serenade than this admirable sextet of musicians are able to furnish. Their repertoire contains an extensive selection of arrangements from German melodies, oratorios, operas, &c., with occasionally an airy Italian cavatina to follow the substantial feast in the capacity of a light dessert.

Finally, Music is taught in all the private families of the individual Moravian congregations, with an assiduity and watchful perseverance which greatly tends to develope the results which we have thus cursorily endeavored to portray. . . .

Much enthusiastic stress is likewise laid upon the cultivation of good music in all of the Moravian boarding schools. Those at Nazareth, Bethlehem, Litiz, and Salem, N.C., possess, in their internal economy, the best arrangements for implanting into the minds of their pupils a thorough and systematic foundation in this heavenly art; and their public entertainments and vacation exhibitions are almost invariably graced with compositions of a very high order of merit. The "Messiah" has been several times most admirably given at the Bethlehem Seminary, under the superintendence of its efficient and accomplished Principal, Rev. Sylvester Wolle.

MANRICO

30. *A Music Teacher Out West*

The Yankee singing master, pictured making his rounds aboard horse or donkey like a circuit rider, had a western incarnation who traveled from place to place by rail. Writing from Aurora, Illinois, Dwight's Chicago correspondent outlines the full seven-day schedule of a typical midcentury singing teacher in the West. The work requires "untiring energy," he notes, but it does pay fairly well.

A later edition of the *Journal* carried a correction of one detail. "Dear Dwight," the correspondent wrote on January 7, 1860, "Tell your printer to put on his 'specs' when he next reads proof for 'Der Freischuetz.' Choirs $100 per annum, (*one*, not *seven*). Did the man think we were made of money out west?" The pseudonymous correspondent—who was to send Dwight further comment from Chicago—probably was W. S. B. Mathews, later music critic of the *Chicago Tribune*, editor of the monthly magazine *Music*, and author of an early history of music in America.

Dwight's Journal of Music, Boston, Saturday, December 24, 1859

Aurora, Ill., Dec. 10.—Perhaps some of your readers may like to know something of a music-teacher's life "out West." For the edification of such I subjoin a memorandum of a week's work of a music-teacher in regular standing.

Monday. Take the cars at 10 o'clock, and go to B., thirteen miles, ten by railroad and three by stage. In P.M. give private lessons from 2 to 4 on Melodeon. Eve, singing class, numbering seventy-five. They will sing the cantata "Daniel" at close of the course as a concert.

Tuesday. 9 to 10 A.M. singing lesson to public school. P.M., two private lessons. Eve., singing class at C, (three miles from B) numbering fifty. The weekly singing school is an event to the most of them and the enthusiasm is proportionately great.

Wednesday. One private lesson. Eve., singing class, numbering seventy, at D, (Five miles from C.) The enthusiasm is good, and they will sing "Esther," by Bradbury, at the close of the course.

Thursday. Take the cars at 3 A.M., and go to E, 17 miles from D, (we came back to D after singing school last eve,) and give private lessons on pianoforte all day, say ten lessons. Return to A. in eve on the cars. This eve, for a wonder, we have to ourself, and luxuriate in going to bed at 8 P.M.

Friday. Give four private lessons on piano. At 1 P.M. lesson in public school, one hour. Eve choir meeting; this is a Catholic choir, and sings Mozart's Masses and such like. This evening is a pleasure.

Saturday. Take the cars at 7 A.M., go to E seven miles, and walk to F, three miles further on. Give six piano lessons, walk back to E, give four lessons, return to A, and sing at choir rehearsal (Baptist) from 7½ to 8½. At 8½ go to Catholic choir, and return home at 11 P.M., thoroughly tired both in mind and body. You retire to rest with comfortable consciousness of being able to sleep until 8 or 9 o'clock the next morning.

Sunday. At 10½ A.M. go to Baptist church and play and conduct singing for first two hymns, which being got along with, must be at Catholic Mass at 11 A.M. This lasts until 1 o'clock, and then hurrah for freedom until 4 o'clock, when Vespers require our attention. This is soon over, and we are free again until 5½ P.M., when the evening service at Baptist must be attended. Finally, at 9 o'clock, P.M., your week's work may be summed up at 28 private lessons, three singing classes, two public school lessons, three choir meetings and four services on Sunday. Sometimes this routine is varied by an application to conduct a three days' session of some county musical association, when we delight in the best of Psalmody, Anthems, and choruses from Mozart and Handel.

"What works do we use?"

Why, for singing classes on Monday and Tuesday eve, the "Shawm;" Wednesday eve, the "Jubilee;" in the public schools, "Mason's Normal Singer;" for the Melodeon, "Zundel's Method;" for the piano forte, "Richardson's New Method," which we like much; for advanced pupils, anything from Grobe to Beethoven.

"Does it pay?"

Well, pretty well; here is the tariff. Private lessons, 50 cents each; public schools, $1.00 each; singing classes, for 12 lessons, $1.00 per scholar. Conventions anywhere from $25 to $100 for three days. The first sum is about the customary price to a local conductor. Choirs, $700 per annum, each.

"Is there much musical taste there?"

Well, yes; pretty good, at least for the country which is so new. We have some fine musicians in the West.

A good knowledge of music, geniality, good humor, knowledge of human nature and "soft sawder," and untiring energy are essential to succeed here, and with them one may do well, as the above (which is the actual week's work of the writer), will show.

DER FREISCHUETZ

31. *From St. Louis*

St. Louis was an important stop for traveling concert parties and opera troupes, and the influx of German immigrants toward midcentury offered them an increasingly hospitable audience. Early issues of *Dwight's Journal* record the beginnings of local musical organizations, which developed along a familiar course from singing clubs to choral societies to the choral-orchestral Philharmonic Society. The latter was led by Koenigsberg-born Eduard de Sobolewski, who had studied with Carl Maria von Weber and had an opera produced by Liszt at Weimar before he came to the United States in 1859. His first stop was Milwaukee, where he produced the opera *Mohega*, with his own libretto (in German) on an American subject: a romantic encounter between General Pulaski and an Indian maiden during the Revolutionary War.

In 1860, Sobolewski was called to St. Louis to be music director of the new Philharmonic Society, which he conducted for the next six years. A correspondent reported to Dwight on the organization of the society, and another later described a concert that took place not long after the outbreak of the Civil War. The presence of Federal troops in the city seems to have dampened the festivity not at all. And too, out west a touring pianist would still leaven a program of music with a bit of magic.

Dwight's Journal of Music, December 8, 1860

St. Louis, Nov. 22.—We once took a young lady to whom we were "devotedly attached" to the opera. She liked music, so did we, though sometimes we prefer to change the key "from long metre and short metre to meet her by moonlight." Overcome by the ravishing allurements of the opera, she exclaimed, *"How well music does go with singing."*

We were not particularly impressed with the remark then, but fully realized its truthfulness, when attending the second concert ever given by our Philharmonic Society on Wednesday evening. A word about its formation.

The St. Louis Philharmonic Society was formed "to advance the study and promote the progress of music in St. Louis, and to encourage the reunion and social intercourse of the lovers of music in our city." There are three classes of members, life members, subscribing members, and performing or active members. The subscribing members pay fifty dollars each. There are now one hundred and three, and only in its second month. These one hundred and three men, represent over twenty-five millions of dollars of this city. Every concert increases the members. They will spend every cent gained this year, over five thousand dollars. The tickets for the concerts are *never* sold, any member selling or disposing of a ticket for gain, forfeits his membership. The performing members number one hundred and ten. They each pay five dollars per year. The musical year consists of eight months from September till May, one concert to be given every month, and the tickets distributed regularly among the members, as many tickets in all being given as there are seats. These concerts are given in our finest hall, and are attended by the finest audiences St. Louis can boast of.

Their leader, Mr. EDWARD SOBELESKI, has a better European than American reputation. A better musician never was west of the Mississippi river, as he can both lead the orchestra and the vocal score. His office and the librarian's are salaried. Of course some of the orchestra are hired, there being no amateur player on the clarionet, horn, &c. They have two rehearsals every week, and the leader gives two extra ones besides, and in addition to all this the leader devotes three hours every day to instructing members not well up in their parts. The rehearsal rooms are the finest for the purpose I ever saw. The first concert was a complete success. The programme being mainly classical music. . . .

The second concert of the Society was given on Wednesday evening, 21st inst., to an audience of over two thousand. I append a programme. Everything went off as well as the most ardent friends of the society could wish.

PART I.

1. Overture, "The Elopement" . . . .   Mozart
2. Chorus, "Blessed is the Lord," from
      the Oratorio of Elijah . . . .   Mendelssohn Bartholdy
3. Trio for Soprano, Tenor and Basso,
      from Fidelio . . . .   Beethoven
4. Symphonie in D, first part . . . .   Beethoven
5. Sextette, "Chi mi frena," from Lucia
      di Lammermoor . . . .   Donizetti

PART II.

1. Overture, "Der Freischütz" . . . .   C. M. v. Weber
2. Double Chorus from Antigone, for
      Male Voices . . . .   Mendelssohn Bartholdy
3. Flute Solo, "Air Allemand" . . . .   Boehm
4. Cavatina, "In tears I pine," from
      "I Lombardi" . . . .   Verdi
5. Solo and Chorus, "Inflammatus est,"
      from Stabat Mater . . . .   Rossini

The Society are determined to cultivate a taste for classical music. The Symphony of Beethoven and Chorus from Antigone, sung by over one hundred and twenty voices were especially fine. As might be expected many could not understand it. One young lady near me, remarked after the symphony was played, "Well, ain't that funny music?" Just so, it was funny to some, but we hope it will not be long.

We would like to make particular mention of the soloists, and of some other things, but somehow no matter how kindly a thing is said, some one is offended. If you criticise they are offended, if you praise they are offended, because some one else is praised more, and so it goes. . . . We have no musical critic in this city at all connected with any paper. It is only a "local" and the motto "cut it short" and praise home talent or "advertising talent." They contract for advertising and so many lines of "notice," and so it goes, and so it always has gone, and will go, I suppose. The Society give their next concert next month.

I can not close without adverting to our system of music in the Public Schools. The "Board" and Superintendent are doing all they can to make music an indispensable branch. The Superintendent is earnestly striving to promote this necessary end. The greatest obstacle is the people who refuse to vote supplies. They see no necessity for buying aught but chalk and black boards, entirely ignoring the ennobling influences of music. But of that more anon.

PHIL.

Dwight's Journal of Music, February 8, 1862

St. Louis, Jan. 25th, 1862.—Our Philharmonic Society gave their fourth Concert, of this season, on Thursday evening, to a crowded house as usual. Queerly enough, notwithstanding the universal and too earnest cry of hard times, and entire want of money, it appears as though places of amusement were never better patronized then they are this winter. It can only be accounted for, by presuming that men in business are so harrassed and annoyed during the day, that they find more need of amusement, to drive care away and make them forget for a time that they are creatures subject to trials and troubles. Be it as it may, our concerts are literally jammed, several hundred being refused admittance last evening. One noticeable feature which attracts the attention of strangers, one which you quiet people in Athens are entirely unaccustomed to, is the pains which the ladies take to dress in such a manner as to make known their Union or "Secesh" principles, and at the same time to be fashionably attired. Red skirts, white waists and red bonnets, white trimmings, white handkerchiefs, red borders, red and white rosettes, &c.

But I am wandering from the concert, which had this fine programme:

PART I.

1. Overture—"Der Wassertraeger,"
   (the Water-Carrier) . . . .   Cherubini
2. Vintage Chorus—from "Dinorah". . . .   Meyerbeer
3. Cavatina—"O Madre del Cielo,"
   from I Lombardi . . . .   Verdi
4. Scherzo—from "First Symphonie" . . .   Beethoven

5. Sextetto—"Words of Sacrilege"
   from Il Poliuto .... Donizetti

PART II.

1. Overture—"Melusina" .... Mendelssohn Bartholdy
2. Chorus—"Crucifixus" .... Lotti
3. Violin Solo—"Homage to Rubini" .. J. Artot
4. Finale—from "Second Symphonie"... Mozart
5. March and Chorus—from
   "Tannhaeuser" .... R. Wagner

The Society gave a grand ball Thursday evening, Feb. 6th, for the benefit of their excellent Librarian, Mr. KUHE.

This gentleman devotes his whole time to the interests of the Society, as you can conceive when I state that for the second concert he copied 2000 pages of music, for the third 1200, and 700 for the last with a prospect of 1600 for the next. This is rendered necessary, as there is a chorus of about 100, and 30 in the Orchestra. . . .

We have been treated to numerous minor concerts, well attended; and ROBERT HELLER has been delighting large audiences nightly with his excellent performances on the piano as well as by his extraordinary feats of legerdemain.

PRESTO

32. From Chicago

The population of Chicago grew tenfold between 1850 and 1870 and musical activity grew with it. Before the Civil War, there were at least three failed attempts to establish a philharmonic society, two of them under the frustrated leadership of former Germania Orchestra members. Somewhat more successful was Hans Balatka, a Moravian-born conductor who came down from Milwaukee in 1860 to lead a new philharmonic society that lasted all of eight years.

Meanwhile, traveling performers had been calling—Ole Bull, Clara Louise Kellogg, Gottschalk—and in 1865 Crosby's Opera House rose to give them an elegant new showcase. In its six years, ending in the Great Fire of 1871, Crosby's was host to virtually every opera company or concert party contrived by Grau or Bateman, Strakosch or Maretzek, interspersed during hard times with popular extravaganzas like *The Black Crook*, as well as Swiss bell ringers, gymnasts, and freak shows.

One of the visiting opera companies of 1869 was that organized by Scottish-born soprano Euphrosyne Parepa and her husband, violinist-conductor Carl Rosa. The Parepa-Rosa company, performing in English, gave important new impetus to American ventures in touring opera.

The tradition of English opera was older in the United States than the Italian, and English troupes like the Pyne-Harrison company and the Seguin Opera Troupe had taken opera on tour in America in the 1830s and 1840s. Later companies like Parepa-Rosa drew less on original English operas (by Bishop, Balfe, Wallace) and more on translations of the newly popular Italian repertoire. Even so, Parepa was carrying on a tradition. Her mother was the sister of Arthur Edward Seguin, the English basso who headed one of the most active of the early companies. And there were Seguins in Parepa's 1869 company: her cousin Edward Seguin and his wife Zelda, both accomplished artists who later appeared with the Emma Abbott Opera Company, one of several that followed on the success of Parepa-Rosa in the 1870s.

In a later report, Dwight's faithful Chicago correspondent discusses performances of the Mendelssohn Quintette Club, which after twenty years of playing in and around Boston had undertaken a western tour. It was the first of many such tours that made the Quintette Club a chamber-music counterpart of the Parepa-Rosa company in opera and the Theodore Thomas Orchestra in symphonic music. Musically too, the West was to be won.

Dwight's Journal of Music, December 4, 1869

Musical Correspondence

Chicago, Nov. 13.—The Parepa-Rosa English Opera troupe is just closing what is probably the most successful opera season ever given in this city. During the season the following works were performed: *Il Trovatore* (2), *Fra Diavolo* (2), *Martha* (4), *Black Domino* (2), *Bohemian Girl* (3), *Sonnambula* (2), *Puritan's Daughter* (1), *Maritana* (2), and Mozart's *Marriage of Figaro*, three times. Of their performance of *Maritana*, *Sonnambula*, *Puritan's Daughter*, and *Bohemian Girl*, I have before written. The *Bohemian Girl* was afterwards twice given, with Mme. Parepa-Rosa and Mr. [William] Castle in the roles originally assigned to Miss [Rose] Hersee and Mr. Nordblom. In respect to singing it was perhaps an improvement to put Mme. Rosa in Miss Hersee's place; but as far as appearance goes, it pleased me more to see Miss Hersee in the role of "Arline." The other substitution, however, was much to the advantage of the performance. No tenor is more admired here than Mr. Castle, and on the occasion of his benefit we had one of the largest houses of the season.

Martha was a great success. The light and pleasing music of this opera, the unobjectionable nature of the plot, and the perfect familiarity of the singers with the music and the requisite stage business, combined to make a very pleasing ensemble. *Martha* is also better known here than any other opera, it having been played in Chicago upwards of thirty times.

But the event of the season was the production of Mozart's *Marriage of Figaro*, for the first time in English, and for the second time in this city. . . . In the present case the roles were taken thus: "Susanna," Mme. Parepa-Rosa; "The Countess," Miss Rose Hersee; "Count Almaviva," Mr. [Alberto] Laurence; "Figaro," Mr. S. C. Campbell; "Don Basilio," Mr. Nordblom; "Antonio," Mr. Seguin; "Cherubino," Mrs. E. Seguin; "Doctor Bartolo," Mr. Gustavus Hall; "Marcellina," Miss Fannie Stockton. On this cast there are a few observations to be made. It admits of question whether Mme. Parepa would not more properly have been the "Countess," and Miss Hersee "Susannah." . . . Miss Fannie Stockton is a good actress, and, I am told, a most estimable person, but she has such a habit of singing out of tune as to render it necessary to omit the duet she sings with Susannah in the first act, and her song, "The hart and hind together," in the last act. The part of "Cherubino" was excellently done by Mrs. Seguin, who is good in everything she undertakes. Mr. Nordblom did well. "Figaro" was hardly lively enough, but the music was well sung. Besides, allowance should be made for the very great demands that this opera makes on the singers, requiring so much of their attention as to render it a labor of time to become easy in the stage business. The other three leading parts were done so well, Mme. Parepa, Miss Hersee and Mr. Laurence being so entirely competent to their respective roles, that it is unnecessary to praise them. . . .

The orchestra did very well indeed, thanks to Carl Rosa. How then was Mozart's music received by our public? Three performances were given. The house was entirely full every night. That is, every seat was occupied and several hundred people were standing. The last night was the fullest. Notwithstanding the enormous houses, there was less enthusiasm than on some less pretentious occasions. The music is so smooth and melodious, there is so little mere noise in the score, the pieces are of such equal excellence, while the arias do not terminate with a grand flourish of cadenzas, that the public were often at loss to know where to applaud. But the crowded houses at the end of the season, and the general interest, spoke more for the appreciation of the public than the most violent applause could have done. . . . The troupe has *Faust, Norma,* and *Oberon* in preparation. I ought also to bear witness to Mme.

Parepa's wonderful endurance. I have never seen a singer capable of enduring so much hard work. . . .

DER FREYSCHUETZ

Dwight's Journal of Music, April 9, 1870

Chicago, March 25.—The Testimonial Benefit tendered to the
Mendelssohn Quintette Club last Saturday, prior to their return to the
East, makes a fitting occasion for me to give your readers a brief outline
of their doings in this department of the "moral heritage" during the
past few months.

As you know, the Quintette Club came West in October, and entered upon an extended tour which has just closed. They visited and
gave concerts in all the principal towns of Michigan, Indiana, Kentucky,
Illinois, Minnesota, Wisconsin, Iowa, Kansas and Missouri. To do this
they travelled more than 9,000 miles, and gave over 150 concerts. In a
large majority of instances their concerts have been the first introduction of really artistic music to the respective audiences; and, when we
consider the power of first impressions, we can hardly over-estimate the
artistic importance of a series of musical entertainments given by so accomplished artists as these, throughout the small cities that are just now
entering upon that stage of existence in which artistic culture becomes
possible. This and the unusually extended provincial tour of the Parepa-
Rosa troupe, bringing the best singing where no true song had ever
been before, seem to determine the present as a musical season long to
be remembered.

In many of these towns the Club gave three or four concerts, and in
some cases, where but one had been intended, they were obliged to return from long distances to give one or two others, so highly were their
efforts appreciated. Of course the programmes were in most cases what
a Boston audience would term light, but every one contained at least
selections from the classics and very often a whole quartet. Beyond this
it was not found possible to carry the attempt to introduce classic music. The remainder of the selections consisted of arrangements of airs
from operas, parts of concertos, short extracts from symphonies, and a

variety of virtuoso doings. About the best appreciated of all these things were the wonderful performances of Heindl on the flute. The immense number of notes that he manages to get out of a flute in little or no time, and his truly wonderful length of wind, in which none but Parepa seems his equal, proved entirely too much for the self-possession of every audience.

Even in Chicago the programmes were no more severe than the Club have been in the habit of giving in the suburbs of Boston, and by no means up to the ultra-classical standard of the soirées in Chickering's Hall. They have given here eight concerts of the regular series, and quite a number of extra ones in churches in various parts of the city. . . .

On the "north side" four regular concerts were given in the Historical Hall, a pleasant, *recherché* little place, holding four hundred or so. Here they have gathered the best Chicago audiences, and here they have played their best western programmes; yet kindly as they did "temper the wind to the shorn lambs" in the matter of classicism, it was made a request that on the occasion of the farewell benefit the programme should be as *light as possible*. Hence it came that the following was the bill of fare:

Overture to the "Poet and Peasant"	Suppe.
Scene and Air, "Il Bacio"	
Miss Jennie Busk.	
Italian Fantasia for Flute	Tersheck.
Edward Heindl.	
Selections from Oberon, for Quintet	Weber.
Fantasie Melodique, for Violoncello	Schubert.
Wulf Fries	

Caprice in B minor, for Piano, Quintet	
accomp't	Mendelssohn.
"Salterella," Solo for Violin	Alard.
William Schultze.	
a) Song without Words No. 9, Bk V	Mendelssohn.
b) Scherzo from "Reformation Symphony"	Mendelssohn.
English Ballad, "Alpine Shepherd"	Glover.
Miss Jennie Busk.	
First Potpourri, an Original and	
Favorite Theme	T. Ryan

Concerning the execution of these selections I do not need to say anything, except that it was in the Club's best style. One of the most interesting features was the Mendelssohn *Caprice*, of which the piano part was played by Miss Tinkham, a young lady of, apparently, sixteen or so. . . .

I have spun rather a long yarn; my excuse is that I fear me it will be many a day before my pen gets afoul of this noble band of musicians again.

Meanwhile I am,

DER FREYSCHUETZ

33. *A Concert Company in Georgia*

A report from Macon, Georgia, describes the visit of one of the better concert companies that toured south and west from New York after the Civil War. The name of Adelaide Phillipps may have been new to a Maconite, but it was well known in the northeast as belonging to one of the most accomplished of American singers of opera and oratorio. The solo concert was still a rarity, so in the 1870s Phillipps traveled with the popular cornet virtuoso Jules Levy and a pianist and a male vocalist only sketchily identified.

Dwight's Journal of Music, February 11, 1871

Macon, (Georgia), Jan. 30.—The Maconites enjoyed last week an entertainment by the "Adelaide Phillipps Concert Company," which was refreshing to music lovers after a season of musical dearth.

Miss Phillipps came unheralded and unadvertised; and as she enjoys a reputation more local than continental, very few had heard of the fair cantatrice. But we presume to say none could have felt any disappointment in her wonderful contralto voice. The compass of her voice, as well as her executive skill, as exhibited in her rendering of that most hackneyed concert aria: "*Una voce poca fa*," was astonishing. It seemed to us a perfect piece of vocalization. She very graciously responded to all the encores, as did the other artists, and we were thereby compensated for a too short programme. A little ballad which she gave as an encore, called, we believe, "*The Angel of the Rosebush*," sung in a hushed, suppressed *sotto voce* (most effectively after a Laughing Song) still haunts us like a tuneful, sad spirit. But let me ask if public singers will never weary of "Comin' thro' the Rye," and if *claqueurs* will never cease applauding it! The coquetry of that bonnie Scotch lass is now acknowledged, and she certainly must be *passée*.

Mons. Levy excited a *furore* with his matchless performance on the Cornet. What a charming instrument it is in the hands of an accomplished player! His skillful producing and sustaining the voluptuous tones of the familiar melody, "The Last Rose of Summer," deliciously excited our musical sensibilities, and enfolded us in a reverie, from which we sighed to be aroused.

Mr. Ed. Hoffman, we suppose, would be startled to hear himself called a great artist or an *homme de genie*. He is neither, but we enjoyed his music notwithstanding. He played several original compositions with a pleasing grace and limpidity, on a light and sweet-toned Knabe Piano, just suited to his style. The "Last Hope," by Gottschalk, however, was rendered by him with less sentiment than we have heard from many amateurs. Mons. Hasler, if he had not been so extravagantly announced, would have astounded us more; but we can say he had a pleasing voice, of no particular strength, compass or cultivation.

We left the hall grateful. Grateful that these refined musicians had not passed us by, and that we had been mildly, not wildly entertained for one evening with music not severely artistic, but adapted to a people as yet untutored in musical classics.

34. *Educating an Audience*

The public for Dwight's kind of music was small, but he and his fellow advocates were certain it could be wider. For them, indeed, increasing it was essential to the moral uplift they felt ought to accompany the nation's growth. "Musical missionaries are wanted," T. had written in the *Journal*'s first year, and time had brought a stream of them, from the early singing masters to the later Sobolewskis and Balatkas, from Jenny Lind to Parepa-Rosa, from the Germanians to the Thomas Orchestra.

But it was no simple matter to win for "better" music a public happily accustomed to hymn singing, sentimental songs, minstrels, and variety shows. Some of the difficulties the musical missionaries faced are suggested in an article by one of Dwight's faithful western correspondents.

Dwight's Journal of Music, May 12, 1877

Travelling Concert Troups as Educators
BY JOHN C. FILLMORE

However discouraging to Eastern music-lovers may be the fact that artists are not well supported even in New York and Boston, we who live in the West ought to be able to feel that we may greatly profit by the necessity of travelling which seems to be laid on the members of the Mendelssohn Quintette Club, and similar organizations. At least, those of us who love music, who believe in the power of the *best* music to make its way among the people, wherever it is properly presented, and who are laboring with all our strength to bring whomsoever we can to a real love and appreciation of the best composers, would like to feel that, whenever a company of Eastern artists comes among us, they will give us really artistic renderings of the best music, to our real edification. We certainly do feel that we have a right to expect this. There are teachers scattered all through the West, who do their best to lead their pupils to Beethoven, Schumann, and all that noble company, and who really succeed in doing so, in a multitude of cases. They give their pupils the best music to study; they cultivate a taste for it; they seek to develop an intelligent, discriminating love for it. The greatest lack they feel is the almost total want of opportunity to hear great compositions interpreted by artists who make it their business to interpret them. The teachers are generally overworked, and in no condition to do justice to anything beyond a very small repertoire; the performance of their pupils is, of course, for the most part inadequate. They look therefore to the travelling artist to meet their needs, and that of their pupils, and, it must be added, of the music-loving public; for, wherever pupils study great composers, parents at home gradually acquire a love for good music, and soon find, to their own surprise, that trash does not please them as it once did. The travelling artist, therefore, has it in his power to render a great service to Art; to supplement the work of the laborious, conscientious teacher, to reinforce his teaching by example, and to kindle enthusiasm for the best music. Nothing can be of more importance to musical culture in America at this juncture, than that travelling violinists, pianists and vocalists shall be real artists and art-lovers, shall have an earnest purpose to educate their audiences and be helpful to them, and shall be above the vulgar temptation of stooping to claptrap. Of course it must be admitted at the outset that the path of virtue, in musical matters as elsewhere, is a difficult one. The travelling musician plays to miscellaneous audiences, composed largely of uncultivated people, totally ignorant of good music, and, what is worse, totally void of any desire to know it, or to improve themselves in any way,—people who go to a concert-room simply to be amused, and to whom any other conception of a concert than that of an "entertainment" would be utterly strange. In playing to such people, the really earnest musician labors under a two-fold embarrassment, and has a double temptation to give them only what they will like best, regardless of what will benefit them most;—he has taken to travelling because he was not well supported at home, and must please his audiences in order to make a re-engagement probable, and he finds it terribly uphill work to play good music to an unsympathetic audience. He remembers an excellent and authoritative saying about casting pearls before swine, and since, whenever he plays the best music, he is not applauded, or the applause is, at best, but faint, he concludes, in disgust, that the public are swine after all, and must have nothing but swill. Far be it from me to underrate the difficulties which such musicians have to meet, or to fail to put myself in their place, or to condemn their shortcomings too severely. But I firmly believe that, in many cases, the discouragements are, after all, more apparent than real: that artists only need to respect themselves and their art to make others respect both; and that noisy applause, or the lack of it, is no index to the pleasure of the audience or the permanent effect produced. I have been for nearly nine years a music teacher in a western town, one so small that I know personally a large proportion of its concert-goers. I have carefully studied this public; have been instrumental in getting outside musicians here, and have watched the effect of their concerts. I think my experience warrants me in holding some positive opinions on this subject; and I have thought that a statement of the results of that experience might be useful. The most important concerts given here within the past three years have been two by the Mendelssohn Quintette Club, one by Mme. [Camilla] Urso, one by Miss Julia Rivé, and one, a few weeks ago, by the Boston Philharmonic Club. Let me briefly state the character of their programmes, and their effect upon the public.

The Mendelssohn Quintette Club played, on both occasions, good programmes; the second being much better than the first. The first was played to an overflowing house, (owing largely to accidental circumstances), and was in all respects, apparently, a most encouraging success. The second was played to a very moderate-sized audience, and was, to all appearance, much less warmly received. I think the Club were much discouraged by their second reception; that they regarded it as decisively against their superior programme, and felt that they could not safely repeat the experiment. . . . I do not believe that any great part of the apparent ill success of the second concert was due to the classical character of the programme, but mainly to two facts;—first, that there were too few solos, and second, that Miss Kellogg, who sang some Schumann songs, and who had before made an excellent impression, was in very bad voice, had to give up entirely the next day, in fact,—and so disappointed the public. At any rate my conversation with average people, of no musical training, has forced me to believe that they enjoyed the best music most, (though they did not applaud noisily, because they did not feel like it;) that the Club is thoroughly respected and believed in here, and that they would be well received and supported here now. The only thing which prevented their engagement this season was a previous engagement with the Boston Philharmonic Club, the date of whose concert would have conflicted with theirs. On the other hand, this last-named club played a programme, a large part of which was sheer trash, and hardly any of which was of any musical significance. For example, Mr. Weiner's flute solo was a medley, containing "Home, sweet home," "Yankee Doodle," and "O Susannah." I was curious to know how this would impress the thoughtful part of the public, some of whom had complained that artists would not play simple things which they could understand. I believe I speak the exact truth when I say that the feeling with which all the better portion of the audience regarded this performance was one of mingled disgust and contempt. They had become familiar with the notion that artists were above that sort of thing; no artist had done it here before, and the incongruity of it was keenly felt. I took pains to ask men who had grumbled at classical programmes whether they liked this concert as well as those of the Mendelssohn Quintette Club, and I invariably got a negative answer. It is not too much to say that people felt that the playing of such a programme by artists involved degradation of themselves and contempt of their audience. . . .

Mme. Urso played last year a respectable, but not a classical programme. It was well received. Miss Rivé played two whole Sonatas of Beethoven, the *Appassionata*, and the one in E♭, Op. 27; three pieces by Chopin; the Marche Funebre, the Scherzo in B♭ minor, Op. 81, and the Rondeau in E♭; three by Liszt: Spinning Song, Tannhäuser March, and 2nd Hungarian Rhapsody, and Tausig's arrangement of "Man lives but once." This is as good a programme as she would have played in Boston, and it was thoroughly enjoyed. People said to me afterwards, "I never got much out of Beethoven before, but I thoroughly enjoyed the Sonata Appassionata." Moreover it was felt to be a compliment to her audience that she would assume that they desired to hear such things, and people like to be complimented. I am sure the public here entertain toward Miss Rivé feelings of strong respect and admiration. . . . She thoroughly respects herself, her art, and her audience, and she makes her audiences respect her. Let other artists mark, learn and inwardly digest these facts, and follow her praiseworthy example. In the long run, honesty, straightforward following of earnest convictions pays best, in art no less than elsewhere, in the matter of bread and butter, and from the lowest point of view from which a real artist can possibly look at his work. The sooner travelling artists become thoroughly convinced of this, the better will it be for musical progress in America.

—Ripon, Wis., April 29, 1877

35. *A Decade of Progress*

From Chicago, a former Bostonian provides Dwight with a review of musical development in the West in the 1870s. Much has been accomplished since T.'s 1852 tour westward, yet the later correspondent, like the earlier one, shows less than complete confidence in the success of the effort to elevate the musical taste of the great American public. True musical institutions are still lacking, he laments, and the question remains when they will emerge.

Dwight's Journal of Music, January 18, 1879

The Progress of Music in the West
BY C. H. BRITTAN

It is now some ten years since the writer of this article, fresh from musical experiences in Boston, began his life in the West. Every indication of musical progress has been carefully noted from that time until the present hour. The great West has bent the full force of her energy to commercial and agricultural life. Yet the development of a love for art and music is being manifested in so marked a manner, and its aspect is so noticeable in the generous support that is given to all that is worthy of recognition, that at last we have reached a position which entitles us to respect and consideration. The condition of music in the West is one that is brighter than ever before. The organization of important musical societies and home orchestras gives evidence of a more extended interest. A better class of music is studied by these societies, and our programmes often bear the marked words, "for the first time in America," even of an important composition. . . .

In three or four of the great cities of the West, we see efforts made in the same direction that was taken by Boston in the earlier years of its musical life. . . . When I first came to the West and attempted to find some of Robert Franz's lovely songs, it was with much difficulty that I made the music clerk understand what I wanted. There was little market for the so-called classical music, and the general tone of musical taste was largely indicated by the trashy compositions that found the largest sale. Yet there were influences at work that soon developed a taste for the better class of musical works, and Shumann's, Schubert's, and Franz's songs got a vocal hearing. The musicians were aided in their work by music lovers, and everywhere the signs were brighter. Should our Eastern friends watch our programmes for a season, and note the works which our local societies are producing, in contrast with their own, they could but admit that in endeavor, at least, we were equal. The first concert of the Beethoven Society of Chicago, this season, gave us "The First Walpurgis Night" of Mendelssohn, the overture and scenes from the *Tannhäuser* of Wagner, besides smaller pieces from Rubinstein and Gade; while the Apollo Club produced Handel's *Acis and Galatea*, and the first part of Mendelssohn's *St. Paul*. The orchestral accompaniments were better performed than last season, while the chorus did its work with more earnestness and a greater finish. When we contrast the programmes given in Cincinnati at the musical festivals with those offered by the Handel and Haydn Society at their triennial performances, we see that the West is in no way behind the East in her endeavors to produce the works of the great masters. The piano and organ recitals, that form no insignificant part of our musical season, are devoted to the performance of the best music. One society had all the sonatas of Beethoven, and the complete piano works of Schumann and Chopin, performed in an artistic manner, for the edification and education of its members, active and honorary. Thus also with the classical song-writers, a wider acquaintance has been made with their beautiful compositions by efforts of the same noble character.

I do not speak of the support given to operatic representations, for where fashion largely reigns, perhaps its motives are other than those which spring from a real love for the beautiful in art. To support an orchestra of excellence at home, to found and endow a music school of an exalted character, and to build noble halls to enable societies to have a proper place to perform great works in, would indeed show an atmosphere in which art could flourish. But, unfortunately, we are as yet in the early years of our development, and the whole country has hardly been able to support one really great orchestra, such as that of Mr. Thomas. Real culture must develop from germs that unfold in the home, and we cannot expect a great Conservatory of Music that can produce noble artists, and be above the low plane of a money-making concern, until we have created that love for music that shall induce the capitalist to part with some of his treasures, expecting no return but that which would come to him in benefiting his country and its people.

The various musical "conventions," "Normal Music Schools," and local gatherings for the performance or study of music, which have been held in the small towns in the West, have presented marked indications of progress during the past few years. Not long ago, a singing-book maker would hold gatherings of the "convention" character for the purpose of introducing his work; give an indifferent concert or two, with the aid of all the church choirs in the town or village, and pass on to another place to do likewise if possible. But of late there has been a great difference manifested in the work attempted at these conventions. Local societies are formed for the study of oratorio or cantata music, and as soon as they are able to perform it a public concert is given. Thus the convention director is obliged to furnish better works for study, if he would obtain an engagement, for the old and crude idea of music is giving way to one that shows a fuller culture. The normal schools that are held all over the western country during the summer months, bring together a better class of teachers and performers. As one notes their programmes, he observes the weekly "recitals" at which classical music is largely given, while the evening chorus rehearsals are devoted to parts of oratorios, or choruses of the better class. Solo talent of no mean order is employed, and year by year improvement is made in the manner of conducting all their public performances. These musical gatherings are but the forerunners of permanent organizations, and leave behind them a local interest that in time will develop into better things. It is no uncommon occurrence to have pupils come into the city for instruction, bearing with them perhaps a sonata of Beethoven, a nocturne of Chopin, or something from Mendelssohn, which they had learned in a far distant little town. Upon being questioned as to their instruction, we hear of some devotee of music, who, having settled in the Far West, made his influence felt by training young fingers to play the noble works of the truly great masters. Thus, in thousands of cases, is the good seed planted all over this western land. It is not alone in the cities that a deeper love for the pure in art is manifested. Not long since a letter was received by one of our local teachers, coming from a little town in the extreme western part of Kansas. The writer mentioned a young daughter who had been studying the piano, with the best assistance that could be obtained in the village, and also stated that the little girl had found Mendelssohn's and Beethoven's letters among the books in a small library in the place, and from her interest in them was eager to have some of their music. "Would it be possible," wrote the father, "for you to send us some little things from these masters, that young fingers might try? for although we are living beyond the reach of the benefits of a city's culture, we do not wish to degenerate in our love for what is beautiful and grand." Any number of pleasing indications of this character are constantly coming to the observer of the advancement of culture in the West.

Yet, notwithstanding our seeming progress, we are far from being, even as a nation, a musical people. Can Boston be really a musical city, when it becomes necessary to send out most earnest appeals to the cultivated part of its people to give a better support to the Harvard Musical Association, that it might go on another season, and furnish orchestral concerts of an artistic character without the danger of financial ruin? Is New York musical, when she allows a fine organization like Thomas's Orchestra to be disbanded for want of enough support to live? Can we be a musical people, and yet have no permanent opera in any city in the country, and no endowed musical school of a high rank anywhere in the land? We force even our best musicians into the teaching rank to earn their bread. Until home organizations in good musical societies, fine orchestras, and convervatories worthy of the name are supported by the great cities of our land, and the musical talent is given proper encouragement, we cannot be more than slowly approaching the rank of a music-loving nation. . . .

Chicago, Dec. 21, 1878

36. *From Cincinnati*

The transitional state of the country's musical development could be seen in microcosm in Cincinnati, where permanent musical institutions were beginning to emerge in a sometimes painful process of growth and reversal. A central figure in the process there was Theodore Thomas, who founded the Cincinnati Music Festivals in 1873 and later gave the Cincinnati College of Music its start. Dwight wrote more than once of the ambiguity he saw in Thomas' influence: On one hand, the conductor unquestionably set standards of performance that excited audiences and inspired musicians; on the other hand, the excellence of his traveling professional orchestra put struggling local bands so far in the shade that the public became (at least in Dwight's Boston) reluctant to give homegrown efforts the support they needed. Even in Chicago, it was charged that the visiting Thomas Orchestra's performances utterly squelched interest in Hans Balatka's Philharmonic Society, a loss uncompensated until two decades later when Thomas returned to found the Chicago Symphony Orchestra.

Cincinnati, too, both benefited and suffered from Thomas' uncompromising professionalism. When the music school's financial benefactor sought to lower standards for business reasons, Thomas resigned as director and returned to New York. In the long run, Thomas' principles prevailed, but in the meanwhile, in 1881, it was a rather sombre report from Cincinnati that Dwight found in a Boston newspaper and relayed to his readers.

Dwight's Journal of Music, March 26, 1881

Music in Cincinnati
CONCORDS AND DISCORDS.—THE THOMAS INVASION.—PAST ORCHESTRAS.—THE OPERA FESTIVAL.

The following is the principal portion of a letter from Cincinnati (March 5) to the Boston *Daily Advertiser*:—

Doubtless many of your readers think of Cincinnati as a great musical centre, a place where symphonies and operas are everyday affairs, a city in which pigs become pork to slow orchestration, and wherein beer is brewed to grand choral accompaniments. Such being the popular notion, it may be well for me to state the facts.

Not many years ago Cincinnati was as barren musically as any other Western town. Theodore Thomas came here with his orchestra, and played to small audiences; but classical music was not appreciated, and it is said that he went away in disgust. Slowly an interest in good music sprang up, however, and in spite of many discouragements some gentlemen of influence organized a musical festival, copied somewhat after the Handel and Haydn triennials. The first experiment was highly successful; it was repeated another season, and the biennial festival became an established institution. In 1875 the festival, finer than ever before, was held in the old, defective Exposition building, a temporary structure built of wood, and in nowise suited to such purposes. The festival was brilliantly successful, and, in consequence of the enthusiasm which it aroused, Mr. Reuben Springer gave a large sum of money towards the erection of a permanent music hall. Other money, upon which the gift of Mr. Springer was conditioned, was raised; the music hall was erected, flanked by permanent exposition buildings, and provided with a huge organ, the largest, if not the finest, on this continent. Here, in 1878, another grand musical festival was held, followed by the last, and thus far the grandest, in 1880.

As an outgrowth of the musical spirit developed by the earlier festivals, a Cincinnati orchestra was organized, and this for several winters gave short series of symphony concerts, which drew fair audiences and were modestly sustained. In 1878, however, a change came. Mr. George Ward Nichols, a prime mover in the great festivals, conceived the idea of organizing a college of music. He secured the cooperation of Mr. Springer and other wealthy gentlemen, and suddenly it was telegraphed all over the country that Theodore Thomas had been engaged to take charge of the enterprise. Thomas came; students flocked to study under the teachers whom he gathered together; the Cincinnati orchestra of

Michael Brand was swallowed up in a grander orchestra, of which Thomas was conductor; two seasons of brilliant concerts were given in the Music Hall; chamber concerts were furnished by a picked string quartet; and Cincinnati was looked up to as the musical stronghold of America. Soon came discord into all this harmony; there were quarrels in the College of Music; one teacher after another resigned; finally there was a grand crash, and Thomas himself withdrew. The college remained, Nichols remained, and the Music Hall remained. Such was essentially the state of affairs at the beginning of the present season.

So much for the past, now for the present. Musically, with one or two important exceptions, the season in Cincinnati has been dull. The foregoing historical sketch suggests a growth in musical interest so rapid and extraordinary that much of it must have been forced; a hotbed product of local pride and western enthusiasm. Early last autumn the Cincinnati orchestra proposed a series of symphony concerts. Seven hundred subscribers were needed to insure success, but only five hundred could be secured, so the enterprise fell through. The quartet from the College of Music has given a few good chamber concerts; there have been two or three other concerts of the promiscuous kind, one oratorio and a little opera; but this, barring the late opera festival, has been all. Such concerts as are given in Boston by the Cecilia, Boylston and Apollo clubs are practically unknown here; pianoforte recitals are rare, and poorly patronized; musical entertainments, in short, to succeed in Cincinnati, must be of the very biggest kind; small affairs are barely tolerated.

This passion for bigness and grandeur has been well exemplified by the opera festival held here last week. The enterprise was conceived by Col. Nichols, and carried out under the auspices of the College of Music. It has been in all essential particulars a most brilliant success. The great Music Hall, which seats nearly five thousand people, was converted into an opera-house; Mapleson came here with all his resources; the Cincinnati orchestra was added to his, and some new scenery was painted. For a week the performances continued. *Lohengrin, The Magic Flute, Mefistofele, Lucia, Sonnambula, Aida, Faust*, and part of *Moses in Egypt*, were magnificently rendered. The audiences numbered something like an average of seven thousand for each performance, and the utmost enthusiasm prevailed. Mapleson made money, the College of Music made money, Nichols won popularity, and nearly every one was satisfied. Now, however, we are far enough away from the festival to see it with a little perspective, and we may properly ask wherein it was great, and wherein it fell short of the advertisements. As regards the performances, they were certainly magnificent. But then they were given by Mapleson's company, with Gerster, Valleria, Cary, Belocca, Campanini, Ravelli, Novara, Del Puente, and all the other fine soloists with whom he travels. His company can be heard in any great city, and there is no reason to suppose that it sang better here than elsewhere. The orchestra, however, was a great addition to Mapleson's forces, and added to the performances a breadth and vigor truly remarkable. The chorus was also somewhat larger than usual, and, furthermore, there was the great Music Hall organ, which in certain scenes—as, for example, in *Lohengrin*, when the bridal party enters the cathedral—was used with magnificent effect. In these particulars the rendition of the several operas excelled; in none did they fall short. From a spectacular point of view, on the other hand, the festival was not quite up to all expectations. The settings were very good, but not extraordinary; the best of the scenery was that which Mapleson carries with him. In fact, the stage was too small and too shallow for the grandest spectacular effects, and it was folly to suppose that as much could be done with a mere temporary arrangement as can be accomplished on a really large and thorough stage like that of the Boston Theatre. As regards scenery, and so forth, the thing could be much better done in Boston; but Boston could not supply the space for that other element of a great spectacle, the enormous audience. In this particular the festival was unique; no better could be done anywhere in the world without the special construction of a building equal to our Music Hall.

Part Four

American Institutions

37. Conventions and Beyond— Lowell Mason

Fifteen years before *Dwight's Journal* appeared, Lowell Mason had succeeded in winning a place for music in the curriculum of Boston's public schools, setting an American precedent. In the process, he had given vital momentum to a movement for music instruction in public schools in other parts of the country. Mason then took on the task of training the teachers who would be needed. He seized on the idea of the convention, the regional meeting of singing clubs that had become popular in the 1840s, and converted it into an occasion for training teachers and chorus masters.

In an early issue of the *Journal*, Dwight reported on a teachers' convention of the kind Lowell Mason had originated, but this one directed instead by Benjamin F. Baker, Mason's successor as superintendent of music in Boston's schools. Dwight takes the opportunity to reprint some ideas he had penned half a dozen years earlier on the subject of conventions. A year later, he addresses the subject again, this time in the context of Lowell Mason's founding the Normal Musical Institute in New York City, which remained in New York only three years before moving to North Reading, Massachusetts, where teachers from all over the country came to attend its three-month courses.

Dwight's and Mason's interests were, to some extent, divergent. Dwight's devoted interest was in the ultimate achievements and significance of music as an art and a profession; Mason, direct spiritual kin of the old New England singing masters, was a church musician and a teacher, bent on such basics as having children learn to sing from notes and training teachers to teach them. His work prospered, and it was said that Mason "provided the United States for a generation with most of its trained music teachers." Dwight looked beyond that and saw in Mason's efforts the seeds of music festivals and conservatories still to be cultivated in the United States.

Dwight's Journal of Music, August 14, 1852

Musical Conventions

The middle of August has now for fifteen years or more been Singing-Masters' and Psalm-Book Makers' Fair in Boston. The custom of "Conventions," or "Teachers' Classes" has grown to be more or less a custom in many parts of our country. Here at least, in New England, for a musical journal, it is of importance enough to be the topic of the month. One of these bodies is just now in the middle of its ten days' session at the Melodeon in this city. It is one of the offshoots, or rather a coalition, consummated last year, of several offshoots, from the original Convention, which has always until this year, constituted the largest and most formidable nucleus under the guidance of Messrs. Mason and Webb and the auspices of the Boston Academy of Music. Unfortunately, owing to the prolonged stay of Mr. Mason in Europe, and to other untoward circumstances (among which the want of a hall as large as the old Tremont Temple may be mentioned), this organization does not take the field at all this summer. It will bring the more singers and music-lovers to the meetings of Messrs. Baker and Johnson, which have opened with a goodly show of numbers, including fine materials for a chorus, and with an increase from day to day, to which apparently only the size of the hall will set a limit. . . .

The present gathering will suggest matter of comment; but we prefer to wait and weigh it well when it is all over. Meanwhile as a basis for such remarks and comparisons as we may have to make, we reproduce some paragraphs (new to most of our readers) in which we noted down six years ago the observations and speculations into which we were led by the Conventions at that time.

"The popular musical movement in this country seems to be tending to something like a great organic unity;—or rather to several unities,—for there are rival organizations, all of which, in the nature of things, must finally be swallowed up in one. Observe, we speak of the *popular* movement, of the music which begins in singing schools and village choirs, and is for the people; proceeding from the first stirrings of the popular want, uneducated, unrefined, rather than from any high artistic centre. This development doubtless is not watched with pleasure by the professionally musical, and by those who have made fond acquaintance all their lives with the artistic productions of the old musical countries. Its rude, homely, puritanic taste; its perpetual drilling in bare elements, and perpetual discussion of them; its cart-loads of psalmody of home manufacture; and the Yankee trading shrewdness and seeming charlatanry of those who conduct it, through the whole hierarchy, from the simple country singing master, and the more metropolitan teachers, up to the 'great Panjandrum,' or Psalm-King, himself:—all this distinguishes the popular movement, as a kind of illegitimate upstart, in the eyes of genuine musicians and amateurs, from what they conceive to be the true derivation and descent of taste in the old way from the highest and oldest reservoirs of musical attainment down through the multitudes. This giving of importance to the vulgar, homely taste for music, by organizing it, even though that taste accumulates the power in this way of improving itself, is naturally regarded by musicians, with whom music is an art, as something as profane musically, as it is orthodox and moral in its social origin. For ourselves, we believe that Music is destined to take possession of this American people in both ways; partly by the natural charm of the beautiful and grand already created in music, drawing congenial natures to itself; and partly by the organized combination of such plain psalm-singing propensities as we have, gradually rising to meet the influence which flows down from the true holy land of Art, now visited by the few alone who can appreciate its glories. In other words we think that the Italian opera, the orchestras of trained musicians, who play overtures and symphonies to such as begin to appreciate, the oratorio-performances in our cities, the accomplished virtuoso pianists and violinists, and *cantatrici* who make the tour of our States, give one great impulse to music in this country; and that the Teachers' Classes and Conventions, the common-school instructions, the multifarious manuals, psalm-books, glee-books, &c., of Lowell Mason, and his hosts of co-operators and rivals, in this field, do also give another impulse, not to be despised, but showing fruits from year to year, and actually converging towards and promising in due time to meet the first-named influence. That furnishes models, this creates audiences. . . .

"There is, then, both good and evil in these great organizations of singing masters and choristers now growing up; but we are sure the good preponderates.

"The Boston Academy of Music originated this plan of holding ten days' conventions of teachers every August, for the purpose of receiving instructions from competent professors in the elements and practice of sacred music, and in the best modes of teaching the same, fourteen years ago. The first class numbered only twelve persons. It soon increased to hundreds. Teachers, choir-leaders, and others flocked from all parts of the country, to Boston, to learn the art of teaching from the most successful masters. Combining, as they did, a considerable power of ready sight-singing in these meetings, they were naturally led to spend much of the session in practising new music, trying the new books which the professors had got ready for them to circulate when they went home, and by timid degrees even venturing upon some of the works of the great masters, to the manifest growth of enthusiasm and good taste. Considered as a speculation, or as a fête, this was too good a thing not to be imitated, and rival Teachers' Institutes sprang up, particularly that of Messrs. Baker and Woodbury, who found ample field without encroaching on the other. Moreover the chiefs of these hierarchies, after holding their grand conventions at home, leave their emporium in the Autumn, and like enterprising bishops visit their respective dioceses among the cities of the West, holding teachers' conventions in Buffalo, Cleveland, Cincinnati, and so forth, and establishing affiliated centres there."

Passing over a description of the musical exercises on the occasion after which this was written, we come to one peculiar feature of the Conventions:

"Handbills were distributed among the audience as they entered the hall, which seemed to be programmes of the concert, but which proved to be catalogues of a large auction sale of music and musical works, to take place in the evening. So that this great annual gathering becomes a fair or market, not only for the conductors who thus circulate their 'methods' and their 'collections,' but also for the music dealers and publishers of the city, who seize upon this rare chance to dispose of what lies dead upon their hands. And this suggests the objection, commonly urged against these conventions, of their trading spirit and the monopoly of the music market likely to be acquired by those who take the lead in them. It becomes no objection if the fact be generally understood. On the contrary it is a great mutual convenience; let the professors and book-makers find their interest in it, if they can. However low the tone which they might set in their writings (we only suppose a case) it is evident that the demand for better music will rise every year, by these opportunities of coming together in a musical centre; and that to satisfy the market it becomes more and more necessary for them to make *good* books. . . .

"The good we anticipate from this organization is threefold.

"First, the influence upon those engaged in it. We could not but feel, as we heard the choruses of Handel and the four-part songs of Mendelssohn sung by this vast assembly of persons, mostly of but ordinary culture and but little leisure, that this was for them the beginning of the highest culture. They had actually made acquaintance with some of the most exalted, most refined productions of the most refining of all arts. They had together shared the emotion of great music, and experienced an enthusiasm of a deeper, finer quality, than their lives before perhaps had furnished. The person who can comprehend, appreciate, feel Mendelssohn, has already won admission to the finer spheres of life. The Unitary sentiment may also be mentioned here; the beneficial consciousness of combined action, of days spent rhythmically, and with orderly enthusiasm.

"Secondly, the influence upon musical taste and practice throughout the country. From their rural, isolated homes, where advantages for hearing higher kinds of music do not exist, these enterprising leaders of choirs and classes come up once a year to Jerusalem, to receive truer notions of their art, and listen to great models, and go back to give the same tone to their respective circles and communities. The standard is thus rising throughout all the land. A musical emulation is excited in the most dull utilitarian places; and each year the leader carries with him more and more of his neighbors, who avail themselves of the increased facilities for travelling, to go up also and rekindle their musical imaginations at the great feast.

"Finally, we see in all this, as we intimated in the beginning of this article, a tendency to organic unity in the multifarious musical aspirations of this people. It is the natural tendency of music, where nothing interferes; it seeks combination, means of broader harmony, grander effects, and the composite enthusiasm of great numbers co-operating to one end. Wherever a considerable unity of this sort becomes once established, it attracts more and more force to it; all related elements gravitate towards it; to the teachers' class of Messrs. Webb and Mason, the choirs of Boston soon came and added themselves, for the numerous chorus thus afforded them; then came finally the orchestra; and accomplished virtuosos also will find a sphere opened for them upon these occasions which they have not at other times. *What then is to prevent these meetings from growing by degrees into great musical festivals, like those of London, Birmingham, and parts of Germany?* And all by a spontaneous accumulation and expansion, from rude beginnings made with simply what we had, taking up the popular taste as it was, and so organizing its first motions that they lend both weight and stimulus to each other, and rise collectively to an ever higher platform?"

Dwight's Journal of Music, May 14, 1853

New York Normal Musical Institute

This novel enterprize commenced its active existence, according to the announcement which has stood for some time in our advertising columns, at nine o'clock on Monday morning, April 25th. The ground was broken in an introductory lecture by Mr. LOWELL MASON, who had only a few days before arrived from Europe, and who may be considered as the father of the plan, as well as of the whole movement of popular musical instruction in this country. Among psalm-book makers and mass teachers there is no one like him; and the Normal Institute is probably to be regarded as his crowning effort, to concentrate and build up into some distinct form of permanency the results and methods of his extensive and in many respects original experience as a pioneer in choirs and public schools throughout our once unmusical New England.

We understand that about fifty pupils of both sexes appeared at the opening, designing to attend the classes and enjoy the privileges of the institution, through its session of three months. The scene of operations is Dodworth's large and beautiful Hall in the building upon Broadway next Grace Church. The class exercises occupy the hours from *nine* to *one* each morning. Mr. MASON lectures from 9 till 10 on the Art of Teaching; Mr. R. STORRS WILLIS from 10 till 11 (Tuesdays and Thursdays) on Harmony and Composition; Mr. G. F. ROOT from 11 till 12 on the Culture of the Voice; and Mr. W. B. BRADBURY from 12 till 1 on Part-Singing. Besides these, Mr. THOMAS HASTINGS, (author of a treatise just published upon "Musical Taste"), communicates "sound and experienced views as to the *side-culture*—mental and physical—of the musician." Private lessons in singing are given by Dr. BEAMES; and those who wish instruction in the use of instruments can be taught the organ by Mr. HOWE, and all sorts of band instruments by Mr. DODWORTH.

The original and distinctive feature of the Normal Institute is that it *teaches the art of teaching*. Its primary end is not, like that of the European Conservatories to train *artists* but rather to raise up and qualify *teachers* of the first elements of music *for the masses*, so that the whole rising generation of American society may grow up in some actual possession of the musical faculties implanted in our common nature. This certainly is a most worthy end; and to its speedier and truer realization the Normal School, or nursery of teachers, is as necessary to the popular musical culture as it has been found to be to our whole general system of Free Schools, so indispensable to a Republican society. It would be hardly reasonable to look to such an institution (at least in the outset) for the ripe artistic culture of the Conservatories in France and Germany, which are presided over by the greatest artists, composers and theoretic professors of the age. Probably our time has not yet come for that. But meanwhile here is a great and important work demanded by the times; and for its accomplishment, or for the first successful trial of the way thereto, we look with no small hope to the school so auspiciously commenced in New York.

A people must owe its musical culture to two main sources: first and principally, no doubt, to the inspiring influence of Art itself, to the presence of true artists and the frequent hearing and enjoying of true works of Art. Handel and Mozart and Beethoven and Mendelssohn, with fit interpreters, are of course our best educators. But there is also need of systematic, elementary teaching. . . . It needs to be proved and practically illustrated that teaching itself, even of the simplest rudiments, may be made an *art*; so that if any have an inborn talent for it they may find it as attractive and as enlivening an employment as the creation of poems, songs or pictures. Perhaps this Institute may do something to present the teacher's function in a more worthy and attractive aspect, to artists who in this country have to live by teaching, as well as by the practice of their art.

The Normal Institute may be regarded as the ultimate consolidation of those summer "Musical Conventions," which for many years have so stimulated the popular interest in music. It offers the best benefits, without the hurry and the crudities of the Conventions. The pupils remain together three months, in the company of those earnestly pursuing the same end with themselves, in a musical metropolis, where there are multitudes of opportunities of hearing such good music as they might never hear at home; and where they are likely to be thrown much in the way of artists and enter circles that are pervaded by an artistic tone: so that, besides learning the mere rudiments and how to teach them, those who are apt for it may possibly receive some deeper notions of artistic culture, and even unfold some germs of a creative talent as composers. Such a school, if liberally and wisely managed, might draw in more or less the aid of all the most accomplished musical teachers and musicians residing in or visiting the city. We see not why such a movement may not gradually grow and ripen into something quite as formidable as a Paris or a Leipsic Conservatory, while it should still retain its distinctive feature of the Normal School, or school for teachers. We shall be glad to receive reports from time to time of its progress.

38. *The New York Philharmonic Society*

Dwight's discussion of the thirteenth annual report of the New York Philharmonic Society reveals clearly that the orchestra of 1855 was not yet the kind of organization that would begin to typify American orchestras before the end of the century. It was more like the groups of "gentlemen amateurs" who, in the first decades of the century, gathered in Boston and Philadelphia to try out Haydn symphonies for their own pleasure and that of their friends. The model of the full-time professional symphony orchestra playing regular concerts for the general public hardly existed, even in Europe, where orchestras generally were adjuncts to a court or an opera house.

The Philharmonic Society of Dwight's period was essentially a cooperative orchestra whose musicians elected and paid a conductor and a librarian and then shared among themselves the expenses and receipts of their concerts. Dwight seems to have sensed that this scheme was not the ultimate answer for American orchestras, but he does not suggest what the answer might be. Meanwhile, he salutes the standards of the country's oldest orchestral organization.

Dwight's Journal of Music, November 3, 1855

New York Philharmonic Society

We have received the Thirteenth Annual Report of this now really flourishing society. Its history is not only full of encouragement to the high-toned musicians, who have labored through its instrumentality to make classical music a permanent institution in that great Babel of a city, and to those among its busy, care-worn population who hunger and thirst after good music, but it may furnish some good lessons to those of like wants and tastes in our own and other cities. The love for great orchestral music is sure to deepen and the audience therefor to widen, where such music can be frequently and well performed, and easily accessible. In each of our large cities there are given the desire for it on the part of many, and the capacity in more; there are given also the musical material and talent for such concerts. The only real problem is of organization, of bringing the demand and supply into some permanent and working form. The New York Philharmonic Society may not be by any means a perfect solution of the problem; its plan perhaps admits of many modifications for the better; yet it has wrought out a result instructive and encouraging.

By the Report it appears that the gross receipts from the four Concerts (with rehearsals) for the season of 1854–'55, amounted to the large sum of $6,400. This, after defraying all expenses, left a dividend of $65.00 to each member of the orchestra of over seventy musicians.— Since the beginning of the society the amount of $1,434.14 has been appropriated for charitable purposes, for the relief of members in distress, of widows and children of deceased, &c. The Report gives a list of 747 "associate members," as the subscribers for season tickets are called, who form for the most part a body of reliable supporters of the concerts season after season. There is also a list of 144 "professional members" and of 51 "subscribing members," whose relation to the affair we do not precisely understand. Some light, however, may be gathered from the opening paragraph of the Report: . . .

> At the time of the formation of the Society we had only *subscribing* members, whose privilege it was to attend the *three concerts* of each season, and who were quite satisfied with listening to our performances on these occasions alone; a few years later, however, a desire was manifested by many to attend also the *rehearsals* of the Society, so as to have an opportunity of hearing the works of the great masters several times before the final performance, in order to be enabled to enjoy and appreciate them more thoroughly, which fact at once induced the Society to create an *associate membership*, the additional advantage of which is, that all such belonging to this class of members have an admission to all the rehearsals of the Society; moreover the annual number of concerts was increased from three to four. From the moment this arrangement was consummated, the *associate* members increased rapidly from season to season, while the list of subscribers as

regularly decreased. You will at once perceive that a most unmistakable proof is thus furnished of the great change which has taken place during the last fifteen years in the musical sense of our community, and of the increased interest that is now felt in our midst for truly good music.

. . . The success of the Philharmonic Society seems due to several causes, prominent among which are these. *First*, it has been fortunate from the start in the composition of its members, and particularly in the fact, that being a self-governing society of musicians, a class so seldom capable of managing the business of a society, it has found musicians gifted with the capacity for leadership, high-toned, gentlemanly, who had the spirit of devotion and of order, and whose wholesome influence was cheerfully seconded by all. *Second*, as regards the musical excellence and completeness of the orchestra, New York has so very large a body of musicians, from which such a society may draw. *Third*, their audience, although it has averaged very much smaller, until the last year, than our Boston audiences for such concerts, has *paid* very much better. The high price system has prevailed. A sort of exclusiveness has even been the policy of the society during the years of its initiation; it has been made a *privilege* to be enrolled among its auditors, like an admission into the true society and sphere of music-lovers:—a thing therefore worth paying well for, for the sake of listening in a somewhat congenial atmosphere and undisturbed. This has not been without its good result; it has given character and basis to the concerts, on the strength of which they can now afford to make themselves more cheap and popular, without catering to lower tastes.

But in and through all and above all is this success due to the high stand taken, and persistently maintained, by the artistic leaders who have given tone to the society; who, notwithstanding some inferior programmes, have ever had a foremost regard to the cultivation of a high and classical taste in music; and who have not compromised the dignity of Art by resorting to the extraneous means of brilliant superficial triumphs, to swelling advertisements and the like Barnumbian clap-trap. Content to persevere in doing a good thing and let the world find them out, they at length have their reward.

39. *Chamber Music*

Chamber music was in the process of moving from the private salon to the public concert hall, and strong roles in the transfer were played by the Mendelssohn Quintette Club of Boston and the Mason-Thomas Quartet in New York.

The Boston group, indeed, carried out the change quite literally. It began in 1849 playing quartets and quintets for friends gathered in their homes, gradually began performing in concert halls in Boston and its suburbs, and finally embarked on national concert tours. Even in its later years the Quintette Club aimed to be entertaining as well as edifying; instrumental solos and singers leavened programs that might otherwise have been intimidating to uninitiated audiences.

William Mason, Lowell's son, formed a chamber ensemble in New York in 1855 expressly to give public concerts. Recently returned from studies in Europe, Mason should by all rights have set out on a career as concert pianist. One season on the road, however, convinced him that the itinerant life of the virtuoso was not for him; besides, it did not appear that the public was ready to appreciate the kind of solo recital he wanted to give, unrelieved by songs or stunts. So he settled in New York to teach, to perform with the Philharmonic Society, and to introduce the idea of regular chamber music concerts.

First, he wanted to give the premiere performance of the new Trio, Opus 8, by young Johannes Brahms, whom he had met in Germany. For that, he called in Carl Bergmann as cellist and, on Bergmann's recommendation, the twenty-year-old Theodore Thomas as violinist. In other music, George Matzka played the viola and Joseph Mosenthal the second violin. Within a year, Thomas' genius as a leader asserted itself; the group took the name Mason-Thomas Quartet and launched on a thirteen-year career that set permanent standards for chamber music performance and program-making.

The musicians of both the Mendelssohn Quintette Club and the Mason-Thomas ensemble also took part in orchestral concerts in their respective cities. The Mendelssohn players tended to form the nucleus of whatever orchestral ventures rose and faded on the Boston scene. Carl Bergmann was the conductor of the New York Philharmonic Society and Thomas, Matzka, and Mosenthal all were members. In 1858 *Dwight's Journal* carried a correspondent's review of a characteristic Mason-Thomas concert in New York and, a month later, surveyed the first nine years of the Mendelssohn Quintette Club.

Dwight's Journal of Music, May 1, 1858

New York, April 19.—Our concerts seem to rise in quality as they decrease in number. MASON's last Matinee, on Saturday, was an entertainment such as we rarely hear anywhere. The five names on the programme were taken from among the highest in Tone-Art. Beethoven, Handel, and Bach, represented different phases of the old school; Mendelssohn and Schumann its more modern development. The "Music of the Future" was left untouched. And various as was the character of the composers who bore these names, so unlike, too, were their works which were laid before us here. Each was a fair type of its creator. First came Beethoven's Quartet, op. 95, No. 11, generally considered, I believe, one of his less comprehensible ones. It was, however, so well interpreted by the excellence of its performance, that it belied its reputation on this occasion at least. The quick passages were played with a clearness and energy, and the slow, serious ones with a pathos, fulness, and depth of feeling, which made it difficult to believe that the performers were the same who "scratched" off this very piece in a most heart and ear rending manner two years ago. The same may be said, too, of Schumann's beautiful Quintet, in which Mr. Mason's uncommonly spirited and expressive playing was most worthily accompanied by the stringed instruments. The solemn, mournful march was particularly beautiful. The two remaining numbers of the programme were solos by Messrs. MASON and THOMAS. The former gave us a Fugue in E minor, by Handel,—the same, I think, which he played repeatedly just after his return from Europe, but now infinitely superior in its rendering—and a most characteristic *Rondo Capriccioso* by Mendelssohn—sparkling, fairy-like, and then again flowing on in lovely melody—a mixture of the "Midsummer Night's Dream" style and that of the Songs without Words. This was loudly *encored*, in answer to which demonstration the pianist gave us his pretty, rippling little "Silver Spring."

Decidedly the most wonderful performance of the concert was Mr. THOMAS's playing of the celebrated *Chaconne*, by Bach. This young art-ist (and *very* young he is, although the stamp of genius matures his al-most boyish face) bids fair to rise high in the musical world. His tone is pure and full, his command of his instrument very great, and his inter-pretation of the music he plays most faithful and artistic. The *Chaconne* is a strange composition, which must be heard often to be thoroughly appreciated; though even in first listening to it, you discover enough to wish to know it better. It is extremely difficult, and must be very fatiguing for the performer. It is intricate and has no regular forms or themes to assist the memory; and yet young Thomas played the whole unfalter-ingly, without notes, and consequently with all the more freedom and *abandon*. His mechanism, too, gave proof of untiring industry in prac-tice; but more than all, his evident enjoyment of what he was playing, and his thorough entering into the spirit of the music, showed the true artist in him. His choice of pieces also betokens real Art-love and rever-ence: he never plays any but *good* music. Such men are and ought to be the Missionaries of Art in this country. Few of them visit it; but in pro-portion as their numbers increase, and they keep steadily on their path, without letting necessity, or flattery, or thirst for fame turn them from it, their own true creed will spread and gain influence. Will the day ever come when Humbug succumbs to true Art in our land! This was once a hopeless question, but of late years a faint light has begun to appear. True, it breaks but slowly, very slowly, and the rays of the rising sun are still dimmed and thickened by the clouds which they shall finally dis-perse; but there is at least hope of fair weather. Of these sun-rays Mason's concerts are among the most effective; and we owe him and his fellow-laborers a vast debt of gratitude for their winter's work. Every one of these quiet, unpretending concerts has brought us something new, and nothing but what was good; and though at first the little hall was but scantily filled, the end of the series found it so crowded that a large room will be needed in its place next winter, when we hope that the ground now broken, will be farther tilled.

Dwight's Journal of Music, June 5, 1858

Mendelssohn Quintette Club—Nine Years' Work

We fulfil our promise of recording here a list of the Classical Chamber Compositions, by the best masters, which have been presented to Boston ears by the Mendelssohn Quintette Club, during the nine years since the Club was organized. The record is significant, and must be valuable to the lovers of violin Quartet and Quintet music hereabouts for reference. It shows in fact, in a sort of tabular view, the history of the growing taste for this kind of music in our community. The love of such music is the surest index of a love of music pure and for itself; that is, of musical Art reduced to its essentials, relying on its intrinsic charm and virtue, devoid of all mere external tricks of effect,—music so constructed that, if there be not worth and beauty in the design, in the ideas themselves, there is nothing like orchestral coloring or mere power of mass, to cover up its nakedness or weakness. It cannot be supposed that the multitude anywhere or ever will appreciate such music. But Quartet parties in all musical communities form the selectest pleasures of the circles that are most musically cultivated. In our young, busy country such a taste is but of recent growth. In this city the nine years' concerts of the Quintette Club, stand (as we have said) for nearly its whole history; for, with the exception of the two courses of Chamber Concerts given under the patronage of the "Harvard Musical Association," in Mr. Chickering's ware-rooms, in the winters of 1844 and 1846, we remember very little of the sort, in public, prior to the first season of the Mendelssohn Quintette Club.

Our list includes only the performances of the Club in Boston, and in their public concerts, leaving out of the account their numerous concerts in the surrounding towns, and their frequent performances before private circles and in private houses.

As our object is to show how much of the famous gallery of masters in this department has been, as it were, lighted up for us and brought directly before us by the labors of the Club, we have been less particular about completeness in the latter portion of our list, which includes works by new or less important European names, and contributions by several of our own native or resident artists, members or close associates of the Club; yet we add what we can recall of these as matters of interest. To each work we add, as nearly as could be ascertained, the number of times that it has been performed. But it is to be considered that in these latter years many of the most important items of the list have also been brought repeatedly to our hearing by other parties, who have followed the example of the Quintette Club. We commence in the order of historical succession:

J. S. BACH

Concerto for three Pianos, &c., in D minor	2	times
Sonata, No. 2, for Violin and Piano	2	"
Chaconne	1	"
Various Preludes and Fugues	3	"

HAYDN

Quartets, Nos. 39, 45, 63, 66, 67, 60, 70, 72, 73, 78, (each)	2	"
Quartets, Nos. 75 & 77 (each)	8	"
Quartets, "Seven Last Words"	1	"
Trios: Piano, violin and 'cello	3	"

MOZART

Quintet, No. 1, in C minor	3	"
Quintet, No. 2, in C	4	"
Quintet, No. 3, in D	4	"
Quintet, No. 4, in G minor	5	"
Quintet, No. 5, in E flat	6	"
Quintet, No. 6, in B flat	2	"
Quintet, with Clarinet	10	"
Quintet, in G minor, arranged for Piano and Quartet .	4	"
Quartet, No. 1, in G	4	"
Quartet, No. 2, in D minor	5	"
Quartet, No. 3, in B flat	4	"

Quartet, No. 4, in E flat 6   "
Quartet, No. 5, in A 3   "
Quartet, No. 6, in C 4   "
Quartet, No. 7, in D 2   "
Quartet, No. 8, in F 4   "
Quartet, No. 9, in B flat 1   "
Quartet, No. 10, in D 2   "
Sextet, for Strings and Horns 2   "
"Musical Joke," for the same 3   "
Trios, for Piano and Strings 4   "

BEETHOVEN

Quintet, in E flat, op. 4 8   "
Quintet, in C, op. 29 10   "
Quintet, in E flat, op. 20 (arranged from Septuor) 7   "
Sextet, for Strings and two Horns, in E flat,
  op. 82 2   "
Sextet, arranged as Quintet 3   "
Quartet, in F, op. 18, No. 1 4   "
Quartet, in G, op. 18, No. 2 3   "
Quartet, in D, op. 18, No. 3 2   "
Quartet, in C minor, op. 18, No. 4 1   "
Quartet, in A, op. 18, No. 5 6   "
Quartet, in B flat, op. 18, No. 6 7   "
Quartet, in F, op. 59 (Rasoumoffsky set) No. 1 4   "
Quartet, in E minor, op. 59, (do.) No. 2 2   "
Quartet, in C, op. 59 (do.) No. 3 4   "
Quartet, in E flat, op. 74 1   "
Quartet, with Piano, arr. from Quintet op. 16 4   "
Trio, (Piano, Violin and 'Cello), op. 1, No. 1,
  in E flat 4   "
Trio, (Piano, Violin and 'Cello), op. 1, No. 2, in G ... 4   "
Trio, (Piano, Violin and 'Cello), op. 1, No. 3, in
  C minor 4   "
Trio, (Piano, Violin and 'Cello), op. 11, in B flat 4   "
Trio, (Piano, Violin and 'Cello), op. 70, No. 1, in D .. 4   "
Trio, (Piano, Violin and 'Cello), op. 70, No. 2,
  in E flat 3   "

Trio, (Piano, Violin and 'Cello), op. 97, in B flat 3   "

Concerto (Piano), in C minor, op. 37 1   "

Concerto (Violin), in D, op. 61 2   "

Sonata (Piano and Violin), in A, op. 47, "Kreutzer" . . 4   "

Sonata (Piano and Violin), in F op. 24 2   "

Sonata (Piano and 'Cello), in G minor, op. 5   2   "

Sonata (Piano Solo), op. 13, "Pathetique" 2   "

Sonata (Piano Solo), op. 57, "Appassionata" 2   "

HUMMELL

Trio (Piano and strings), in E, op. 83 3   "

Trio (Piano and strings), in E flat, op. 93 2   "

Trio (Piano and strings), in E flat minor 1   "

Concerto (Piano, &c.), in A minor 3   "

Concerto (Piano, &c.), in E major 2   "

CHERUBINI

Quartet, in E flat 4   "

MOSCHELES

Sonata (Piano and 'Cello) 2   "

"Homage à Haendel" (2 Pianos) 1   "

FERD. RIES

Quintet (Piano and Strings), in B minor 2   "

SCHUBERT

Quartet, in D minor 3   "

Quartet, in A minor 2   "

Trio (Piano and Strings), in E flat 3   "

Trio (Piano and Strings), in G 1   "

WEBER

Quintet (with Clarinet) 4   "

Trio (Piano, Flute and 'Cello) 2   "

"Concert-Stueck" (Piano and Accomp.) 2   "

SPOHR

Quintet, No. 6, in E minor 4   "

Quintet, No. 4, in A minor 2   "

Quintet, (with Piano) 2   "

Concerto (Clarinet) 2   "

ONSLOW

Quintets, Nos. 8, 15, 16, 18, 32, 33, 34, 38, (each)	2	"
Sonata (Piano, 4 hands)	2	"

MENDELSSOHN

Quintet, in A, op. 18	12	"
Quintet, in B flat, op. 87	10	"
Quartet, in E flat, op. 12	4	"
Quartet, in A minor, op. 13	3	"
Quartet, in D op. 44	6	"
Quartet, in E minor	5	"
Quartet, in E flat	4	"
Quartet, in E, op. 81 (Posthumous)	3	"
Quartet, in F minor, op. 80, (Posthumous)	3	"
Quartet (with Piano), in C minor, op. 1	1	"
Quartet (with Piano), in F minor, op. 2	4	"
Quartet (with Piano), in B minor, op. 3	3	"
Trio (Piano and Strings) in D minor	7	"
Trio (Piano and Strings) in C minor	4	"
Ottetto (Strings)	3	"
Sonata (Piano and 'Cello), in F	3	"
Sonata (Piano and 'Cello), in B flat	4	"
Sonata (Piano and 'Cello), in D	4	"
Sonata (Piano and Violin) in F minor	1	"
Sonata (for Organ) in F	1	"
Variations, in D (Piano and 'Cello)	3	"
Cappriccios (Piano)	4	"

SCHUMANN

Quintet (with Piano) in E flat, op. 52	5	"
Quartet, in F, op. 44, No. 2	1	"
Quartet, in A, op. 44, No. 3	2	"
Romanzas (Piano and Clarinet)	3	"

CHOPIN

Concerto, in E	2	"
Polacca (Piano and 'Cello)	3	"
Notturnes, Etudes, Polonaises, &c., &c		

GADE

Quintet, in E minor, op. 8	2	"
Sonata (Piano and Violin)	1	"

KALLIWODA

Trio and Quartet, in G	2	"

LACHNER, V.

Quintet, in C	3	"

VEIT

Quintet, No. 5	2	"

CORTICELLO

Trio (Piano, Clarinet and 'Cello)	2	"

CRUSEL

Concerto and Quartet (for Clarinet)	3	"

FERD. DAVID

Concerto (Violin)	1	"

GOUVY

Trio, in E, op. 8	1	"

BRAHMS

Trio (Piano and Strings), in B, op. 8	2	"

RUBINSTEIN

Quartet, in C minor, op. 17, No. 1	3	"
Quartet, in F, op. 17, No. 2	1	"
Quartet, in C, op. 17, No. 3	1	"

T. RYAN

Quintet, in F	3	"
Quartet, in D, No. 2	2	"

C. C. PERKINS

Quintet, in D	2	"
Quartet	4	"
Quartet (with Piano), in B flat	2	"

J. C. D. PARKER

Quartet, No. 2	2	"

40. *The Handel and Haydn Society*

The first Triennial Festival of Boston's Handel and Haydn Society was both a culmination and a signpost pointing toward the future. It brought together a number of historic elements in Boston's and New England's musical life, and like the society itself, it became a model for similar efforts elsewhere.

When the society was formed in 1815, two of its founders typified the sources that converged in it. The initiator was Johann Gottlieb Graupner, who as early as 1810 had organized the Philo-Harmonic Society in Boston to play symphonies of Haydn, Gyrowetz, Pleyel, and even Beethoven. One of his associates, and the Handel and Haydn Society's first president, was Thomas S. Webb, who had actually been a pupil of William Billings and thus was a direct link to the old singing-school tradition. The combination meant that the Handel and Haydn Society was not to be an old-style singing club with its rudimentary hymn practice and religious aim. It was organized as a performing group, to give public concerts of music from the great oratorios of those masters whose names it had adopted.

Lowell Mason also played an important role in the society's history. In 1821 he offered it a collection of hymns that he had compiled and, in part, composed. The *Boston Handel and Haydn Society Collection of Church Music* turned out to be a landmark in American hymnody. As a result the society prospered and young Mason was persuaded to give up banking and devote himself to music.

There was a connection, as well, between the new festival and the older convention tradition. Singing societies in nearby Worcester County had for some years been meeting in annual conventions to demonstrate their new accomplishments and, inspired by the Handel and Haydn Society, to combine in performing larger choral works. By 1866 the convention had become a virtual music festival, conducted by Carl Zerrahn, who brought in the Mendelssohn Quintette Club to accompany a full performance of Handel's *Judas Maccabaeus*. Zerrahn represented another historic force: He had come to the United States as flutist with the Germania Orchestra, and when that dissolved, settled in Boston, where he became conductor of the Handel and Haydn Society and also, over the years, conducted one after another of the concert series that were launched in the city's repeated attempts to establish a symphony orchestra.

In the Triennial Festival, Zerrahn combined choral and orchestral forces on a scale that had not been attempted before in the United States. And though the Handel and Haydn Society abandoned its festivals after the sixth one in 1883, it had set a precedent soon to be followed in other parts of the country.

Dwight's Journal of Music, May 9, 1868

First Triennial Festival of the Handel and Haydn Society

Musical interest has its centre for this week at least in Boston. Five great Oratorios in one week, grandly given by a well balanced, well trained force of 750 voices, with an orchestra of more than a hundred instruments, the best solo singers in the country, and one of the grandest organs in the world, as well as in the noblest Music Hall in the whole country—besides four Symphony Concerts, with splendid programmes and by such an orchestra:—this may indeed be called a Festival. Now there might be more of smoke than fire in all this; the American people often err in the ambition to do things on a bigger scale than others, to compel cheap wonder by display of quantity, with too small regard to quality. So this great Festival might have been a windy, unsatisfactory, self-glorifying enterprise, a piling of Ossa upon Pelion of imposing "monster" concerts, of doubtful influence on musical taste and culture, compared with the usual more quiet influences. But both the spirit and the matter and the manner of it forbid that supposition. The musical matter chosen is all of the highest intrinsic worth, deserving large interpretation, and to be received with ears and souls quickened by a general sympathy; the means of execution are adequate in every sense; the labor of arrangement, organization and rehearsal has been earnest and continuous, and all prompted by an artistic desire to make all these means cooperate with ease and certainty in a performance as nearly perfect as possible in this busy and distracting world, and in an inclement season particularly trying to singers' throats and to the whole musical and moral temper of any but an utterly unsensitive "harp of a thousand strings."

Our old Handel and Haydn Society made a brave first experiment of musical festivals in May, 1857. In spite of bad weather, of the amount of public scepticism or indifference then to be overcome, and of the comparatively small means then at their command (although unprecedented in this country for that time), the measure of success was, to say the least, convincing; the play was *destined* to succeed, after a few more trials, with more means and experience, and growing taste in the community to meet the invitations half way. A prime condition of that effort was our possession of a worthy Music Hall. Three years ago, May, 1865, the Society chose the occasion of its fiftieth anniversary for another and more matured attempt, and on a larger scale. By that time the Great Organ stood in the Hall, a proud hope realized. The love of chorus practice had spread more among our people, not a few of the most cultivated families contributing a voice or two to the vocal ranks, and the Society, under zealous and judicious management, was in better condition than ever before. Public interest, too, in great music of all kinds had grown more and more encouraging, and a bolder, higher aim (this time instead of a three days' Festival, as in '57, it was for a whole week, the chorus at its fullest numbered 700 voices, and the orchestra of 75 had been raised to 100), yet cautious as it was bold, secured a signal success. Though it cost more than $17,000, not only were the guarantors not taxed as before, but there was left a balance of $4,000, to be divided between the two great War charities and the Societies own fund for further musical usefulness.

This week the Society inaugurates the custom of a great Triennial Musical Festival. It has felt the musical temper of the community and the musical means of the country clearly and long enough, and now feels its own strength and tendency and temper well enough to be able to resolve, that this thing, now, on the third trial, done with something like completeness and with the sure instinct of success in it through every stage of its preparation, is not for once, but from this time forward shall become the custom, a great feast of music to come round, as regularly as that in Birmingham, every third year in Boston.

The present Festival goes as far beyond that of 1865, as that went beyond the one of 1857. The foundations have been laid broad and deep, and all the preparation made with judgment, energy and skill. The guaranty fund, subscribed by 200 individuals and firms, amounts to nearly $50,000; but there is not the slightest fear that any one will be called upon to pay a dollar; the sale of tickets for the season and for each single Oratorio and Concert soon made the thing financially sure. The chorus of the Society, never averaging so well before in numbers, or in quality of voices, or in the right sort of musical spirit, has been kept in rehearsal nearly all winter on the oratorios, and lately on the choral parts of the Ninth Symphony, and Mr. ZERRAHN's drill has been more critical and searching, as well as more inspiring, even than before. The parts are uncommonly well balanced. According to the printed list contained in the handsomely printed and convenient Book Programme of the Festival, the Soprano singers number 230, the Alto 171, the Tenor 142, and the Bass 204, making a total of 747 voices. For several weeks past there have been four rehearsals in a week, and so nearly filled have been the wide half circles of the lower (Bumstead) Hall with actual singers, that there has been small room for listeners. For solo singers, although the hopes which for some time rested upon one or two of the famous English singers and upon the great German baritone Stockhausen, were disappointed, the government have been able to present a goodly list, headed by Mme. PAREPA-ROSA and Miss ADELAIDE PHILLIPPS, each a host in herself, and continuing with such names of good assurance as Miss J. E. HOUSTON, Mrs. CARY, Mr. GEORGE SIMPSON, of New York, (who sang also in our first Festival), and Messrs. JAMES WHITNEY, J. F. WINCH, H. WILDE, J. F. RUDOLPHSEN and M. W. WHITNEY. Two distinguished instrumental solo artsits were engaged, too, for the afternoon concerts,—Miss ALIDE TOPP, the young German Pianiste, pupil of von Bülow, and Mr. CARL ROSA, the violinist. The grand orchestra is even finer than that of three years ago, and numbers

115 musicians. To the sixty odd of our own, who have been moulded together and consolidated and refined during the last three years by the good exercise afforded by the Harvard Symphony Concerts, are added about 40 of the best members of the New York Philharmonic Society and several from Philadelphia,—among them many welcome faces of the old "Germania." The proportions are excellent,—22 first violins, headed by our own WILLIAM SCHULTZE, with JULIUS EICHBERG as Lieutenant; 20 second violins; 12 violas; 10 violoncellos; 13 double basses; 4 flutes, besides piccolo; 4 oboes; 4 clarionets; 4 bassoons; 6 horns; 4 trumpets; 1 cornet; 3 trombones; 2 ophicleids; 1 serpent; 4 instruments of percussion. . . .

The New York and Philadelphia quota of the orchestra having arrived, Sunday (May 3) was devoted to rehearsals:—in the morning, of the grand orchestral symphonies and overtures, and of the Schumann Concerto with the Fräulein Alide Topp;—in the evening, of the opening concert of the Festival for Tuesday morning. This last was a public rehearsal, each of the nearly 800 singers being allowed to bring a friend, while all the remaining space of the great Hall was more than filled by those who paid a dollar for admission. For the first time the full force, vocal and instrumental, was brought together; when lo! a curious difficulty, there was too much of a good thing! As the Sopranos on the one side, and the Contraltos on the other, filed in upon the platform, the human tide kept rising rank upon rank up either slope, until it even trenched upon the side balconies; where were the gentlemen Tenors and Basses to find room? They bestowed themselves in the corners round the organ, in the balconies and finally away up in the second balcony above, and still more remained outside, to wander about the hall finding no place or "coigne of vantage" whence to join their voices with their brethren, while the great choir and orchestra and organ rolled out their mighty floods of harmony. But this was an evil not irremediable; better err on the safe side, and have too many rather than too few; a natural shrinkage has to be allowed for; and it is a fact of choral, at least of Handel and Haydn Society experience, that to make sure of 600 singers, at least 800 must be invited. What, should they all accept! Well, many evils cure themselves,—as Tuesday morning showed.

Opening of the Festival.

Tuesday, May 5, was in all respects a bright, auspicious day. Even the weather of this so far black and wintry Spring for once was sunshiny and delightful. By the appointed hour of eleven, the large and eager audience were in their places; presently the tide of orchestra and singers— the latter reduced to a convenient 700—flooded all the stage again, and only the adjoining lower balconies; and at that moment the Music Hall indeed presented a beautiful and brilliant aspect, yet with wise abstinence from extra ornament. . . .

As Dr. Upham ended his brief and judicious preface, the curtains which had been hanging against the rear wall of the Music Hall were let fall, and there were disclosed the busts of Palestrina and of Mozart, poised upon their symbolical brackets, one at the right and the other at the left of the Apollo Belvidere. Many of the audience rose eagerly in their places, the chorus waved their handkerchiefs, and Charlotte Cushman's gift was acknowledged with many a token of appreciation and pleasure. . . .

Then ZERRAHN waved his baton, and all the voices and the instruments and the great Organ, at which sat Mr. B. J. LANG, burst at once upon the ear, *fortissimo*, in all their weight and splendor, in the Choral, "*Ein feste Burg*," with which Nicolai begins his Festival Overture. We have only room now to say that the whole concert was a magnificent success, and that the three works, the Choral Overture, the 95th Psalm and the "Hymn of Praise" by Mendelssohn, were indeed admirably rendered, Mme. ROSA and Miss PHILLIPPS being in fine voice and mood, and Mr. SIMPSON well up to his task in the tenor solos. Indeed, we think we never heard an Oratorio performance on the whole so perfect, so electrifying, as that of the "Hymn of Praise" on Tuesday, both in the opening symphonic movements and the vocal part which follows.— "Samson" went almost equally well in the evening; and glorious was the Symphony Concert of Wednesday afternoon, of which the sensation was the wonderful piano performance (Schumann's Concerto and one of Liszt's *Rhapsodies Hongroises*) by Miss ALIDE TOPP. . . .

41. *American Conservatories*

In his issue of February 16, 1867, Dwight wrote a brief notice of the opening of the Boston Conservatory of Music and appended a hasty paragraph reporting that "scarcely was the above announced when by a sudden *coup d'etat* a 'New England Conservatory of Music' dropped down from the clouds, captured the Music Hall, flooded Boston with grandiloquent Circulars, created 'professors' by the score, and, gathering up pupils fast, is ready to open next Monday. . . . Perhaps the more the merrier," Dwight mused at the end, "but we must pause, observe, and think."

Indeed, it appeared that the time had come for American conservatories, and they opened in quick succession not only in Boston but also in Cincinnati, Chicago, and Baltimore. The Oberlin Conservatory in Ohio had opened two years earlier, under the leadership of two teachers from the music department of Oberlin College. The difference between a conservatory and a college music department of that time was crucial.

The first mission of American colleges, in their early days, was to prepare young men for the ministry. Accordingly, the earliest college music departments, like the one begun at Oberlin in 1837, concentrated on church music and produced principally organists and choir directors. The young man or woman who wanted to take up music as a secular profession simply took lessons from the available practitioners of the art, most often immigrant Germans who eked out a living as teachers while performing occasionally at the local theater or concert place. In the 1850s and 1860s some of the more ambitious or determined students went to Europe for their training.

After the Civil War, qualified musicians and opportunities for them to practice their craft became numerous enough that the idea of organizing American conservatories began to look promising, even profitable. Music had been taught in girls' schools as one of the social graces, in colleges as in adjunct to the church. Now came independent schools of music to teach the art for its own sake, as a profession.

If not for the war, the first conservatory might well have been the Peabody Conservatory in Baltimore, for the Massachusetts-born philanthropist George Peabody endowed it in 1857 as part of a larger institute for the advancement of the arts. The Peabody Institute finally opened in 1868, its conservatory complete with a resident orchestra and a public concert series. Two years later a correspondent described for Dwight its impact on a city that was, the reporter's complaints notwithstanding, one of the main music centers on the eastern seaboard.

Dwight's Journal of Music, June 18, 1870

Baltimore, June 10.—Music, in Baltimore, or at least good music, seems by nine-tenths of the public to be looked at, when they condescend to look at all, in the light of a very secondary matter; not to be for a moment compared to the merits of politics, horse racing or prize fights! One may look till he is gray in the four daily papers, without finding so much as a hint that any decent music is to be heard: except it may be in the advertisement columns. It would seem as though nothing but one of Gilmore's earthquakes would turn the attention of the public to the fact of there being such a thing as "the divine art."

Previous to the formation of the "Peabody Institute," four years ago, the amount of music which could be heard outside the churches and theatres was extremely small. There are amateur concerts, confined as to programmes mostly to opera selections: and as they seem to have had very few really good vocal teachers, the style of singing can be better imagined than described. Then there are performances of the "Independent Blues" Band, which seems to have been the "Germania" of Baltimore. Then occasional visits from Opera companies (the Richings troupe being here at present), and concerts from most of the travelling concerns; and lastly, occasional Piano Recitals by resident professors. . . .

I come now to a much more promising subject, viz.: the Peabody Institute. Probably most of your readers are aware that Mr. Peabody left, or gave rather, a very large sum, to establish an institution for the higher artistic education of the people of Baltimore. The interest of this,—after erecting the magnificent building of white marble, in a beautiful situation, near the Washington monument, and forming one side of the square—amounts to something over $50,000 per annum. This immense sum is in the hands of a Board of 200 Directors, one of whom is General Grant.

So far the interest of the fund has been expended on two departments only: the Library and the Academy of Music, of which latter Mr. L. H. Southard, formerly of Boston, is the director. I have just stated that the fund is expended (or so much as the board think proper) on two departments. Such is the fact. But I beg the reader not to suppose for a moment that it is *equally* divided: by no means. Nothing could possibly show more clearly the estimation in which music is held in Baltimore, than the proportion of this fund of $50,000 which is set apart for the Academy of Music, which consists of a Conservatory, having a building of its own, next to the Institute, and organized something after the manner of our Boston Conservatories, and the formation of a grand orchestra, and a series of orchestral concerts yearly. Any one acquainted with the details of the management of good orchestral performances, does not need to be told how very expensive it is. The pay of members of the orchestra in Baltimore is about the same as in Boston, and as the orchestra numbers some 40 or more, the expense must be very large.

As Mr. Peabody directed that only a nominal sum should be charged at the door, and as great liberality is exercised by the management in this respect (for instance, no one who comes *without* having purchased a ticket of admission is ever refused entrance!), very little can be realized from this source. Also the concerts are not advertised as with us; merely an announcement being inserted in one or two daily papers on the day of the performance.

For all this outlay the directors appropriate the sum of $5,000 of the above fund, which must carry on the Conservatory, pay the salary of the Director, pay the members of the orchestra, copying, new music, instruments, &c, &c.! And this notwithstanding the expressed wish of the giver (in writing) that music should be one of the principal features of the Institute!

It is almost unnecessary to affirm that none but a Yankee and a Bostonian would be able to do much with so miserable a pittance.

But Mr. Southard has organized a complete orchestra (the largest number they had got together before of their own performers, being from 13 to 20, with which they used to *do* Beethoven's Symphonies!) consisting of 11 violins (6 first and 5 second), 4 violas, 2 violoncellos, 3 double basses, 2 flutes, 2 oboes, 2 clarinets, 2 bassoons, 2 trumpets (cornets), 4 French horns, 3 trombones, tuba, and full set of drums.

It will be seen at a glance that the band is weak in the string department, there being brass and wood enough for three times the number of violins. . . . On the other hand, the hall in the Peabody Institute is not very large, holding only about 1,000 people, and the wind instruments are placed in a recess at one end, which has the effect of muffling them somewhat, while the strings are in front, and brought out into the hall, rendering the whole orchestra tolerably well balanced. . . .

It is perhaps unnecessary to add that the latest "improvements" introduced by Mr. Theo. Thomas in Boston, of symmetrical bowing, a real pianissimo, terracing the performers, &c., have not yet reached Baltimore. (They were a long while reaching Boston, for that matter!)

A glance at the programme for the past two seasons will show what has been done in the way of introducing good music to the people of Baltimore: Beethoven's 1st, 2d, 5th and 7th Symphonies have been given, and his E-flat Concerto twice; Mozart's Symphonies in C and E♭, and his Concerto in D minor; Gade's Symphony in C twice or more; the Scotch Symphony of Mendelssohn; two movements of the great Schubert Symphony in C, (the 9th); two symphonies of Haydn, one in E♭ and one in D; two movements of Spohr's Symphony, Op. 78, &c.

Of Overtures a great variety have been given: 3 by Mendelssohn ("Ruy Blas," "Fingal's Cave," and "Midsummer Night's Dream"); 4 by Weber; 2 by Mozart; 6 by Rossini; 5 by Auber; 2 by Boieldieu; 2 by Suppé; and one each by Meyerbeer, Cherubini, Reinecke, Nicolai, Spontini, Donizetti, Balfe, Flotow, Reissiger, and Onslow. Also Mendelssohn's *Cappricio Brillant* (with Orchestra), Op. 22; his *Serenade and Allegro giojoso*, Op. 43, and the whole of his "Midsummer Night's Dream" music. Besides these, a great number of smaller pieces have been given, some of them arranged in a really effective manner by the director.

I have been greatly interested in examining this trial of *an American* in a sphere, where but very few (in this country at least) are placed. There seems to be no doubt but that we have got to have, sometime, (and that not far distant), orchestras manned and directed by Americans:—that is, if we are to have orchestral music at all.

In England it was formerly as with us; they relied on German performers; but now their orchestras are largely made up of Englishmen, and to any one who has heard the best London concerts, it is needless to state that the performances have lost nothing in quality by the change.

As to the best means for bringing about this most desirable state of things, it is not the purpose of the writer to inquire, but I think one thing has been fully proved by this experiment in Baltimore, and that is: that, given even a small amount of support, a good musician will acquit himself creditably at the head of an orchestra, be he of what nationality he may.

42. *A Musical Professorship*

In 1875 Harvard instituted the first chair in music in an American university. Dwight had long urged his alma mater to take the step, but his welcoming article has much more in it than self-congratulation or home-team enthusiasm. He foresees a special role for the university music department, as opposed to the conservatory, in cultivating musicians for the "many-sided universal culture" he imagines for America.

Before Dwight closed the *Journal*, music departments had been established not only at Oberlin and Harvard but also at Vassar College (1872), the University of Pennsylvania and Smith College (both in 1875), and in the state universities of Illinois (1877) and Michigan (1879). The new music departments did not all necessarily conform to the ivory-tower model Dwight posed (any more than the conservatories followed the commercial path he anticipated for them), but a century later the United States, unlike European nations, looked to universities rather than to conservatories to train the preponderance of its professional musicians.

Dwight's Journal of Music, August 21, 1875

A Musical Professorship at Harvard
I.

At last our venerable University has made up her mind to establish a Professorship of Music,—on a full and equal footing, as to dignity at least, with the existing chairs of literature and science. The "President and Fellows" made the proposition, and the board of Overseers, at their last meeting, voted that it should be done. . . . For the material wherewithal, the funds, it may safely go for granted that these will promptly be forthcoming, now that Alma Mater has given notice to her sons and to the world, that she must have Music formally installed and recognized among the rest of the "humanities" with equal honor.

Who is to be the man? Although some formal steps are wanting (during the vacation period) to complete the action, it is perfectly well understood that he will be no other than the learned, earnest, and devoted musician, yet in the prime of life, who has for the past fourteen years labored so assiduously, in spite of very moderate encouragement, as musical instructor in the College, (holding for the past year the rank of Assistant Professor),—Mr. JOHN KNOWLES PAINE. So far as a single man may fill the place, we know not one who would be more competent. He certainly has earned his title to it there, having made the most of the small means and narrow opportunities at his disposal. At home in all the science and the ready use of counterpoint; a composer, who has produced his proofs in many of the largest forms of composition with a good measure of success, he was prepared to teach, if there were any ready to be taught. There may be others of a more brilliant genius, a more marked individuality, a more quickening, magnetic power, more tact and ready art in intercourse with men; of this we do not presume to judge; but there is that in his deep, earnest love of art, his thorough training and his knowledge, his singleness of purpose and simplicity of character, his fidelity to the high *morale* of his calling, and his hearty love of work, which goes far to offset all that may be imagined to be wanting.—Of course this musical professorship will be what he will make it; he has to create it as the sculptor moulds the clay; indeed he has been creating it these fourteen years, by humble means and processes, which it is to be hoped will now blossom to the light and bear good fruit.

Here then is a good beginning,—a first *bona fide* University professorship of Music; not hastily arrived at, not at all premature; not an empty name, the cheap resolution of an ignorant ambition, such as has hitherto conferred degrees of Doctor in Music on the part of Colleges by no means musical; but a live fact, well rooted, that has grown up from the germ. But we trust it will be considered only the beginning. Music, to be fitly and fully represented in the University, needs more than one professor, needs in fact a complete Faculty, or School, as fully equipped as those of Law and Medicine and Natural History are now. . . .

There is some education derived, of course, from the whole multifarious opera and concert business, from the hearing of so much music good, bad and indifferent. There is also a loosening of the soil, over wide tracts where naught would grow before, by means of the numerous "Conservatories," so called, which have sprung up in this country of late years, some of which count their pupils by thousands. But *numbers* are of too great account with them, and "business," far more than Art or Culture, seems to be the genius and the mainspring of their organization. Let these do all the good they can in their own way; but there is still wanting an *authority*; something established, and respected, far above mercenary motives, which may set a higher tone and an example for them also, so that there may be something to refer to, something standard, in the midst of all their differences, and superficialities and caterings to the fashions and the idols of a day. Where can this be found so well as in an ancient University. . . . where culture is pursued purely, and for its own sake; a University so placed as to be as far above and independent of all speculative, mere business arts and influences, as any Church can be? . . . Here the standard of pure taste would not have to be dragged down into the market place continually, to compete with the new fashions, the passing excitements and cheap popularities of those with whom *enterprise* is regarded as the one thing needful, and constitutes their entire talent. Moreover, in the University, Music will dwell in sweet companionship with sister arts, and stand in living, daily, true relationship with all the branches of a many-sided universal culture. The study of the Art could hardly fail, in such a liberal and genial sphere. . . .

We have opened a great subject, and one which, to discuss fully, would lead us far beyond our present means or purpose. Yet, in another paper, we hope to develop the theme a little further, as well as to give some brief account of how much actually *has* been accomplished in the university at Cambridge toward building up a musical character for itself.

Dwight's Journal of Music, September 18, 1875

A Musical Professorship at Harvard
II.

In congratulating our old University on its making room at last for a Chair for Music among the other "humanities," we promised some account of what actually *has* been accomplished there in this direction within a few years. . . .

The College began with a very moderate recognition of the importance of the subject about twenty years ago, in the employment of the late Levi P. Homer as "musical instructor," in which office he was succeeded by Mr. Paine in 1861. His functions were few, and his sphere of labors exceedingly small. In fact there was little for him to do, beyond directing the chapel music, training a few short-lived voluntary singing classes, and giving a few private lessons on the piano and organ, or in harmony, &c. And there was small pay for that. In course of time the instructor, of his own impulse, gave one or two courses of lectures on musical history and aesthetics before a very meagre audience of students and townspeople. Four or five years ago, however, when the system of "Electives" came in force, Music was placed on the list of elective studies, and Mr. Paine formed his first class, of only six or eight young men, who "elected" to devote some three recitation hours per week to exercises in Harmony and simple Counterpoint. The next year a new class was formed, equally small, while the old class went on in studies more advanced, getting somewhat initiated into Imitative Counterpoint, and the study and practice of the various musical *forms* (Song, Rondo, Sonata, &c., &c.) Last year the course was further extended into the mysteries of Fugue and Canon, and even somewhat into the study of Instrumentation. The exercises and attempts at original composition of a number of the pupils were highly creditable, and two or three of the young men seemed to show great promise; one of them, Mr. Arthur Foote, of Salem, of the Class of 1874, is devoting himself to the study of Music as a life profession. But the examiners (and the very appointment of such a Committee, must be counted among the signs of a recognition of Music on the part of Alma Mater), suggested in their report of 1874, whether perhaps Mr. Paine was not trying to cover too much ground, considering the limited time the students have for it amid so many other studies, and whether it would not be wiser to give more time to making them more thoroughly grounded in the earlier stages of Harmony, plain Counterpoint, the harmonizing of Chorals, &c., rather than attempt to carry them into Instrumentation, when no orchestra or opportunity of trial of their exercises existed in the college. And also whether the teacher's influence need be limited to the inducting of a very few students into the dry theory of Counterpoint; whether he could not do something also toward interesting the mass of undergraduates in music as a matter of taste and refined social culture, accustoming them to the *hearing* of the best works of the masters.

—We are happy to say that during the past year both of these suggestions have been adopted by the "Assistant Professor" (the title which Mr. Paine has worn for one year preliminary to his receiving the full professorship.) The study of Harmony, the Choral, &c., has been dwelt upon more thoroughly, throwing the second and third classes into one, while at the same time one or two students who were exceptionally advanced have received special instruction in the higher branches of Imitation, Fugue, &c. . . .

During the year, too, Mr. Paine has instituted a fourth class, in the *history* of Music, which has been somewhat larger than the others. The Professor lectures on some period of the history in a familiar conversational way, while the students take notes. The next time, having consulted authorities meanwhile as recommended by the teacher, they are questioned on the points of the last lecture, and take notes on a new instalment of the history.

But the new feature of most interest undoubtedly has been the Thursday Evening social musical performances, which Mr. Paine, aided by some of the best singers and players of instruments among the students, has held weekly through the year in the class room,—a small and very uninviting place for it, to be sure, and the poor *square* piano being not eminently sympathetic or responsive to the best artistic intentions; it is to be hoped that a better place and better means to work with will be provided when the Professor is inaugurated! These "Abendsunterhaltungen," as they call such occasions at the Leipzig Conservatory, have proved very interesting and instructive. The attendance has been quite large, and the programmes choice and historically significant. On one evening when we had the pleasure of being present, Mr. Paine played first a group of pieces, consisting of a Fugue by Handel, a Sarabande by Bach, and a Gigue by Mozart, preceded by brief historical and critical notices of those masters. Then came an Aria of Mozart: *Dalla sua pace*, from "Don Giovanni" beautifully sung by the young tenor Szemelenyi, who graduated this year; then *Lieder ohne Worte* by Mendelssohn; Piano pieces by Schubert and Schumann, followed by Songs of the same; and finally a Sonata of Beethoven. We were struck by the very close attention of the students who composed the larger part of the audience; they evidently were bent on *knowing* something about the several composers, and the forms and styles in which they wrote.—We understand that the number of students who have given notice of their intention to take up one or more of these musical "electives" in the next term is at least double what it was last year. . . .

43. *The Boston Symphony Orchestra*

On the front page of the *Evening Transcript* of March 30, 1881, appeared a historic notice. "The Boston Symphony Orchestra" it was headed—an instance of what the historian Daniel J. Boorstin has called "nouns in the future tense." The item was, in effect, a promissory note signed by H. L. Higginson, who pledged to bring such an orchestra into being for the fall season. The Boston Symphony Orchestra, as Henry Lee Higginson conceived it, was to be the first permanently endowed American orchestra.

New York by this time had three orchestras competing for the musical public: the Philharmonic Society, the Thomas Orchestra, and, since 1878, Leopold Damrosch's Symphony Society. Of these, the first was a cooperative venture that returned its members less than a pittance; the second was always close to the brink financially, saved from going over only by its leader's personal sacrifice; the third, lacking any stable financial base, depended on a group of wealthy patrons to provide necessary support, *ad hoc*. So it went, too, for orchestral organizations in St. Louis, Cincinnati, Louisville, Milwaukee, Philadelphia, and Chicago. And so it had gone in Boston, where the concerts that Carl Zerrahn conducted for the Harvard Musical Association barely scraped by, year after year, unable to pay musicians enough to win the best, hence unable to maintain a standard of performance that would attract and hold a sustaining audience.

The new Boston Symphony Orchestra would be a different story. Higginson planned to provide an endowment of a million dollars, the interest from which would be enough to cover the $50,000 deficit that could be expected in a season of concerts. The orchestra's treasury thus guaranteed, the conductor would be free to concentrate wholly on musical matters: on the personnel and training of the orchestra, and on the music to be performed.

Henry Lee Higginson was a Harvard-educated banker who, as a youth, had spent a year in Vienna studying music. The catalyst that converted him from music lover to orchestral patron was Georg Henschel, a young German singer-composer who came to the United States in 1880 to appear in concerts as soloist and in company with his fiancee, Lillian Bailey, a gifted soprano who had grown up in Boston. The couple had met in London, where Henschel was well launched on a career when Bailey arrived from studies in Paris.

Henschel made a strong impression in Boston, not only as a singer and composer, but also, at a concert of the Harvard Musical Association, as a conductor. In a surprise appearance, he led the orchestra in his own "Concert Overture," and even John S. Dwight was struck by "the revelation (from the very first measures of the work) of that *rara avis*, a born conductor." Higginson evidently was impressed, too: That concert took place March 3, 1881; within the month he had conceived a new orchestra and engaged Henschel as its conductor.

Dwight had campaigned so long and ardently for a permanent Boston orchestra, he must have been stunned to have it thus created by fiat. Perhaps the blow was softened by Higginson's thoughtful acknowledgment, in his published notice, of Dwight's role in educating the Boston public in "music of a higher character." In any case, Dwight reprinted the notice in the earliest possible issue of the *Journal*, and gave the project his wholehearted blessing. In a later number, he reprinted an article from a London journal hailing the American example in musical patronage. The Boston Symphony Orchestra played its first concert October 22, 1881. *Dwight's Journal of Music* had ceased publication less than two months before.

Dwight's Journal of Music, April 9, 1881

The Orchestral Problem Well-Nigh Settled

In most of the daily papers suddenly appeared, one day last week, the following "word," with noble motive, power, decision, and wise plan behind it. Every one has read it, yet none the less we wish to have it stand recorded here:—

A WORD IN THE INTEREST OF GOOD MUSIC

To the Editor of—

Notwithstanding the development of musical taste in Boston, we have never yet possessed a full and permanent orchestra, offering the best music at low prices, such as may be found in all the large European cities, or even in the smaller musical centres of Germany. The essential condition of such orchestras is their stability, whereas ours are necessarily shifting and uncertain, because we are dependent upon musicians whose work and time are largely pledged elsewhere.

To obviate this difficulty the following plan is offered. It is an effort made simply in the interest of good music, and though individual inasmuch as it is independent of societies or clubs, it is in no way antagonistic to any previously existing musical organization. Indeed, the first step as well as the natural impulse in announcing a new musical project, is to thank those who have brought us where we now stand. Whatever may be done in the future, to the Handel and Haydn Society and to the Harvard Musical Association we all owe the greater part of our home education in music of a high character. Can we forget either how admirably their work has been supplemented by the taste and critical judgment of Mr. John S. Dwight, and by the artists who have identified themselves with the same cause in Boston? These have been our teachers. We build on foundations they have laid. Such details of this scheme as concern the public are stated below.

The orchestra is to number sixty selected musicians; their time, so far as required for careful training and for a given number of concerts, to be engaged in advance.

Mr. Georg Henschel will be the conductor for the coming season.

The concerts will be twenty in number, given in the Music Hall on Saturday evenings, from the middle of October to the middle of March.

The price of season tickets, with reserved seats, for the whole series of evening concerts will be either ten dollars or five dollars, according to position.

Single tickets, with reserved seats, will be seventy-five cents or twenty-five cents, according to position.

Besides the concerts, there will be a public rehearsal on one afternoon of every week, with single tickets at twenty-five cents, and no re-served seats.

The intention is that this orchestra shall be made permanent here, and shall be called "The Boston Symphony Orchestra."

Both as the condition and result of success the sympathy of the public is asked.

H. L. HIGGINSON

Here is the orchestra question suddenly settled, it would seem, and over all our heads; settled by one-man power, a *coup-d'etat*, with no pre-tence of any *plebiscite*. But in this surprise there lurks no mischief. Here the one-man power means only good; means music of the highest kind, accessible to all the people, and a plenty of it. Nothing could be more modest, simple and direct than Mr. Higginson's announcement of what he has resolved to do and how he has arranged to do it. Loving music, and having spent some of his younger years in Germany, where he enjoyed the best, it has been one of his dreams to be able some day to make this enjoyment and this culture cheap and common in his na-tive city. Connected with the well-known banking-house of Lee & Higginson, and having recently become possessed of ample means, he now finds himself in a condition to realize the dream. He is prepared and willing, if need be, to sustain large losses in the enterprise, in which artistic excellence, completeness, and the elevation of the public taste are evidently of more account to him than any saving of expense, pecu-niary profit being wholly out of the question. Probably the appearance here of Mr. Henschel was what crystallized the project long held in solution in his mind, and brought the whole thing to a practical de-cision now.

Nothing ever came more timely. Among the musical signs of the times here in Boston for some months past, has been the remarkable preoccupation of the whole community with what is called the perma-nent orchestra problem. For sixteen years the Harvard Musical Associa-tion (of which, by the way, Mr. Higginson is a member) has, through good report and ill report, in spite of insufficient means, and many obstacles (unsparing criticism, prejudices, party feeling, and capricious patronage), upheld the cause of classical Symphony Concerts, as well as it was able, losing not a dollar, to be sure, in the long run, but constrained to such economy as sadly interfered with its ideal in the matter of performance, although not of repertoire and programme. Still it has not secured the general confidence and sympathy enough to concentrate the general support upon its efforts; it has persevered in faith, trusting that the good time would come when money would not be wanting to enable it to do what from the first it has aspired to do. Of late, divided (not to say rival) movements in the same, or a similar direction have sprung up, until the prospect was that by another year we should be flooded with orchestral concerts, yet no one series of them strong enough singly to do much toward the "permanence" of an orchestral organization. Mr. Higginson's decided movement, while it may take the wind out of the sails of all these, both the old and new, is on a larger scale than all of them combined, and is a very strong one, offering such positive advantages that we must all wish it God-speed and a long continuance.

Among these advantages are the following: (1) It is free from all taint of speculation; art being made of more consequence than money-making. (2) It places the best of music within frequent and easy reach of all who love it and cannot afford to pay the prices usual heretofore; and it tends to bring down the scale of prices for all such pure and elevating entertainments. (3) It has the advantage of unity of plan and will, backed by abundant means;—although for permanence, and for consistent loyalty to a high idea, we still believe that such idea had better be embodied in an organized society, standing for a bulwark in this field, like our old Handel and Haydn Society (for instance) in the field of oratorio. (4) It antagonizes no other organization, although it yet remains to see what special field is left for each to cultivate and make its own *par excellence*. (5) It ensures a plenty of good orchestral music for next season, and a plenty of occupation for all good musicians, going farther than any promise yet held out toward the realization of a "permanent orchestra," that is, an orchestra whose members shall make that their one, at least their chief, occupation and support. And the very rumor of a Boston so full of music and of good work for musicians will draw other good ones to us. (6) Last, not least, it makes Mr. Henschel one of us, and that will be a great gain indeed to Boston. Therefore, Success to the Boston Symphony Orchestra, and thanks to Mr. Higginson!

Dwight's Journal of Music, July 16, 1881

The Boston Symphony Orchestra

The noble movement of Mr. Higginson has found admiring recognition abroad. The July number of the London *Musical Times* (Novello, Ewer & Co.) pays him the just tribute which we print below. . . . When will a millionnaire be found to give America the large, strong, many-sided, but high-toned Musical Journal which the present development and prospect of the art in this great country calls for? But for the London greeting!

A TRUE MUSICAL PATRON.

. . . Patronage in art—and more especially in music—is good; but the timely help proffered to a struggling genius, however much it may become a valuable personal benefit, is rather the patronage of artists; and he, therefore, who, disregarding individuals, helps to found institutions which shall spread a knowledge of the standard works amongst the people, is the true missionary, for he sets in action, by the magic power of wealth, those grand creations, the beauties of which can alone be revealed by the engagement of a large number of performers at an outlay beyond the means of a private speculator. Disinterested patrons of this kind are rare, but their rarity increases their value; and as it is in the nature of these benefactors of the art to shrink from any demonstrations of gratitude which their actions must necessarily call forth, it is the duty of all who become acquainted with such actions to reveal the name of the actor, not only that justice may be given to whom it is due, but that a worthy pattern may be held up to the world for others to imitate.

Let us then at once say that such a person as we have attempted to describe has recently appeared, not in this country, but at Boston, in the United States. Quietly and unostentatiously—as all earnest workers in a cause they have at heart invariably proceed—he has devoted himself to the task of organizing performances of the greatest compositions in musical art, and admitting the public at a price thoroughly within the reach of all. Our readers will, we are certain, be interested in knowing how this work is to be carried out; and as the facts are in our possession, we will briefly state them. At the last Harvard Concert, Herr Henschel conducted an overture, which went remarkably well. Amongst the audience was Mr. Henry Lee Higginson, son-in-law of Professor Agassiz, and one of the most prominent citizens of Boston, who, struck with the excellence of the performance, immediately resolved, not only to found an orchestra, with the desire of its becoming a permanent institution of the city where he resides, but to place Herr Henschel at the head of it. It appears that Mr. Higginson had for twenty years resolved to carry out this idea, and waited only for the right time and opportunity. Presuming even that he had also put himself forward as chairman of a board to determine how such an undertaking should be directed, and to suggest, if not actually to command, what music should be performed, the Boston public would owe him a deep debt of gratitude. But to prove—for it scarcely would be believed without proof—how, after making himself responsible for the large outlay which must be involved, and intimating his desire that all classes shall be enabled to share the benefits of his generosity, he modestly retires from the scene, we now give the business details of the plan.

Herr Henschel was commissioned to engage an orchestra of from sixty-five to seventy performers, which, as we have already said, is to be permanent, under the title of "The Boston Symphony Orchestra," and at the time of the publication of this article is complete, and ready for the first rehearsal. The sole charge of the orchestra rests with Herr Henschel, who is to be the conductor, and who, without the slightest supervision or control, is to make out the programme of each performance. The concerts are to take place on twenty Saturday nights between October 15, 1881, and March 15, 1882. Three rehearsals are to take place for every concert, each rehearsal of three hours' duration. There are to be no committees, nor any kind of criticism upon the actions of the conductor. Mr. Higginson pays all the artists and every expense connected with the concerts. We may also say that he has bought a splendid library for this orchestra, which already includes fifty symphonies, seventy overtures, and ninety miscellaneous pieces, all the best editions, in full score, and with the orchestral parts. Herr Henschel has on his programmes all the nine symphonies of Beethoven, two of Mozart, two of Haydn, two of Schumann, one of Mendelssohn, one of Schubert, two of Brahms, and one of Rubinstein, besides a varied selection of overtures and pieces; and it is his intention to produce novelties at not less than fifteen of the concerts. In addition to the orchestral performances—the main feature of the enterprise—the most talented solo vocalists will be engaged at every concert. The entrance fee for the performances are twenty-five and fifty cents (1s. and 2s.). Season tickets, with reserved seats, will also be issued for the twenty concerts, for five and ten dollars (£1 and £2).

Here, then, are the authentic particulars of a plan which we believe we are safe in saying has no parallel in musical history. We have many instances of wealthy patrons of art helping young composers, not only to make a reputation, but to partially free them from the great battle of existence, so that they can sustain and add to that reputation in maturer years. Help of this kind came to Beethoven, for example, in Germany; and in England we may cite the case of the Duke of Chandos, who appointed Handel to the place of Chapel-master at Cannons, and encouraged him to compose, placing an orchestra and vocalists at his disposal. But all this kindly aid, although indirectly benefiting the art, was mainly directed towards the fostering of a special gift for composition which had already decisively developed itself in the two great artists we have named. The object of our Boston patron is avowedly to further the knowledge of the art itself,—not to draw forth new treasures from rising composers, but to make thousands acquainted with the treasures lying around them. The realization of this object is still in the future; but meantime we cannot withhold the expression of our admiration at the noble manner in which the project has been organized. Let us indulge the earnest hope that wealthy lovers of art on this side of the Atlantic may take this lesson to heart. America has shown us that she can practise as well as preach. Here, the "precept" has long, very long, been set before our artistic capitalists, but we have yet to wait for the "example."

H. C. L.

Part Five

Songs of the Blacks

44. *A Letter from Georgia*

While Dwight was above all devoted to the idea of an American musical culture based on European models, he clearly was fascinated by occasional glimpses of an Afro-American musical culture just beginning to show through the obscurity of slave life in the South. In the 1850s, northerners knew hardly anything of the actual music of plantation blacks. What they did know—for Dwight, all too well—was a parody invented by northern entertainers. In immensely and persistently popular blackface minstrel shows, white performers wantonly burlesqued supposed ways and music of southern blacks in comic and sentimental "scenes of plantation life."

Ignorant of the real thing, northerners unthinkingly accepted the minstrel confections as authentic Negro melodies. And in an early issue of *Dwight's Journal*, a "down east music teacher," writing from Georgia, provides evidence that blacks accepted them, too: In addition to the music they created, they picked up songs popular among the whites and sang them in a way so much their own that "Old Folks at Home," heard in a southern cottonfield, could sound like a spontaneous creation of the fieldhands rather than of Stephen Foster's imagination.

The letter actually sets out to make a different point. It is a reply to charges, made in an earlier letter from Mississippi, that in the South "there is not the least cultivated taste for music—nothing beyond strumming a waltz or polka on the piano, or singing a Negro melody. . . . You at the North are mainly responsible for this evil," the Mississippian had written, placing the blame on northern music teachers. In defending the fraternity, the Georgia-resident teacher compares musical environments, in the North and South, and in the process describes a kind of black-white interchange that was to be a vital factor in the later development of all kinds of American music.

Dwight's Journal of Music, February 26, 1853

Letter from a Teacher at the South

MR. DWIGHT:—In a recent number of the *Journal* was an extract from the New York *Musical World and Times*, entitled "Music in Mississippi," which, with your permission, I wish to notice. . . .

Never having been in Mississippi, I cannot answer for the condition of the musical education there, but if in sixteen years the lady has never found a "*tolerably* taught" scholar, it seems to me her opportunities for observation must be somewhat limited, or in this respect pupils in Mississippi must be much inferior to those in Georgia. During two years' residence in this State I have found many pupils not only well-taught but full of talent and enthusiasm, who with *time* and *study* might compete with the best scholars in New York or Boston. That they do *not* give this time can hardly be the fault of Northern musicians, I think.

The country *is* rich and beautiful as a whole, and the people are rich and liberal as a class. They are willing and do spend large sums for the education of their children, and music is considered of the highest importance as—an amusing accomplishment—nothing higher. In nine times out of ten this study is reserved for the last year of school as part of the finishing, nor is this custom confined to the South. . . .

Numerous young ladies *are* sent from the South to the North to school—some for one year, some for two and some for several—be the time long or short they are expected to return proficient. A mechanic produces work according to the orders and materials furnished him. Can a teacher do more? . . . I have known girls in New York and Boston, who have studied under the best masters, "do nothing beyond strumming a Waltz or Polka on the piano, or singing a negro melody;" yet in those cities they are surrounded by music all their lives—at home or at school, at church and at play. There is music for the mass as well as the few. That this *is a fact*, I must deeply regret; but that it is the fault of teachers exclusively, I cannot believe. Whilst "Negro Vocalists," "Ethiopian Serenaders," and low priced third and fourth rate concerts are patronized by cultivated people it would take a legion of teachers to raise the musical taste of all their pupils to a high standard. Here, the early advantages are greatly inferior—their domestic music is made by the Negro. Church music among the Methodists, who are by far the largest denomination, is Congregational singing, after the obsolete, and to many Northerners, unheard of fashion of *lining* the hymn. With such early preparations girls are sent to school with the expectation that they will return accomplished musicians. . . .

The Mississippi lady objects to "Negro Melodies," and certainly as a part of musical education they are about as appropriate as "Mother Goose's Melodies" would be for a reading book in one of your Grammar Schools—they are justly considered too as equivocal proofs of taste. But if they may be allowed anywhere, it is in this section, where the sentiment, language, expression of them is so familiar. Although first published at the North, you there know nothing of the power and pathos given them here. The whites first learn them—the negroes catch the air and words from once hearing, after which woods and fields resound with their strains—the whites catch the expression from these sable minstrels—thus Negro Melodies have an effect here not dreamed of at the North. I have spent an evening of as hearty, if not as high enjoyment, seated in state on the wide piazza, listening to a negro singing his melodies accompanied by his banjo, now grave now gay, as I ever did in Tremont Temple or the Melodeon, and as I expect to in the new Music Hall. When I heard Jenny Lind sing "Home, sweet Home" it caused such an emotion as I never before experienced; it might be *exquisite home-sickness.* "Old Folks at Home," as I hear it shouted from house to house, from the fields and in the vallies, has an effect scarcely inferior. I find myself often humming the chorus and even dream at night,

> "Oh, comrades, how my heart grows weary,
> Far from the dear friends at home."

This has little to do with musical education in the main, but much in effect. A thing that speaks so to the heart is hard to be reasoned down. We might teach all the New England songs ever published, and sing with the expression that none but a Northerner thus far from home *can* feel, "I love, I love the snow," without the effect that one of these simple melodies has. These are by no means part and parcel of the lessons taught, although they will be learned. . . .

It is greatly to be regretted, I think, that teachers of such inferior stamp only should be found in Mississippi as to give the Lady Correspondent so much disgust for the class. Would it not be well to send some real Professors as missionaries musical to that land, for the benefit of the rising generation and to raise the reputation of the fraternity at home.

Respectfully yours,
"A Down East Music Teacher."

45. *Songs of Captivity*

An article Dwight discovered in a Christian journal interested him enough that he published it in 1856 and again, verbatim and without explanation, in 1859. We can only guess what he found so attractive in it, but more than a century later, despite its foggy racial assumptions, it nonetheless suggests much about the place of music in American society at the time, white as well as black.

Like many another northern missionary working in the South, the writer was moved to eloquence by the music of plantation blacks, which was rapidly becoming legendary in the North. The reference to love songs is unusual. Contemporary reports generally give the impression that almost all the slaves' songs were inspired by religion.

Dwight's Journal of Music, November 15, 1856

Songs of the Blacks

The only musical population of this country are the negroes of the South. Here at the North we have teachers in great numbers, who try to graft the love of music upon the tastes of our colder race. But their success is only limited. . . . We are still dependent on foreigners for our music. Italian singers fill our concert rooms, and German bands parade our streets.

Throughout the country the same holds true. Singing masters itinerate from village to village, to give instruction in the tuneful art, but the most they can muster is a score or two of men and maidens to sing in church on Sunday. Brother Jonathan is awkward at the business, and sings only on set occasions. . . . He makes little music at home, or at most only on the Sabbath day. During the week his melodies are unheard. He does not go to his labor singing to himself along the road. No song of home or country, of love or war, escapes his lips as he works in his shop or follows the plough. Our people work in silence, like convicts in a Penitentiary. . . .

Compared with our taciturn race, the African nature is full of poetry and song. The Negro is a natural musician. He will learn to play on an instrument more quickly than a white man. They have magnificent voices and sing without instruction. They may not know one note from another, yet their ears catch the strains of any floating air, and they repeat it by imitation. The native melody of their voices falls without art into the channel of song. They go singing to their daily labors. The maid sings about the house, and the laborer sings in the field.

Besides their splendid organs of voice, the African nature is full of poetry. Inferior to the white race in reason and intellect, they have more imagination, more lively feelings and a more expressive manner. In this they resemble the southern nations of Europe. Their joy and grief are not pent up in the heart, but find instant expression in their eyes and voice. With their imagination they clothe in rude poetry the incidents of their lowly life, and set them to simple melodies. Thus they sing their humble loves in strains full of tenderness. We at the North hear these songs only as burlesqued by our Negro Minstrels, with faces blackened with charcoal. Yet even thus all feel that they have rare sweetness and melody.

Mingled with these love songs are plaintive airs which seem to have caught a tone of sadness and pathos from the hardships and frequent separation of their slave life. They are the Songs of their Captivity, and are sung with a touching effect. No song of a concert room ever thrilled us like one of these simple African airs, heard afar off in the stillness of a summer night. Sailing down the Mississippi, the voyager on the deck of the steamer may often hear these strains, wild, sad and tender, floating from the shore.

But it is in religion that the African pours out his whole voice and soul. A child in intellect, he is a child in faith. All the revelations of the Bible have to him a startling vividness, and he will sing of the judgment and the resurrection with a terror or a triumph which cannot be concealed. In religion he finds also an element of freedom which he does not find in his hard life, and in these wild bursts of melody he seems to be giving utterance to that exultant liberty of soul which no chains can bind, and no oppression subdue. As hundreds assemble at a camp meeting in the woods, and join in the chorus of such a hymn as

"When I can read my title clear,
To mansions in the skies,"

the unimpassioned hearer is almost lifted from his feet by the volume and majesty of the sound.

No voices of well trained choir in church or cathedral, no pealing organ, nor mighty anthem, ever moved us like these voices of a multitude going up to God under the open canopy of heaven. Blessed power of music! that can raise the poor and despised above their care and poverty. It is a beautiful gift of God to this oppressed race to lighten their sorrows in the house of their bondage.

Might not our countrymen all learn a lesson from these simple children of Africa? . . . Americans are the most favored people on earth, and yet they are the least expressive of their joy. So that we almost deserve the severe comment of a foreigner, who on seeing the great outward prosperity, and yet the anxious look of the people, said that "in America there was less misery, *and less happiness*, than in any other country on earth."

Let us not be ashamed to learn the art of happiness from the poor bondman at the South. If slaves can pour out their hearts in melody, how ought freemen to sing! If that love of music which is inborn in them, could be inbred in us, it would do much to lighten the anxiety and care which brood on every face and weigh on every heart. The spirit of music would beguile the toilsome hours, and make us cheerful and happy in our labor. . . .

Evangelist

46.   *Who Wrote the Negro Songs?*

Before the Civil War, "Negro songs" meant popular songs with verses written in a parody of Negro dialect. They might come from the blackface minstrel shows or from the books of sentimental songs that lay on so many parlor pianos. They might be called "Ethiopian songs" or "plantation melodies." Who wrote them? Hardly anyone stopped to think about it; maybe some people thought that the songs actually came from southern plantations.

In a brief, unsigned item in 1857, *Dwight's Journal of Music* posed the question and furnished an answer. Two years later, Dwight reprinted an article from the New York *Evening Post* in which virtually the same question is given the same answer, though at greater length.

Dwight's Journal of Music, March 21, 1857

WHO WROTE THE NEGRO SONGS.—The principal writer is Stephen C. Foster, author of "Uncle Ned," "O Susannah," &c. Mr. Foster resides near Pittsburg, where he occupies a moderate clerkship, upon which, and a percentage on the sale of his songs, he depends for a living. He writes the music of his songs, as well as the poetry. These are sung wherever the English language is spoken, while the music is sung wherever men sing. In the cotton fields of the South, among the mines of California and Australia, in the sea-coast cities of China, in Paris, in the London prison, everywhere in fact, his melodies are heard. "Uncle Ned" was the first. This was published in 1845, and reached a sale unknown till then in the music publishing business. Of "The Old Folks at Home," 100,000 copies have been sold in this country, and as many more in England. "My Old Kentucky Home" and "Old Dog Tray," each had a sale of about 70,000. All his other songs have had a great run. All his compositions are simple, but they are natural, and find their way to the popular heart.

Dwight's Journal of Music, May 14, 1859

Who Writes Our Songs?

(From the New York Evening Post)

The musical composer who really furnishes the great majority of our songs, and whose productions have the widest popularity among the masses of our people, is known to very few of them, even by reputation. The new melodies that greet the public ear, month after month, and are sung, whistled and hummed by thousands—that are thumped on pianofortes, thrummed on banjos, breathed on flutes, tortured into variations, and enjoy a wide, though, after all, evanescent popularity, are chiefly the product of one of fertile brain—and that brain, as Mr. Micawber would say, is the brain appertaining to Mr. Stephen C. Foster. This gentleman is a native of Pittsburgh, and has spent all his days there, excepting three years at Cincinnati, and two at New York. He was born on the 4th of July, 1826, (the very day that John Adams and Thomas Jefferson died) and is therefore, now in his thirty-third year. . . .

It would render this article too much like a "catalogue of popular and standard music" to give a list of Mr. Foster's songs. "Massa's in the Cold Ground," "Old Kentucky Home," "Hi! Boys, Carry me 'Long," "Nelly was a Lady," and "Old Folks at Home," may be mentioned as among the most popular. His "Susanna" melody has been seized by many pianists, (among whom may be mentioned Herz and Thalberg) as a melodic theme peculiarly suited for treatment with variations, and some of the other negro melodies have obtained an equal popularity. Nor is this popularity merely a local one. In many of the Southern States Mr. Foster's songs have been adopted by the slaves to enliven them at their huskings and field labors. . . .

Ethiopian minstrelsy, as it is called, has, however, culminated, and is now in its decline. Appreciating this fact, Mr. Foster has somewhat changed his style, and abandoning the use of negro jargon, he now writes songs better adapted for general use. While the melodies exhibit a decided improvement, the words are rhythmical, always unexceptionable in point of moral, and as good, poetically considered, as the majority of songs. We do not say that Mr. Foster's "melodies" can be compared with those that have immortalized the names of Burns, Barry

Cornwall, or Thomas Moore; but we do maintain that the composer who produced such popular and pleasing songs as "Gentle Annie," "Willie, we have Missed You," "Maggie by my Side," "I see her still in my Dreams," "Old Dog Tray," "Jeannie with the Light Brown Hair," &c., deserves an honorable mention, as one of those who has enlarged the pleasure of thousands. . . .

And, as Mr. Foster is still young, he may improve and elevate his style, till he attains a musical reputation that will be more than ephemeral.

47. *Minstrels*

In the next issue of *Dwight's Journal*, a dispatch from Hartford, Connecticut, makes it clear that any report of minstrelsy's demise was exaggerated. In fact, traveling minstrel troupes continued to make their circuit almost to the end of the century. After the Civil War, some even included real Negroes. In Hartford in 1859 blackface minstrels evidently had no difficulty in competing with Eliza Biscaccianti, who was back home after ventures in San Francisco and Peru. Dwight's correspondent, in his report, makes a choice juxtaposition of the popular and the genteel offerings that vied for the musical audience in mid-nineteenth-century America.

Dwight's Journal of Music, May 21, 1859

Hartford, Conn., May 16.—What should we do without the negro minstrels—the "Buckley's," the "Campbell's," the "Sanford Troupe," the "New Orleans Serenaders," and a host of other companies—who always draw immense audiences wherever they perform—none greater, I understand, than those at the South, in the midst of the very ones whom they caricature and burlesque? There is a strange fascination about them, which has proved itself for over twenty years—from "Jim Crow Rice" to the present time; and still the attraction is unabated. Think of the fortune E. P. Christy has made in New York, through the agency of banjos and "burnt cork!"—riding on Broadway like a prince; and "Matt Peel," too, one of the very best of the Ethiopean delineators, who lately died in Buffalo, leaving a large fortune from "rattling the bones!" In England these negro bands "take" immensely, and even in Paris, the "Christy" entertainments have been crowded. How a Frenchman can enjoy any thing of the kind, I cannot understand; but it is told that their appreciation of the jokes hardly falls short of our own, purely from imagination; so much so that when "Pompey" merely cries out, "All right," it is enough to bring down tremendous applause from the Gallic audience. Just as it is in the German theatres, whenever in a play, an English character exclaims, "Gott tam," it is received with intense delight, and is always considered a great "hit."

Well, we have had the "minstrels" here, lately, in profusion. The "Sandford Troupe" came first, and Town Hall was completely packed with people to see and hear them. They were here two evenings, and met with great success. The next week appeared the "New Orleans Metropolitan Troupe," and they, too, attracted crowded houses. A day or two since the exciting and important news burst upon us that the "Campbells are coming!" They have "come," and are filling their hall every night. And now again today, as I passed along the street, I was highly gratified to learn that the "Morris, Brothers" celebrated troupe will shortly appear! And still I don't believe that they will go away penniless.

Friday evening, while American Hall was crammed to listen to the "Campbells," Town Hall was also filled to hear Madame BISCACCIANTI and her assistants, Mr. WILLIAM H. DENNETT, Basso, Mr. G. T. EVANS, Pianist, and Sig. A. BISCACCIANTI, violoncellist. It was one of the finest and most select audiences that has been seen in Hartford for a long time. Mme. Biscaccianti sang most delightfully, and was received with tumultuous applause every time she appeared, being *encored*, as is the present outrageous fashion, at the close of each of her pieces named on the programme, thereby making the second part of the concert quite tedious. . . . Mr. Evans is one of the very best accompaniests upon the piano-forte I ever heard. His solos, such as Mason's "Silver Spring," Thalberg's "Home, Sweet Home," &c., were well played. By close practice he might become one of the finest performers in the country. No singer, since Jenny Lind, has pleased the Hartford people to such a high degree as Madame Biscaccianti. As a testimonial of appreciation of her powers, she was presented, at the close of the concert, with an immense floral star, made up of the choicest flowers, by one of our choicest damsels.

H.

48. *Contraband Singing*

The Civil War brought to an end the experience that had given rise to the real Negro songs, the songs of the slaves. It also brought the beginning of a wider awareness of those songs among Americans at large. Early in the war, fugitive slaves made their way into Union army encampments and there found protection as "contrabands of war." First in Fortress Monroe, Virginia, then in the Sea Islands of South Carolina, northern observers heard the freedmen sing their spirituals and were moved to copy them down. Some understood immediately that a musical and poetic treasure was being uncovered and that it would disappear unless an effort were made to preserve it.

The contrabands of Port Royal, South Carolina, became the most important source for the first collectors of the slave songs. Taken early by the Union and then isolated from the turmoil of battle, Port Royal became a proving ground for volunteer workers who came from the North to look after the welfare and the education of the island's freed blacks.

James J. McKim, one of the volunteers who was particularly struck with the singing of the former slaves, was quick to report his discovery to the North. Fortuitously, traveling with him was his daughter Lucy, a trained musician, who attempted to notate the music of the songs as she heard them in 1862. Lucy McKim's transcriptions were the first to show an intuitive grasp not merely of the spirit of the songs she wrote down but of the unconventional musical turns of phrase that give that spirit substance.

With two like-minded collectors, Charles P. Ware and William Francis Allen, Lucy McKim (by then, Mrs. Wendell Phillips Garrison) compiled *Slave Songs of the United States*. With their own gleanings from Port Royal, they incorporated some two dozen songs collected by Thomas Wentworth Higginson, a fiery antislavery preacher who had gone to war and become commander of the First Regiment of

South Carolina Volunteers, made up of freed slaves mustered into the Union army.

In June, 1867, the *Atlantic Monthly* published an article by Higginson (then working in the Freedmen's Bureau), giving the texts of songs he had managed to copy down as he had heard them sung around the campfire by his freedmen soldiers. The music appeared at last when *Slave Songs of the United States* was published later that year. *Dwight's Journal of Music* followed step by step the emergence of the slave songs from obscurity.

Dwight's Journal of Music, September 7, 1861

CONTRABAND SINGING.—It is one of the most striking incidents of this war to listen to the singing of the groups of colored people in Fortress Monroe, who gather at their resorts after nightfall. Last evening, having occasion to "visit" an officer of the garrison sick in his tent, I passed around by the fortress chapel and adjacent yard, where most of the "contraband" tents are spread. There were hundreds of men of all ages scattered around. In one tent they were singing in order, one man leading, as extemporaneous chorister, while some ten or twelve others joined in the chorus. The hymn was long and plaintive, as usual, and the air was one of the sweetest minors I have ever listened to. It would have touched many a heart if sung in the audiences who appreciate the simple melody of nature, fresh and warm from the heart. One verse ran thus:

> "Shout along, children!
> Shout along, children!
>   Hear the dying Lamb:
> Oh! take your nets and follow me
> For I died for you upon the tree!
>   Shout along, children!
>   Shout along, children!
>   Hear the dying Lamb."

There was no confusion, no uproar, no discord—all was as tender and harmonious as the symphony of an organ.

Passing into the yard, I found a large company standing in the open air round a slow fire. One young man sat on the end of a rude seat, "with a little book in the hand." It had been much fingered, and he was stooping down towards the dim blaze of the fire, to make out the words, as he lined them for the singers. Where he had learned to read I know not, but where some of his companions *will* learn to read I *do* know. The singers were dressed in all manner of garbs and stood leaning around in all kinds of attitudes. As the reader progressed one young man threw a few fresh hoops on the fire, and then as the reading became more distinct, I caught the words:

> "Could I but climb on Pisgah's top
>   And view the promised land,
> My flesh itself would long to drop,
>   At my dear Lord's command.
>
> "This living grace on earth we owe,
>   To Jesus' dying love;
> We would be only his below,
>   And reign with him above."

At this moment the tattoo drum sounded the parade, and a distant bugle reminded me of my duty in another direction. With a word of counsel to the company, and a gentle encouragement, I withdrew.

Who shall dare say that these fellow-inheritors with us of the image of the Father and the love of the Son are fit only to be slaves?— C. W. D.—*N. Y. Com. Ad.*

Dwight's Journal of Music, August 9, 1862

Negro Songs.

Mr. J. McKim, of Philadelphia, an agent of the Port Royal Relief Society, who last month visited the Sea Islands of South Carolina, makes the following remarks upon the negroes' songs:

That the present condition of these people is in favorable contrast with that under their masters is evident from their songs, which constitute a striking feature in their manifestations of character. They are a musical people. When they work in concert, as in rowing or grinding at the mill, their hands keep time to music. Their boat songs are the ones most frequently heard. The islands are made and permeated by rivers and creeks, and the boat furnishes the most common mode of locomotion.

When the negroes begin to row, they at the same time begin to sing. All their songs are in the minor key. If one chances to begin on the major, it quickly saddens and passes into the minor. Their songs are all religious, barcaroles and all. I speak without exception. So far as I heard or was told of their singing, it was all religious. None of their songs express mirth or present joy. The only joy expressed or implied is that of hope. "Rest at last" was their general burthen; "Heaven is my home;" "Have a little patience;" "God will deliver"—these and the like were the refrains of all their ballads.

There was one which on shore we heard more than any other, and which was irresistibly touching. It was a sort of ballad, known as "Poor Rosy, Poor Gal." It is almost impossible to give an idea of the effect of this or any of their songs by a mere recital or description. They are all exceedingly simple, both in sentiment and in music. Each stanza contains but a single thought, set in perhaps two or three bars of music; and yet as they sing it, in alternate recitatives and choruses, with varying inflections and dramatic effect, this simple and otherwise monotonous melody will, to a musical ear and a heart susceptible of impression, have all the charm of variety. Take, for instance, a few stanzas from the dirge of "Poor Rosy." Fancy the first line sung in the major key, and the two following changed by an easy transition, and with varying inflections, into the minor, and you will have some idea of the effect.

> Poor Rosy, poor gal!
> Poor-Rosy-poor-gal!
> P-o-o-r R-o-s-y, p-o-o-r gal!
>> Heaven shall be my home.
>
> Hard trial on my way!
> Hard-trial-on-my-way!
> H-a-r-d t-r-i-a-l o-n m-y w-a-y!
>> Heaven shall be my home.
>
> Wonder what de people want of me,

Wonder-what-de-people-want-of-me,
W-o-n-d-e-r w-h-a-t d-e p-e-o-p-l-e w-a-n-t o-f m-e,
   Heaven shall be my home.

When I talk I talk with God!
When-I-talk-I-talk-with-God!
W-h-e-n I t-a-l-k I t-a-l-k w-i-t-h G-o-d!
   Heaven shall be my home.

I asked one of these blacks—one of the most intelligent I had met—where they got these songs. "Dey make em, sah." "How do they make them?" After a pause, evidently casting about for an explanation, he said, "I'll tell you; it's dis way. My master call me up and order me a short peck of corn and a hundred lash. My friends see it and is sorry for me. When dey come to de praise meeting dat night dey sing about it. Some's very good singers and know how; and dey work it in, work it in, you know; till dey get it right; and dat's de way." A very satisfactory explanation.

I said these songs were all in the minor key. This was a mistake. They have one that has a cheerful, and, as it sounded when I first heard it, a hilarious ring. It is a new one, made, as they said, "since secesh times." It runs thus:

No more driver call for me,
   No more driver call;
No more driver call for me,
   Many a thousand die!

No more peck of corn for me,
   No more peck of corn;
No more peck of corn for me,
   Many a thousand die!

No more hundred lash for me,
   No more hundred lash,
No more hundred lash for me,
   Many a thousand die!

and so on, recounting all the incidents of slave life.

When I first heard this song I was going up from Hilton Head to

Beaufort in a boat rowed by a half dozen men detailed from the first regiment of South Carolina volunteers. They were in fine voice and spirits, and the echoes came back from the inlets of Ladies' and St. Helena with fine effect. As we passed along we encountered a boat load of black people rowing in the opposite direction. They were acquaintances of our oarsmen, and after the first salutation, asked what those clothes meant? Our crew were dressed in the blue blouse and pants and felt hat, which constitutes the uniform of the regiment. They explained—one of them adding, in a tone of laughing triumph,

"We'se Uncle Sam's chil'n now; we'se Uncle Sam's chil'n; we're none of your fiel' hans."

The others looked envious and passed on. The fact that these people are thought worthy to be enlisted as soldiers, adds to their self-respect.

I dwell on these songs not as a matter of entertainment but of instruction. They tell the whole story of these people's life and character. There is no need after hearing them, to inquire into the history of the slave's treatment. Recitals of this kind one will hear enough of, whether he desires it or not; for these people, having now, for the first time in their lives, sympathetic listeners, pour out their hearts in narrations which nothing but flint can resist. I ought to add before leaving this subject, that their songs, like their talk, are couched in a barbarous, Africanized sort of English, and are sometimes quite unintelligible. In the specimens I have here given I have not followed their pronunciation.

Dwight's Journal of Music, November 8, 1862

Songs of the Port Royal "Contrabands."

We have received No. 1 of "Songs of the Freedmen of Port Royal, collected and arranged by Miss LUCY MCKIM," with the following interesting letter, which speaks for itself. We trust we violate no confidence in printing it. The melody has a simple and touching pathos, a flavor of individuality which makes one desire to know more of these things; and we trust that "Poor Rosy" will be followed by other specimens as genuine.

Mr. Dwight,

Sir:—In a recent number of your journal there appeared an article relating to the music of the slaves of Port Royal, taken from an address delivered by my father before the members and friends of the Port Royal Freed-men's Association of this city. The extract included the words of one of their songs, beginning "Poor Rosy, poor gal!"

My chief object in writing to you, is to say, that having accompanied my father on his tour to Port Royal, and being much struck with the songs of its people, I reduced a number of them to paper; among them, the ballad referred to. I send you herewith a copy of it, hoping it may interest you. Whether to have the others printed, is as yet, a question with me.

It is difficult to express the entire character of these negro ballads by mere musical notes and signs. The odd turns made in the throat; and the curious rhythmic effect produced by single voices chiming in at different irregular intervals, seem almost as impossible to place on score, as the singing of birds, or the tones of an Æolian Harp. The airs, however, can be reached. They are too decided not to be easily understood, and their striking originality would catch the ear of any musician. Besides this, they are valuable as an expression of the character and life of the race which is playing such a conspicuous part in our history. The wild, sad strains tell, as the sufferers themselves never could, of crushed hopes, keen sorrow, and a dull daily misery which covered them as hopelessly as the fog from the rice-swamps. On the other hand, the words breathe a trusting faith in rest in the future—in "Canaan's air and happy land," to which their eyes seem constantly turned.

A complaint might be made against these songs on the score of monotony. It is true there is a great deal of repetition of the music, but that is to accommodate the *leader*, who, if he be a good one, is always an improvisator. For instance, on one occasion, the name of each of our party who was present, was dexterously introduced.

As the same songs are sung at every sort of work, of course the *tempo* is not always alike. On the water, the oars dip "Poor Rosy" to an even andante; a stout boy and girl at the hominy-mill will make the same "Poor Rosy" fly, to keep up with the whirling stone; and in the evening, after the day's work is done, "Heab'n shall-a be my home" peals up slowly and mournfully from the distant quarters. One woman,—a respectable house-servant, who had lost all but one of her twenty-two children, said to me:

"Pshaw! dont har to dese yer chil'en, misse. Dey just rattles it off,—dey dont know how for sing it. I likes "Poor Rosy" better dan all de songs, but it cant be sung widout a *full heart and a troubled sperrit*!"

All the songs make good barcaroles. Whittier "builded better than he knew" when he wrote his "Song of the Negro Boatman." It seemed wonderfully applicable as we were being rowed across Hilton Head Harbor among United States gunboats,—the Wabash and the Vermont towering on either side. I thought the crew *must* strike up

> "And massa tink it day ob doom,
> And we ob jubilee."

Perhaps the *grandest* singing we heard was at the Baptist Church on St. Helena Island, when a congregation of three hundred men and women joined in a hymn—

> "Roll, Jordan, roll, Jordan!
> Roll, Jordan, roll!"

It swelled forth like a triumphal anthem. That same hymn was sung by thousands of negroes on the 4th of July last, when they marched in procession under the Stars and Stripes, cheering them for the first time as the "flag of *our* country." A friend writing from there, says that the chorus was indescribably grand,—"that the whole woods and world seemed joining in that rolling sound."

There is much more in this new and curious music, of which it is a temptation to write, but I must remember that it can speak for itself better than any one for it.

Very respectfully,

LUCY MCKIM.

Dwight's Journal of Music, July 20, 1867

THE SONGS OF THE FREEDMEN. Our readers may remember that about five years ago we published a letter from Miss McKim, of Philadelphia, (now the wife of Mr. W. P. Garrison,) describing the songs which she had heard (and partly taken down) among the recently freed people of the Sea Islands. Much larger collections were afterwards made by Prof. Wm. F. Allen, of West Newton, and his cousin, Mr. Chas. P. Ware, of Milton. These three are now united, by common agreement, and have been very largely increased by accessions from all parts of the South. The basis still remains the "spirituals," such as were furnished the *Atlantic* by Mr. Higginson, who has kindly turned them over to the persons named above, that they may publish them, words and music, in one volume. The collection will be edited by Prof. Allen, who has written a preface of some length to illustrate the songs. Messrs. A. Simpson & Co., of the Agathynian Press, 60 Duane Street, New York, intend to give the work their imprint (a guaranty of the highest style of typography), provided they meet with sufficient encouragement. The cost per volume will probably not exceed $1.75, and will be much less to those taking several copies. Orders may be sent to the firm with the above address. No one will question the urgency of preserving these transient productions of a highly musical race, and they will commend themselves for actual enjoyment to all lovers of music, as well as to lovers of the curious.

The *Nation*, of May 30th, alludes to the excellent project in these terms:

"The proper folk-songs of this country should be sought, we suppose, among the aborigines; but the capacity of the Indian for music does not appear to be equal to his reputed capacity for eloquence. The negro possesses both these gifts in a high degree, and it is singular that no one up to this time has explored for preservation the wild, beautiful, and pathetic melodies of the Southern slaves. Their secular songs, or what purported to be such, have in times past made their way into all mouths; but their 'spirituals'—the genuine expression of their eminently religious nature—have only recently claimed attention. We are able to announce a collection, based on the Port Royal hymnody, and including the songs of as many Southern States as are obtainable, which will be published either in the course of this year or at the beginning of the next. The words and (whenever possible) the music will be carefully reproduced, and it is the aim of the editors to make the volume complete in both respects. Any information relating to this subject will be very acceptable to them, and may be sent to Mr. W. P. Garrison, Box 6732, N.Y. Post-office."

49. The Fisk Jubilee Singers

Northerners who read and sang through *Slave Songs of the United States* could only imagine what the music sounded like when sung by the people who had created it. They were able to gain a more vivid idea when a group of nine students from Fisk University traveled from Nashville to give concerts in the North in 1871.

The aim of the tour was not to acquaint northerners with the slave songs but to raise money needed for the survival of the first university founded primarily for the education of freed slaves. At the outset the programs planned for the young singers by their New York–born mentor, George L. White, were a potpourri of familiar airs of the kind performed by popular singing families like the Hutchinsons: favorites like "Old Folks at Home" and "Home, Sweet Home," hymns, and such patriotic, sentimental, and temperance songs as would make polite entertainment for the most respectable society.

Black performers had to prove themselves in the accepted white repertoire if they were to appear in a white church or on a proper concert stage. In the 1850s *Dwight's Journal* carried reports of performances of Elizabeth Taylor Greenfield, evidently a singer of remarkable gifts, who was paraded as "the Black Swan" in concert and opera. In the 1860s Dwight followed even more closely the strange career of Thomas Greene Bethune, a slave boy who may have been a musical prodigy; he was dubbed "Blind Tom" and crassly exploited by masters and managers who exhibited him as a pianist in concerts verging on freak shows.

Northern audiences at first hardly knew what to make of the young singers from Fisk. Some thought they might be an odd kind of minstrel troupe; some were hostile. One lesson the students learned early, as they were refused hotel accommodations in Ohio, was that northerners too could despise black skin. Even the more sympathetic audiences listened to their polished singing, for the most part, with a polite reserve that turned to enthusiasm only at the end of their program, where they introduced a spiritual or two—"Steal Away," for example, and "Go Down, Moses." George White, in his determination to make his students' performance acceptable, had not only polished their singing, he had also disciplined the native dialect out of their pronunciation; but the beauty of the songs and the fervor of the singing nonetheless moved audiences in a wholly unaccustomed way.

It soon became plain that in the spirituals the Fisk singers (all but one of them born into slavery) were sharing a unique musical experience, and as audiences responded to its poignancy and power, White changed the balance of their programs to include more of the slave songs. Before they left Ohio for New York, the group took the name Jubilee Singers, the slave songs became the distinguishing feature of their concerts, and a tour that had begun tenuously ended in triumph in the Northeast.

In 1873 Dwight took notice of the publication of a book recounting the Fisk Jubilee Singers' history and including a collection of their songs. By this time, the Hampton Institute of Virginia had formed a singing group patterned after the Fisk group, and the Jubilee Singers themselves were embarked on a tour of England, Scotland, and Wales. The British venture was so successful that the Jubilee Singers extended their touring to the Continent, and in 1877 made their first appearances in Germany.

Dwight's Journal of Music, April 5, 1873

Negro Folk Songs
SLAVE MELODIES OF THE SOUTH—THE JUBILEE AND HAMPTON SINGERS

The Editor of the *New York Weekly Review*, in the article which follows, shows a just interest in the untutored religious melodies of the ex-slaves of our Southern States. The collection to which he alludes of these songs, set down in notes by Mr. Seward, may be found appended to an interesting volume just published by Lee & Shephard of this city, entitled "The Jubilee Singers of Fisk University," presenting, in a couple of hundred pages, an account of that institution and its teachers, the personal history and portraits of the singers, a chronicle of their successful musical and missionary tour through the Union, and, as we said before, an Appendix containing the words and notes of about sixty of the songs.

At last the American school of music has been discovered. We have had accomplished virtuosi, skilful vocalists and talented composers. They have, however, all trodden the beaten track. It has remained for the obscure and uncultured Negro race in this country to prove that there is an original style of music peculiar to America. This school is found in the songs of the Southern blacks and they have been but lately made familiar to Northerners by the efforts of two groups of colored singers who have lately given concerts in our principal cities. Both of these bands of wandering minstrels are working in aid of meritorious educational institutions.

The Jubilee Singers who appeared here some months ago represent the interests of Fisk University, of Nashville, Tennessee. They are nine in number, including: Ella Sheppard, pianist and soprano; Jennie Jackson, soprano; Maggie Porter, soprano; Minnie Tate, contralto; Eliza Walker, contralto; Thomas Rutling, tenor; Ben. M. Holmes, tenor; I. P. Dickerson, bass; and Greene Evans, bass. They have sung in most of our Eastern cities with excellent pecuniary success; and the quaint, weird melodies in which their natural talents and acquired skill have been exercised, have been further made familiar to the public, through a collection of some fifty of their favorite songs which were reduced to musical notation by Mr. Theodore F. Seward of this city. Of these songs the editor of the little book containing them, and published by Bigelow and Main of this city, says:

"The Songs—Of these neither the words, or the music have ever before been published, or even reduced to written form, at least, to the knowledge of the Jubilee Singers.

"The most of them they learned in childhood—the others, which were not common in the portion of the South in which they were raised, they have received directly from those who were accustomed to sing them. These songs, therefore, can be relied upon as the genuine songs of their race, being in words and music the same as sung by their ancestors in the cabin, on the platform, and in the religious worship.

"By the severe discipline to which the Jubilee Singers have been subjected in the schoolroom, they have been educated out of the peculiarities of the Negro dialect, and they do not attempt to imitate the peculiar pronunciation of their race. They have also received considerable musical instruction, and have become familiar with much of our best sacred and classical music, and this has modified their manner of execution. They do not attempt to imitate the grotesque bodily motions or the drawling intonations that often characterize the singing of great congregations of the colored people in their excited religious meetings.

"It is true, however, both of the words and the music, that whatever modification they have undergone, has been wholly in the minds of the Singers under the influence of the training and culture they have received in the University of which they are members."

The music of these songs is generally strikingly wild. Some of them at once recall the "breakdowns" made familiar to us by the negro minstrel troupes. Others suggest ordinary Sunday School hymn tunes; but the majority are unique in construction, rhythm and melody. The cultivated musician will at once perceive that they are crude and childish, but he cannot deny their originality.

The success of the Jubilee Singers seems to have inspired a number of the pupils of the Hampton, Va. Academy to "go and do likewise," and a band of nineteen members have started out on a similar mission. Being greater in force, they are more efficient in choral effects, and if less cultured than their predecessors, their performances are even more characteristic. They have given three concerts in New York (at Steinway Hall) and have, on each occasion been greeted by large and enthusiastic audiences.

The institution in whose aid their concerts are given is amply described in their programmes. It is situated in the town of Hampton, Virginia, near Fort Monroe, and the mouth of the Chesapeake Bay, and by one of the curious coincidences of history, close to the spot where the first slaves brought to this country were landed. Here, too, the famous order declaring black fugitives to be "contraband of war" was issued, and here was established the first school for Freedmen, from which, in the providence of God, this existing institution has been developed, beginning under the auspices of the American Missionary Association and the Freedmen's Bureau, and drawing its support mainly from Northern benevolence. . . .

Dwight's Journal of Music, November 29, 1873

The Jubilee Singers

(From the North British Daily Mail, Glasgow, Oct. 27)

There must be something in the music or in the manner of singing of these friends from the Far West not usually to be heard in our concert halls, judging not merely by the hearty welcome they receive from crowded audiences everywhere, but also from the fact that these audiences are composed of all ranks and classes of our people, the great majority of them being such as are not usually known in the musical world. The hearts of the people have been touched in a wonderful manner, and as the music is quite simple, and the singing modest and unassuming, it is interesting to try to ascertain why such unpretending performances should produce so great an effect. It has long been the subject of general remark that the fashionable music of our day has got into a rut of its own, and has to a great extent ceased to have any hold upon the affections of our people. To them it has little or no interest. It is run after only by the musical world, who in general care little for the music, and understand it still less, their chief object being to hear this, that or the other great star sing—for it is the fashion. . . .

Among the jubilee singers, there is no grand occidental star to dazzle an audience; therefore it is manifest that the charm of their music does not depend upon individual voices. In their singing the voices are so beautifully blended that individuality is nearly lost. Some of their solos are sung with great beauty, but usually these are not of their own peculiar music. One exception must be particularly noticed—the song of

> "Bury me in the east, bury me in the west,
> I'll hear the trumpet sound in the morning."

is a strain so peculiar, so touching, so solemnizing that its effect is quite indescribable. The first thing that strikes us in the singing of the Jubilee Singers is its intense earnestness. The subject of their songs is to them a reality, something they have themselves realized and not a mere sentiment or imagination; they feel the words, and therefore they sing the music. The words are very simple, usually they contain one striking idea. At first sight they may sometimes appear to be childish, if not ir-reverent, but to the singers they have a deep and vivid meaning. Every line tells something of their people's history and experience—they are the simple and natural expressions of wrong, suffering, and slavery, wrung from the hearts of an uneducated, trodden down, and long suf-fering race. When we remember and realize the circumstances under which these songs were born (for they never were composed in the ordi-nary sense of the term), instead of denouncing them as silly and absurd, we cannot help being impressed by their power and depth of meaning. Still more when such songs as—"Children, we shall all be free," "No more auction block for me," "Turn back Pharaoh's army, Hallelu," are sung by those who have tasted the bitterness of bondage, who have been sold like any other chattels, and have suffered all the indignities of slavery—how is it possible that such songs should not be sung by such singers with a fervor and reality which it is in vain for other vocalists to attempt to imitate? Further, we must consider the deep religiousness of feeling which underlies most of their songs. This is often the true secret of their power, though not usually appreciated by critics. It is hardly possible to express Gospel truth in words more touching and effective than in the simple songs, "O, sinner man, where are you going?" "My good Lord's been here," and "Keep me from sinking down." Such strains put us irresistibly in mind of the oldest song of which we have any record—and it was a slave song—it is written in the 88th Psalm—the song of Heman, son of Zerah, grandson of Judah, expressing the groaning of the people of Israel under that Pharaoh who knew not Joseph. Others, as "Go down Moses, tell old Pharaoh let my people go," "Did not old Pharaoh's army get lost?" and "Turn back Pharaoh's army, hallelu!" re-echo the song of Moses, of Miriam, and of all the people after the passage of the Red Sea. Simple as those songs and melodies appear, they are purely natural—they cannot be imitated. Let any one try to compose one such as "Nobody knows the trouble I see," and he will find how hopeless is the task. Like the truly national songs of our own country, they are the spontaneous growth of genius—the composition of them cannot be traced. Some of them have come down from generation to generation. Others are of recent origin. We know the circumstances which called forth such songs as "John Brown's body," "No more auction block for me," and "Steal away;" and are therefore able to understand how truly they express the story of the country to which they are indigenous, and how powerfully they are calculated to stir up the religious and patriotic feelings of a people with whose very existence they are identified. . . . The character of the music is purely natural as contradistinguished from artistic—hence one great cause of its popular power; and any one conversant with the characteristics of our Scottish music will see at once, in these peculiarities, how much there is in common between them. Further, as the "Scotch snap" frequently occurs, and either the fourth or seventh of the scale are often wanting, and sometimes both, it is no wonder that we constantly find in the structure and cadences of these Negro melodies much that we feel to be very closely akin to ourselves. . . . As to the manner of their singing it must be heard before it can be realized. Like the Swedish melodies of Jenny Lind, it gives a new musical idea. It has been well remarked that, in some respects, it disarms criticism, in others it may be as truly said that it almost defies it. It was beautifully described by a simple Highland girl—"It filled my whole heart." Such singing, (in which the artistic is lost in the natural) can only be the result of the most careful training. The richness and purity of tone, both in melody and harmony, the contrast of light and shade, the varieties of gentleness and grandeur in expression, and the exquisite refinement of the piano, as contrasted with the power of the forte, fill us with delight, and at the same time, make us feel how strange it is that these unpretending singers should come over here to teach us what is the true refinement of music, and make us feel its moral and religious power. Another most important and special lesson they have brought to us, and one which it is to be hoped will not be lost upon us, is—how in their most plaintive or most impassioned songs, the words are so distinctly enunciated. Both the pronunciation and articulation of the language are more perfect than we almost ever hear, and put to shame our most highly trained and artistic singers, whether public or private. The object on account of which these friends have paid us a visit deserves, and will surely receive, all the support and encouragement that our country and people can give them.

C. B.

Andersonian University

Dwight's Journal of Music, February 2, 1878

A Letter from Berlin.
THE "JUBILEE SINGERS." . . .

The *Independent* publishes the following letter from the Rev. Joseph P. Thompson in Berlin:—

The musical season, which begins here in November, opened this year with a novelty—the appearance of the "Jubilee Singers," of the Nashville University, whose successes in England and Holland are well known in America. There were grave reasons for doubting that they would receive a like encouragement in Germany. For here there is no old-time, anti-slavery sentiment and no spontaneous philanthropy— such as was prepared to give them a considerate and sympathetic hearing in England; but they must pass the trying ordeal of German musical criticism. That they have passed this successfully; that the musical critics of the Berlin press, without exception, have awarded to them the praises of fine voices, and of clearness, harmony and effect of execution, is worth far more to the success of their enterprise in Germany, than would have been a handsome philanthropic subscription to Nashville University, headed by the Imperial family. What the singers receive they earn and richly deserve: and the financial success of their concerts, which is already considerable, is a higher compliment to themselves than any words of royal patronage.

But these they have also had. Before appearing in public, they were invited to sing at the "New Palace" in Potsdam, in the presence of the Emperor, the Crown Princess, and a number of distinguished guests; and the kindly, hearty approbation of such an audience was a certificate of character, as well as of musical merit. They were received at the palace not as a strolling band of singers, but as ladies and gentlemen; and the degree of culture and politeness of manner which they exhibited were gracefully recognized by their illustrious hosts. How marvellous the contrast between that scene in the palace of Frederic the Great, when a negro woman expressed so appropriately the disappointment of Americans that His Imperial and Royal Highness had not visited the Exposition at Philadelphia, and the old scenes of the plantations upon which she was born a slave! Here the pleased and complimentary answer of the Crown Prince of Germany; there the oath and lash of the overseer! I do not hesitate to say that these emancipated slaves, in propriety of demeanor and politeness of address, appeared to better advantage in the highest circle of Germany than would many a former slaveholder and his family.

I had the opportunity of noting the social manners of these singers at a *soirée* given by Baron George von Bunsen (who so worthily bears the name of his illustrious father) where the *élite* of Berlin were assembled as guests. The singers mingled easily and freely with the company, but always modestly; and I heard from the foremost men of science and culture, expressions of astonishment at their discreet and polished bearing, and the frank admission that it would be impossible to take the same number of German peasants and in the same time to raise them to a like degree of cultivation. Let those ponder this who fancy that the Negro race is incapable of high civilization; and especially let Southerners consider what a wealth of economic improvement lies in the culture of their former slaves. The success of the "Jubilee Singers" in Germany is now assured; and this is due in no small degree to the wisdom and energy with which President Cravath has managed their affairs.

It is of great advantage to these singers that while in Berlin they can hear some of the best choral music which Germany affords—as, for instance, the famed choir of the Dom and the perfect rendering of such music as Mozart's "Requiem" and Bach's "*Gottes Zeit*" by the Academy.

In orchestral and chamber music Berlin now rivals Leipsic and Stuttgart. The symphony concerts of the royal orchestra and the quartette *soirées* of Joachim and his colleagues are unsurpassed in the rendering of the highest classical compositions.

The opera has fallen behind its standard of ten years ago. Not in the orchestra, nor the chorus, nor the setting of pieces, nor the balancing of the whole; but in the conduct of the leading parts. Niemann is declining and seldom appears; Lucca was long ago lost to Berlin; Mallinger is losing her voice and her charms; none of the newer leaders can yet compete with these, and the Berlin public will not pay the Tietjens, Patti, Nilsson, Albani, Gerster prices, which London, Paris, Petersburg are so ready to meet. Gerster I hope you may soon hear in New York—the purest gem of modern song. Do not strain her tender voice in the Academy; but learn its sweetness in Steinway or Chickering Hall.

But why should Americans covet the singers of the Old World, when Miss Kellogg, Miss [Emma] Thursby, Minnie Hauck, and others of native birth are proving that America may yet rival Italy as a nursery of song? . . .

—*Berlin, Prussia, Nov.* 23d, 1877

Biographical Register

The following entries are not intended to stand independently as biographical sketches, but to supplement without repeating information given in the main body of the text.

Alboni, Marietta. b. 1826 in Città di Castello, Italy; d. 1894 in Paris. Contralto. Chosen by Rossini for leading roles in his operas; rival of Jenny Lind for favor of London audiences in the 1840s; toured the United States in 1852.

Anschütz, Karl. b. 1815 in Koblenz; d. 1870 in New York. Left Prussia for London (1848); moved to New York (1857) as conductor of Ullman-Strakosch Italian Opera company at Academy of Music; conductor of Arion Singing Society, New York (1860–62).

Apthorp, William Foster. b. 1848 in Boston; d. 1913 in Switzerland. While at Harvard (graduated 1869), studied music theory with John Knowles Paine. Wrote music criticism for the *Atlantic Monthly* (1872–77) and the *Boston Transcript* (1881–1903); annotated Boston Symphony Orchestra programs (1892–1901).

Arbuckle, Matthew. b. 1828; d. 1883 in New York. American cornet virtuoso and bandmaster.

Badiali, Cesare. b. 1805, d. 1865 in Imola, Italy. Basso. A leading singer in Italian opera houses and in London, Spain, Portugal before appearing with Havana company in New York (1850); returned in Maretzek company (1851–53), Ole Bull company (1855), concerts (1856).

Bailey, Lillian June. b. 1860 in Columbus, Ohio; d. 1901 in London. American soprano. Pupil of Hermine Rudersdorff in Boston; studied in Paris (1878) with Pauline Viardot-Garcia, in London (1879) with Georg Henschel (*q.v.*), with whom she appeared in duo-recitals; with Henschel, returned to U.S. (1881), where they were married and he was appointed conductor of the newly founded Boston Symphony Orchestra.

Baker, Benjamin Franklin. b. 1811 in Wendham, Mass.; d. 1889 in Boston. Singer, choir director, teacher. Officer of and soloist with Boston Handel and Haydn Society in 1840s; succeeded Lowell Mason as supervisor of music in Boston Public Schools (1842–47); founder and principal teacher of Boston Music School (1857–68). Compiled tune books, textbooks; composed three cantatas; edited *Boston Music Journal* (1855–57).

Balatka, Hans. b. 1827? in Moravia; d. 1899 in Chicago. Came to the U.S. in 1849; settled in Milwaukee, where he founded Musikverein; conducted performances of German choral, symphonic, operatic works, and presented chamber music (1851–60); continued his pioneering work in Chicago, where he became conductor of the Philharmonic Society (1862), founded Liederkranz and Mozart Club, conducted Symphony Society; led German music festivals (Sängerfeste) in Indianapolis, Cleveland, Detroit, and elsewhere.

Balfe, Michael William. b. 1808 in Dublin; d. 1870 in England. Irish singer, conductor, composer of light operas, including *The Bohemian Girl* (1848), widely performed by English companies in the United States.

Belletti, Giovanni. b. 1813, d. 1890 in Sarzana, Italy. Baritone. Associated with Jenny Lind, with whom he appeared in opera in Sweden, England, and on the tour arranged by Barnum in the U.S.

Benedict, Julius. b. 1804 in Stuttgart; d. 1885 in London. Conductor, composer. Music director of the Drury Lane Theater, Her Majesty's Theater, and Norwich Music Festivals in England; accompanied Jenny Lind as conductor in her American tour. Knighted (1871).

Bergmann, Carl. b. 1821 in Saxony; d. 1876 in New York. Joined the Germania Orchestra in the U.S. as cellist (1850), then became its conductor. When the orchestra disbanded (1854), moved briefly to Chicago, then to New York (1855) where he became associated with the Philharmonic Society, first as co-conductor with Theodore Eisfeld, then as sole conductor (1866–76); conducted Boston Handel and Haydn Society (1852–54). Cellist in first Mason-Thomas chamber music concerts (1855).

Bettini, Geremia. b. 1823 in Novara, Italy; d. 1865. After appearances in Havana and U.S. (1850–51), became leading tenor in Italian and other European opera houses.

Biscaccianti, Eliza (née Ostinelli). b. 1825 in Boston; d. 1896 in Paris. After early vocal training in Europe, appeared in *La Sonnambula* at Astor Place Opera House, New York (1849); returned to Europe, appeared in Paris, Milan, St. Petersburg, London; performed in San Francisco (1852) then toured South America; unable to repeat earlier success on return to San Francisco (1859), fell on hard times, and for a while sang in the entertainment parlor Bella Union Melodeon; sailed for Lima (1865), revived career for ten years in South America. Taught in Milan, but after unfortunate marriage died in poverty at Fondation Rossini, a home for artists and musicians.

Bosio, Angiolina. b. 1830 in Italy; d. 1859 in St. Petersburg, Russia. Soprano.

After early successes in Copenhagen and Madrid, appeared in Havana and from there went (with Havana company) to New York, Philadelphia, and Boston (1850–52), before returning to Europe for most brilliant phase of career cut short by her death during her third tour to Russia.

Bradbury, William B. b. 1816 in New York; d. 1868 in Montclair, N.J. Organist, teacher. Pupil of Lowell Mason; associated with George F. Root and Thomas Hastings in organizing singing schools, conventions, singing festivals; compiled some fifty psalmbooks, including widely used *Shawm* (1853), *Jubilee*, and *Fresh Laurels* (1867), of which three million copies were sold. With brother and a German piano maker, established firm (1854) which later became Bradbury Piano Company.

Brignoli, Pasquale. b. 1824 in Italy; d. 1884 in New York. Tenor. Came to U.S. (1855) under Maurice Strakosch's management; became favorite of audiences at New York's Academy of Music. Returned three times to Europe, but eventually made his home in New York where, despite popularity, he died in poverty.

Bristow, George Frederick. b. 1825 in Brooklyn; d. 1898 in New York. Violinist, composer, conductor. Studied with father, an English-born conductor, and in London with G. A. MacFarren. After early experience in New York theater orchestras, joined Philharmonic Society (1842); played in orchestra accompanying Jenny Lind in her first New York concerts (1850); recruited by Jullien for his monster concerts (1853). Briefly resigned from Philharmonic Society (1854) to protest orchestra's neglect of American composers; the Society, which had earlier rehearsed his first symphony, subsequently performed two more of his six symphonies. Opera *Rip Van Winkle* produced in New York (1850, 1870). Church organist; conductor of the choral Harmonic Society (1851–62); visiting teacher of music in New York public schools.

Buck, Dudley. b. 1839 in Hartford, Conn.; d. 1909 in Orange, N.J. Organist, composer. Son of shipping merchant; self-taught to age sixteen, when he won parents' consent to prepare for musical career; studied in Leipzig, Dresden, Paris (1852–56). Became church organist in Hartford, Chicago (1869–71), Boston (1872–75), Brooklyn (1877–1903); also toured as concert organist. Theodore Thomas chose him to be official organist of Cincinnati May Festival (1875) and appointed him assistant conductor of Thomas Orchestra's summer concerts at Central Park Garden, N.Y. Composed many anthems, cantatas, hymns, vocal solos, works for organ, also comic opera *Deseret* (1880).

Bull, Ole Borneman. b. 1810, d. 1880 in Norway. Violin virtuoso. Largely self-taught; appeared in U.S. in five extended visits (1843–45, 1852–57, 1867–69, 1870–72, 1876–80). Second wife (1870) was American, Sara Chapman Thorp, who wrote *Ole Bull: A Memoir* (Boston, 1883).

Bülow, Hans Guido Freiherr von. b. 1830 in Dresden; d. 1894 in Cairo. Having established himself as a pianist, became chief conductor of Munich Royal Opera (1864) and director of conservatory in Munich (1867); in 1870s, following divorce from Cosima Liszt, toured widely as pianist and conductor; under his direction (1880–85) Meiningen Court Orchestra was regarded as best in Europe; resigned Meiningen post to resume touring, also to teach in Frankfort and Berlin.

Campanini, Italo. b. 1845, d. 1896 in Italy. Tenor. First attracted attention in Italian premiere of *Lohengrin* (1871); after New York debut (1873), returned to U.S. with Mapleson company (beginning 1878); headed cast of *Faust*, opening first season of Metropolitan Opera, New York (1883); remained leading tenor on American scene for a decade. Conductor Cleofonte Campanini was his younger brother.

Cary, Annie Louise. b. 1842 in Maine; d. 1921 in Conn. Contralto. Studied in Boston, then with support of friends went to Milan (1866) for further training; made debut as Azucena (*Il Trovatore*) in Copenhagen (1867), but continued to study while appearing in Scandinavia, Hamburg, Paris, London. Returned to U.S. (1870) in company with Christine Nilsson; sang Amneris in first American performances of *Aida* (1873); in great demand at opera houses in London, St. Petersburg, New York, until she retired (1882) because of throat trouble.

Cranch, Christopher Pearse. b. 1813 in Alexandria, D.C.; d. 1892 in Cambridge, Mass. Poet, painter. Friend of Dwight's from Harvard days; frequent visitor at Brook Farm; contributor to *Dwight's Journal of Music*.

Curtis, George William. b. 1824 in Providence; d. 1892 at Staten Island. Essayist, orator, civil service reformer. Political editor of *Harper's Weekly* (from 1862); wrote "From the Editor's Easy Chair" column in *Harper's Monthly* for forty years. Admirer of Emerson, lover of music, was student at Brook Farm, where began long friendship with Dwight. Penname Hafiz, used in writing for *Dwight's Journal*, recalls his published accounts of travels in Near East (1846–50). *Early Letters of George Wm. Curtis to John Sullivan Dwight* (New York, 1898) has foreword by Dwight's biographer, George Willis Cooke (rpr. New York, 1971).

Damrosch, Leopold. b. 1832 in Prussia; d. 1885 in New York. Violinist, conductor. Liszt's concertmaster at Weimar; concert partner of von Bülow and Tausig; conductor of Breslau Philharmonic before emigrating to New York (1871) to conduct Arion Society (men's chorus).

Founded New York Oratorio Society (1873). Elected conductor of Philharmonic Society for one season (1876); when ousted in favor of Theodore Thomas, founded rival New York Symphony Society (1878). Saved fledgling Metropolitan Opera from financial disaster (1884) by producing season of German opera. Son Walter (1862–1950) succeeded him as conductor of Symphony Society and Oratorio Society.

Del Puente, Giuseppe. b. 1841 in Italy; d. 1900 in Philadelphia. Baritone. First appeared in the U.S. (1873) in concert company with Nilsson, Campanini, and Cary; sang role of Escamillo in American premier of *Carmen* (1878) with Hauk and Campanini; Valentin in *Faust* for the inaugural performance of the Metropolitan Opera in New York (1883).

De Meyer, Leopold. b. 1816 near Vienna; d. 1883 in Dresden. Piano virtuoso. Pupil of Czerny; appeared in U.S. 1845–1847.

Dwight, John Sullivan. b. 1813, d. 1893 in Boston. See Introduction. See also, George Willis Cooke, *John Sullivan Dwight, Brook-farmer, Editor, and Critic of Music: A Biography* (Boston, 1898).

Eichberg, Julius. b. 1824 in Düsseldorf; d. 1893 in Boston. Violinist, composer, conductor, teacher. Professor at Geneva Conservatory before emigrating to New York (1857); moved to Boston (1859), where he conducted orchestra concerts, and was a founder of the Boston Conservatory of Music (1867), of which he headed the violin department. Prepared textbooks of violin playing and composed four operettas.

Eisfeld, Theodore. b. 1816 in Wolfenbüttel; d. 1882 in Wiesbaden, Conductor. Resident of New York 1848–66; conductor of Philharmonic Society (1848–54), co-conductor with Carl Bergmann (1855–66); presented programs of chamber music in New York from 1851.

Foote, Arthur. b. 1853 in Salem, Mass.; d. 1937 in Boston. Awarded Harvard's first Master of Arts degree in music (1875) after studies with John Knowles Paine. Organist of First Unitarian Church, Boston, for more than thirty years; appeared frequently as pianist in chamber music. Perhaps the first wholly American-trained composer of lasting quality, wrote three orchestral suites, chamber music, choral works, some one hundred songs, and numerous solos for organ and piano.

Formes, Karl. b. 1816 in Mülheim; d. 1889 in San Francisco. Basso. Had established a reputation in Mannheim, Vienna, and London before appearing in New York (1857); highly regarded figure on American opera and concert stage for twenty years. Retired from stage at sixty to teach in San Francisco.

Foster, Stephen Collins. b. 1826 in Lawrenceville, Pa.; d. 1864 in New York.

Fries, Wulf. b. 1825 in Holstein; d. 1902 in Roxbury, Mass. Came to Boston (1847) with older brother, August; when Mendelssohn Quintette

Club was formed (1849), was cellist and August violinist. Member of orchestras of Musical Fund Society and Harvard Musical Association; played chamber music concerts with Rubinstein and von Bülow; toured widely with Mendelssohn Quintette Club until 1870.

Fry, William Henry. b. 1813 in Philadelphia; d. 1864 in the West Indies. Composer, lecturer, music critic.

Gade, Niels. b. 1817, d. 1890 in Copenhagen. Composer. Friend of Mendelssohn, whom he succeeded as conductor of Leipzig Gewandhaus concerts (1847); returned to Copenhagen (1848), where he became court Kapellmeister and director of conservatory. Among most renowned composers of his time, wrote eight symphonies, orchestral overtures, suites, chamber works, piano music, cantatas.

Garcia, Manuel. b. 1775 in Seville, Spain; d. 1832 in Paris. Operatic singer, composer, teacher. Taught in Europe before establishing Italian opera company in New York (1825), with casts including members of his family; taught his daughters, soprano Maria Malibran and mezzo-soprano Pauline Vairdot-Garcia and his son, Manuel, basso, who in turn became professor of singing at Paris Conservatoire (where Jenny Lind was his pupil) and London's Royal Academy of Music.

Gerster, Etelka. b. 1855 in Hungary; d. 1920 in Italy. Coloratura soprano. Began a short but brilliant career in Venice (1876), where Verdi had recommended her for role of Gilda in *Rigoletto*; appeared successfully in Italy, France, Germany, London before coming to U.S. with Mapleson's company (1878); returned in 1883, sharing top billing with rival Adelina Patti, in company assembled by Mapleson at New York's Academy of Music to compete with the new Metropolitan Opera; made her final American appearance in concert (1887–88).

Gilmore, Patrick Sarsfield. b. 1829 in Ireland; d. 1892 in St. Louis. Organized World Peace Jubilee in Boston (1872), more gigantic but far short of the success of the 1869 spectacle. Became leader (1873) of 22nd Regiment Band in New York, enlarged it, took it on tour throughout the United States and in Europe (1878), achieving fame and popularity unmatched by a concert band until emergence of Sousa Band in 1890s.

Gottschalk, Louis Moreau. b. 1829 in New Orleans; d. 1869 in Rio de Janeiro. Pianist and composer. See his autobiographical *Notes of a Pianist*, published in an informative edition by Jeanne Behrend (New York, 1964).

Grau, Maurice. b. 1849 in Brno; d. 1907 in Paris. Opera and theater impresario. Came to U.S. at age five; educated for a career in law but was attracted to activities of uncle Jacob Grau, theatrical and musical manager, who put him in charge of Rubinstein-Wieniawski tour (1872); in next years, organized Clara Louise Kellogg's English Opera

Company, managed touring companies in operetta and French opera, had role in American visit of Jacques Offenbach (1876); organized first season of Metropolitan Opera (1883), a financial failure, but returned in 1891 with greater success; between 1898 and 1903, was responsible for some of Metropolitan's most brilliant seasons.

Hastings, Thomas. b. 1787 in Connecticut; d. 1872 in New York. Teacher, composer of hymn tunes. Wrote *Dissertation on Musical Taste* (1822, rev. 1853); published fifty collections of hymns, including well-known "Rock of Ages."

Hauk, Minnie. b. Amalia Hauck, 1852, in New York; d. 1929 in Switzerland. Soprano. As child in New Orleans, first appeared in concert at age twelve. Taken to New York to study, heard Clara Louise Kellogg in *Fra Diavolo*, and resolved to be an opera star; before age fifteen had learned leading roles in a half-dozen operas, appeared publicly in *La Sonnambula* and, with Kellogg, in *L'Etoile du Nord* in Manhattan, created role of Juliette in American premier of Gounod's *Romeo et Juliette* at Academy of Music under Maretzek (1867). A grant from music publisher Gustav Schirmer enabled her to go to Europe, where an engagement in Paris was soon followed by appearances in London, Holland, Russia. In Budapest, created roles of Aida and Mignon, studied Wagnerian roles with Hans Richter. In 1870s won great popularity in Berlin, appeared widely in German opera houses before going to Belgium to sing her first *Carmen*; was immediately engaged by Mapleson to sing at Her Majesty's Theater, London, and to participate in his company's first American tour. After 1878 divided time between America and England, with occasional appearances in Paris, until she retired at forty. Perhaps first American-born and American-trained singer to be ranked among all-time greats, she was particularly important for her conception of diva's role as that of singing actress.

Hayes, Catherine. b. 1825 in Ireland; d. 1861 in England. Soprano. Studied with Garcia and Ronconi. Appeared widely in Europe in 1840s, then toured in America and traveled to India, Australia, Polynesia; extremely popular not only in opera but in concert, where she charmed audiences with Irish ballads. It was said her success in San Francisco in the 1850s eclipsed career of Eliza Biscaccianti, her American rival there.

Henschel, Georg. b. 1850 in Breslau; d. 1934 in Scotland. Baritone, composer, conductor. First appeared in England (1877) as singer; engagements during the following years included those with the Bach Choir (1878) and at London Philharmonic (1879), where he sang a duet with American soprano Lillian Bailey (her London debut), who became his pupil and later his wife (1881). After three years as conductor of the

Boston Symphony (1881–84), made his home in England, where he succeeded Jenny Lind as professor of singing at Royal College of Music (1886–88); established London Symphony concerts; appeared in Britain and on Continent as both conductor and singer. Composed numerous choral, vocal, and instrumental works, two operas and an operetta. Knighted (1914). His autobiography is *Musings and Memories of a Musician* (New York, 1919; rpr. 1979).

Higginson, Henry Lee. b. 1834 in New York; d. 1919 in Boston. In the Civil War, commissioned major and breveted lieutenant-colonel of 1st Massachusetts Cavalry; member of banking firm Lee, Higginson & Co. (1868); in 1918, turned control of Boston Symphony over to board of directors.

Higginson, Thomas Wentworth. b. 1823, d. 1911 in Cambridge, Mass. Reformer, author. Descended from first minister of the Massachusetts Bay Colony, was himself Harvard-trained Unitarian minister; left pulpit to become radical advocate of abolition, women's suffrage, temperance. At outbreak of Civil War, helped raise and drill Massachusetts Regiment, then commanded first black regiment, 1st South Carolina Volunteers (1862–64), until wounds forced him to leave army. Wrote *Army Life in a Black Regiment* (1870), the novel *Malbone* (1869), biographies of Margaret Fuller, Longfellow, Whittier, and books of U.S. history.

Jaell, Alfred. b. 1832 in Trieste; d. 1882 in Paris. Pianist. First appeared as child prodigy in Venice (1843); then studied with Moscheles in Vienna; toured extensively in Europe; toured widely in U.S. (1852–54), then resumed European career.

Joachim, Joseph. b. 1831 in Hungary; d. 1907 in Berlin. Violinist. Pupil of Mendelssohn; friend of Brahms; director of Berlin conservatory; leader of Joachim Quartet; among most famous and respected musicians of his time.

Jullien, Louis Antoine. b. 1812, d. 1860 in France. Conductor and composer. Studied at Paris Conservatory; conducted concerts of dance music in Paris, but fled creditors to London (1838), where he organized and conducted concerts with mounting popular success. After American visit, returned to London but was dogged by misfortune—his music was burned in Covent Garden fire (1856), and he lost heavily in business ventures. After series of farewell concerts with reduced orchestra, went to Paris, where he was briefly imprisoned for debt (1859), released, then ended his days in an insane asylum.

Kalliwoda, Johann Wenzeslaus. b. 1800 in Prague; d. 1866 in Karlsruhe. Violinist. Composer of seven symphonies, overtures, concertos for violin, quartets, violin duets, songs. Conductor of Prince Furstenburg's private band at Donaueschingen.

Kellogg, Clara Louise. b. 1842 in South Carolina; d. 1916 in Hartford, Conn. Studied in New York (1857–60); appeared in concert with Pauline Colson and Pasquale Brignoli before operatic debut (1861). Made European debut as Marguerite in *Faust* at Her Majesty's Theater (1867); appeared also in *La Traviata, Linda di Chamounix, Martha, Don Giovanni* (Zerlina). Back in U.S., costarred with Pauline Lucca in touring Lucca-Kellogg Opera Company (1872); started her own company, Kellogg English Opera Company (1873–76), singing as many as 125 performances in a year in addition to supervising translations and sets, rehearsing chorus, training young soloists. Again toured Europe, singing in music centers as far east as St. Petersburg. Returning to U.S. (1881), appeared mainly in recital until her retirement (1887). See her *Memoirs of an American Prima Donna* (New York, 1913).

Lang, Benjamin Johnson. b. 1837 in Salem, Mass.; d. 1909 in Boston. Pianist, conductor, composer, organist. After study in Europe with Jaell and others, made Boston debut as pianist (1858); appeared in concerts of Harvard Musical Association and Mendelssohn Quintette Club. Co-conductor with Carl Zerrahn of concert marking Emancipation Proclamation (1863); conductor of Boston's Apollo Club (chorus) for thirty years, from its inception (1871); also conducted Handel and Haydn Society (1895–97). Among his pupils were Arthur Foote, W. F. Apthorp, Ethelbert Nevin, Margaret Ruthven Lang (his daughter).

Levy, Jules. b. 1838 in London; d. 1903 in Chicago. Cornet virtuoso. Member of H. M. Grenadier Guards Band before coming to U.S. (1864); soloist with Patrick S. Gilmore's bands (from 1868), also frequently taking part in concerts by touring singers. Directed his own American Military Band (1892–1895).

Lind, Jenny. b. 1820 in Stockholm; d. 1887 in England. Leading operatic singer in Sweden, Germany, and England when in 1849 she decided to limit her appearances to concerts and oratorio. Continuing her practice of generous philanthropy, donated most of the proceeds from American tour to Swedish charities, including art scholarships. After returning to Europe with husband, composer-pianist Otto Goldschmidt, resided first in Dresden (1852–55), then in England, where she sang frequently for devoted public until 1883, when she retired from the stage and became professor of singing at Royal Academy of Music.

Lucca, Pauline. b. 1841, d. 1908 in Vienna. Dramatic soprano. Began her career as chorister at Vienna Opera, made her solo debut as Elvira in *Ernani* at Olmütz (1859). At Meyerbeer's suggestion, was engaged at Berlin Opera (1861), soon appointed Court Singer for life. Appeared frequently in London (1863–72); broke with Berlin opera to tour in

U.S. (1872–74). On return to Europe, became leading singer of Vienna Opera (1874–89).

Mapleson, James Henry. b. 1830, d. 1901 in London. Opera manager. Began as singer; first managed opera company at London's Lyceum Theater (1861), then took charge of Her Majesty's Theater (1862), moved to Drury Lane (1868), then reopened Her Majesty's (1877). Brought company to U.S. between seasons at Her Majesty's annually (1878–86), introducing many important singers and operas on both sides of Atlantic. See his *Mapleson Memoirs* (London, 1888; new edition, London, 1966).

Maretzek, Max. b. 1821 in Moravia; d. 1897 at Staten Island. Impresario, conductor, composer. Assistant conductor to Balfe at Her Majesty's Theater, London, before going to New York (1848) as conductor of Italian opera at Astor Place Opera House; when company failed, took it over as manager-conductor; for thirty years, continued to present opera in New York, Cuba, Mexico. Opened New York Academy of Music (1854) with London stars Mario and Grisi in *Norma*. Retired (1879) to teach, coach opera singers. Autobiographical sketches *Crotchets and Quavers* (1855), *Sharps and Flats* (1890) are combined in *Revelations of an Opera Manager in 19th Century America* (New York, 1968).

Marini, Ignazio. b. 1811 in Bergamo, Italy; d. 1873 in Milan. Sang at La Scala, in Vienna, and in London before appearing in Havana and U.S. (1850–51); later was leading bass at St. Petersburg (1856–63) and Milan.

Mason, Lowell. b. 1792 in Medfield, Mass.; d. 1872 in Orange, N.J. Music educator, composer, conductor. Though musically inclined, began professional life as bank clerk in Savannah, Ga. (1812); as avocation, studied music, gave singing lessons, was church organist. Compiled collection of hymn tunes (some original, others adapted), published—at first without credit to the compiler—as *Boston Handel and Haydn Society Collection of Church Music* (1822, with twenty-one subsequent editions). Success of book persuaded him to adopt music as profession; returned to Boston to become church organist, president of Handel and Haydn Society (1827–32); organized Boston Academy of Music (1833) to promote music instruction in public schools, with "normal class" to train teachers in methods derived from Pestalozzi. Taught first music class in Boston public school as volunteer (1837); following year became first paid teacher and supervisor of music for all Boston schools (1838–41); thereafter devoted himself to developing conventions and normal schools for training music teachers, and to compiling songbooks, of which he published more than fifty.

Mason, William. b. 1829 in Boston; d. 1908 in New York. Pianist, composer.

Son of Lowell Mason (*q.v.*). Made debut in Boston (1846); went to Europe to study (1849–54) with Moscheles, Dreyschock, Liszt; on return to U.S., toured as far west as Chicago, possibly first to tour in U.S. giving recitals exclusively of solo piano music. After 1868, devoted himself mainly to teaching; wrote and compiled "methods" of piano playing, and composed short piano pieces. His autobiography is *Memories of a Musical Life* (New York, 1901; rpr. 1970).

Mathews, William Smythe Babcock. b. 1837 in New Hampshire; d. 1912 in Denver. Studied in Boston, taught in South and Midwest; church organist in Chicago. Music critic of *Chicago Tribune* (1878–86); founded *Music* monthly (1891–1902); wrote *A Hundred Years of Music in America* (Chicago, 1889); contributed to *Dwight's Journal of Music* under pen name Der Freyschuetz.

Matzka, George. b. 1825 in Coburg; d. ?. Violist. Member of Philharmonic Society from time of arrival in New York (1852); member of Mason-Thomas Quartet (1855–68); conducted Philharmonic Society (1876) in interim between Damrosch and Thomas.

Mendelssohn Quintette Club. See Fries, Ryan, Schultze. Other members, at various times, for whom biographical information is lacking, were Francis (Franz) Riha, violin; Edward Lehmann, flute and viola; Carl Meisel, violin; and Edward Heindl, flute.

Moscheles, Ignaz. b. 1794 in Prague; d. 1870 in Leipzig. Pianist, composer. Virtuoso performer who, as professor of piano at new Leipzig Conservatory (from 1846), was highly influential teacher.

Mosenthal, Joseph. b. 1834 in Kassel; d. 1896 in New York. Violinist in Spohr's orchestra at Kassel before emigrating to New York (1853), where he was member of the Philharmonic Society for forty years and of Mason Thomas Quartette (1855–68); organist of Calvary Church (1860–87); leader of Mendelssohn Glee Club (1867–96).

Nilsson, Christine. b. 1843, d. 1921 in Sweden. Soprano. Studied with Franz Berwald in Stockholm, then in Paris, where she made debut (1864) at Theatre Lyrique. Sang in London, at Paris Opera (1868–70); in U.S. 1870–72, 1874, 1883, 1884; meanwhile appearing regularly in London and in tours of Continent until her retirement (1891).

Onslow, George. b. 1784, d. 1853 in France. British-French gentleman-composer. Studied with Reicha in Paris; wrote 34 string quintets, 36 quartets, trios, duos, sonatas. Elected to the Institut (1842).

Paine, John Knowles. b. 1839 in Portland, Maine; d. 1906 in Cambridge, Mass. Composer, organist, educator. Revisited Berlin (1867) to conduct Singakademie in premiere of his Mass in D. Oratorio *St. Peter* performed at Portland (1873); Symphony No. 2 ("To Spring") in Boston (1880). Retired from Harvard in 1905.

Parepa Rosa, Euphrosyne. b. 1836 in Edinburgh; d. 1874 in London. Soprano. Leading singer in European opera houses, also in oratorio and concert, especially England. First toured in America (1865) in concert company with violinist Carl Rosa (*q.v.*), whom she married (1867). With her husband, formed Parepa-Rosa Opera Company which toured four years in U.S. (1867–71).

Parker, James Cutler Dunn. b. 1828 in Boston; d. 1916 in Brookline, Mass. Organist, teacher, composer. Studied law; turned to music; went to Leipzig (1851) to study with Moscheles, Richter. After return to Boston (1854) was church organist, organist of Handel and Haydn Society, teacher at New England Conservatory.

Patti, Adelina. b. 1843 in Madrid; d. 1919 in Wales.

Patti, Carlotta. b. 1840 in Florence; d. 1889 in Paris. Soprano. Sister of Adelina. Made her debut in New York (1861); although lameness hampered operatic career, became a favorite concert singer in North and South America, England, Europe.

Perkins, Charles Callahan. b. 1823 in Boston; d. 1886 in Vermont. Studied painting in Italy, Paris. Active in organizing musical activities in Boston (1849–57), with leading role in Handel and Haydn Society (of which he began writing history) and in building of Music Hall (1852).

Phillipps, Adelaide. b. 1833 in England; d. 1882 in Carlsbad, Bohemia. Contralto. Grew up in Boston, first appeared on stage there at nine. After studies in London with Manuel Garcia (1852–53) made debut in Italy. Returned to U.S. (1855); made debut at New York's Academy of Music (1856) as Azucena (*Il Trovatore*); sang with Maretzek company in Havana; returned to Europe; appeared in U.S. with Parepa-Rosa company (1867–71); was heard widely in concert, oratorio, operetta (1879–81).

Raff, Joachim. b. 1822 in Switzerland; d. 1882 in Frankfort. Pupil of Liszt and Mendelssohn; highly respected composer in his day; director of Frankfort Conservatory (from 1877), where Edward MacDowell was among his American pupils.

Reinecke, Carl Heinrich. b. 1824 in Altona; d. 1910 in Leipzig. Composer, conductor, performer, teacher. Settled in Leipzig (1843) where he was associated with Schumann and Mendelssohn. Taught at Cologne and Breslau before becoming conductor of Gewandhaus Orchestra and director of conservatory at Leipzig (1860).

Reissiger, Karl Gottlieb. b. 1798 in Wittenberg; d. 1859 in Dresden. Composer, conductor. Succeeded Weber as conductor of Dresden Opera (1827); director of Dresden conservatory (1856–59).

Ries, Ferdinand. b. 1784 in Bonn; d. 1838 in Frankfort. Pianist, composer, conductor. Pupil and early biographer of Beethoven.

Rivé-King, Julie. b. 1857 in Cincinnati; d. 1937 in Indianapolis. Pianist, composer. Studied first with her mother, then William Mason and English pianist S. B. Mills in New York, and in Europe with Reinecke and Liszt. Debut in Leipzig (1874), with New York Philharmonic Society (1875); performed in Europe (until about 1880); she returned to U.S.; toured coast-to-coast, playing some four thousand concerts and recitals, over five hundred with orchestra (Theodore Thomas and Anton Seidl among the conductors); then taught in Chicago (1905–36).

Romberg, Andreas Jakob. b. 1767 in Westphalia; d. 1821 in Gotha. Violinist, composer. Composed operas, operettas, choral works, including "Das Lied von der Glocke" (Song of the Bell), popular with singing societies in U.S.

Ronconi, Giorgio. b. 1810 in Milan; d. 1890 in Madrid. Baritone. Leading singer in opera houses of Italy, Paris, London, appeared in U.S. (1866–74).

Root, George Frederick. b. 1820 in Massachusetts; d. 1895 in Maine. Teacher, organist, composer. Associate of Lowell Mason in public school music in Boston, New York Normal Institute. Settled in Chicago (1858) as member of brother's music-publishing firm (Root & Cady), wrote many popular sentimental songs and Civil War songs including "Battle Cry of Freedom," "Tramp! Tramp! Tramp!"

Rosa, Carl. b. 1842 in Hamburg; d. 1889 in Paris. Violinist, opera manager. Appeared in U.S. (1865) as violinist in concerts with soprano Euphrosyne Parepa (*q.v.*). After Parepa's death, founded Carl Rosa Opera Company, which toured British Isles performing opera in English.

Rubinstein, Anton. b. 1829 in Volhynia, Russ.; d. 1894 in Peterhof, Russ. Pianist, composer. Founder (1862) and director (1862–67, 1887–91) of St. Petersburg Conservatory. First appeared in Moscow (1839) and Paris (1840) as child prodigy; after period of further preparation (1845–53), won acclaim as a leading virtuoso throughout Europe (1854–87).

Ryan, Thomas. b. 1827 in Ireland; d. 1903 in New Bedford, Mass. At fifteen played clarinet in Belfast orchestra while studying violin. Emigrated to Boston (1845); played in theater orchestra while continuing studies of classical music; with Fries brothers (*q.v.*) founded Mendelssohn Quintette Club (1849); member of new Boston Symphony Orchestra. See also his autobiography, *Recollections of an Old Musician* (Boston, 1899).

Salvi, Lorenzo. b. 1810 in Ancona, It.; d. 1879 in Bologna, It. Tenor. Had major career in Italy, St. Petersburg, London, before appearing in

Havana and U.S. (1850). Toured U.S. with Jenny Lind (1850–51); returned in Maretzek company (1852).

Schultze, William Heinrich. b. 1828 in Hanover; d. 1888 in Syracuse, N.Y. Came to U.S. (1848) with Germania Orchestra; first violinist of Mendelssohn Quintette Club (from 1858); professor of music at Syracuse University (from 1877).

Seguin, Arthur Edward. b. 1809 in London; d. 1852 in New York. Sang Italian and English opera in England; appeared in New York (1838); formed the Seguin Troupe which toured and performed opera (English) in U.S. and Canada till his death. His wife, Ann, was member of company.

Sobolewski, Eduard de. b. 1808? in Königsburg; d. 1872 in St. Louis.

Sontag, Henriette. b. 1806 in Koblenz; d. 1854 in Mexico. Dramatic soprano. Sang in first performances of Weber's *Euryanthe* (1823) and Beethoven's Ninth Symphony (1824). Had been leading opera, concert singer in Europe for quarter-century before she appeared in U.S. (1852).

Southard, Lucien H. b. 1827 in Vermont; d. 1881 in Georgia. Composer, teacher. Supervisor of music in Boston schools (1851–58); first director and conductor of orchestra of new Conservatory at Peabody Institute, Baltimore (1868–71).

Strakosch, Maurice, b. 1825 in Moravia; d. 1887 in Paris. Studied at Vienna Conservatory; came to New York (1848); taught, performed as pianist, and (from 1856) presented Italian opera. Managed appearances of his pupil, sister-in-law Adelina Patti, in U.S.; Patti's agent in Europe until her marriage (1868). Opera impresario in Paris (1873–74) and Rome (1884–85). His opera *Giovanni Prima di Napoli* was produced in New York (1851).

Strakosch, Max. b. 1834; d. 1892 in New York. Continued U.S. opera and concert ventures begun by brother Maurice after latter's departure for Europe (1860).

Thalberg, Sigismond. b. 1812 in Geneva; d. 1871 in Italy.

Thayer, Alexander Wheelock. b. 1817 in South Natick, Mass.; d. 1897 in Trieste.

Thomas, Theodore. b. 1835 in Esens, Hanover; d. 1905 in Chicago. See biography by Charles Edward Russell, *The American Orchestra and Theodore Thomas* (New York, 1927).

Tietjens, Therese. b. 1831 in Hamburg; d. 1877 in London. Dramatic soprano. Leading opera singer in Europe, especially England, when she appeared in U.S. (1875–76).

Tourjee, Eben. b. 1834 in Warwick, Mass.; d. 1891 in Boston. Music educator. Developed system of class teaching at Musical Institute which he established in East Greenwich (1859); founded New England Conservatory (1867); first president of Music Teachers National Association (1876).

Ullmann, Bernard. *Fl.* 1845–65. Managed U.S. tours of visiting virtuosos (Henri Herz, Thalberg); joined with Thalberg and Strakosch in managing opera at New York Academy of Music (1857); manager there with Maretzek when Patti made her operatic debut (1859).

Urso, Camilla. b. 1842 in France; d. 1902 in New York. Violinist. At age nine studied at Paris Conservatoire; appeared in concerts in U.S. (1852); settled with parents in Nashville, Tenn. (1855). After further study, reappeared (1860) with New York Philharmonic Society; embarked on long career as concert artist touring in U.S., Europe, Australia, and South Africa (1895).

Valleria, Alwina (real name Schoening). b. 1848 in Baltimore; d. 1925 in Nice. Dramatic soprano. Studied at Royal Academy of Music, London (1867). After debut in St. Petersburg (1871), sang in Germany, Italy, England before American debut (1879) as Marguerite in *Faust*, with Mapleson's company at N.Y. Academy of Music; first American to sing at new Metropolitan Opera, as Leonora in *Il Trovatore* on third night of opening season (1883).

Vieuxtemps, Henri. b. 1820 in Belgium; d. 1881 in Algiers. Studied in Paris and Vienna. Toured in Germany before appearing in U.S. (1843) at beginning of career as one of great violinists; returned in 1857 (with Thalberg) and 1870 (with Christine Nilsson).

Webb, George James. b. 1803 in England; d. 1887 in Orange, N.J. Singing teacher, organist, conductor. Went to Boston (1830); associate of Lowell Mason in founding Boston Academy of Music (1833), conducting children's singing classes; composed songs, hymns, collaborated with Mason in publishing tune books.

White, George L. b. 1833 in Cadiz, N.Y.; d. 1895 in Ithaca, N.Y. Village blacksmith's son; taught school (including singing) before joining Union Army in Civil War; after war, worked in Freedmen's Bureau in Nashville, Tenn., taught singing classes at Fisk school, predecessor of university; at opening of Fisk University (1866) was its treasurer; continued singing classes, from which he selected singers for fund-raising tour in 1871; retired for reasons of health after Jubilee Singers' first visit to Britain.

Whitney, Myron. b. 1836 in Ashby, Mass.; d. 1910 in Sandwich, Mass. Bass. After Boston debut in *Messiah* (1856), sang in oratorio and concert in U.S. for ten years; went to Italy for operatic training. After singing in Great Britain, returned to U.S.; appeared prominently in concert, oratorio and opera.

Wieniawski, Henri. b. 1835 in Lublin; d. 1880 in Moscow. Violinist, composer. Studied in Paris; gave first concert in 1848; toured in Poland, Russia, western Europe. Solo violinist to Czar (1860); taught at St. Petersburg Conservatory (1862–69); succeeded Vieuxtemps as professor at Brussels Conservatory (1877).

Wilhelmj, August. b. 1845 in German Duchy of Nassau; d. 1908 in London. After childhood debut (1854) in Wiesbaden, studied further in Leipzig (1861–64); toured in Europe, Russia, Scandinavia before his visit to U.S.; professor of violin at Guildhall School of Music, London (from 1894).

Willis, Richard Storrs. b. 1819 in Boston; d. 1900 in Detroit. Composer, writer on music. Studied at Yale and in Germany; in New York, edited *Musical World* (1852–60); published church music, songs, handbook *Our Church Music* (1856).

Zerrahn, Carl. b. 1826 in Mecklenburg-Schwerin; d. 1909 in Milton, Mass. Came to U.S. (1848) as first flutist of Germania Orchestra; conducted Boston Handel and Haydn Society (1854–95); organized Boston Philharmonic Orchestra (1855–63); conducted concerts of Harvard Musical Association (from 1865), Worcester Music Festivals (1866–97); taught at New England Conservatory (to 1898).

Bibliography

A comprehensive bibliography is not within the scope of this volume. The Biographical Register includes some bibliographic references of particular usefulness or interest. Listed below are some of the more general sources used in preparing the text. Where there were discrepancies of fact, the most recent source was usually taken as most authoritative.

d'Amico, Silvio, dirretore. *Enciclopedia dello Spettacolo*. Rome, 1956.

Bohle, Bruce, and Oscar Thompson, eds. *International Cyclopedia of Music and Musicians*. 10th ed. New York, 1975.

Curtis, Edith R. *A Season in Utopia: The Real Story of Brook Farm*. New York, 1971.

Dictionary of American Biography. Vols. I–X.

Lovell, John. *Black Song: The Forge and the Flame*. New York, 1972.

McAleer, John. *Ralph Waldo Emerson: Days of Encounter*. Boston, 1984.

National Cyclopedia of American Biography. Vols. I–V, VII, VIII, X.

Odell, George C. D. *Annals of the New York Stage*. New York, 1927.

Pratt, Waldo Selden, ed. *Grove's Dictionary of Music and Musicians: American Supplement*. New York, 1947.

Sablosky, Irving. *American Music*. Chicago, 1969.

Sadie, Stanley, ed. *The New Grove Dictionary of Music and Musicians*. London, 1980.

Slonimsky, Nicholas, ed. *Baker's Biographical Dictionary of Musicians*. 6th ed. New York, 1978.

Thompson, Oscar. *The American Singer: A Hundred Years of Success in Opera*. New York, 1937.

Index

DATE DUE

AG 13 '86			
GAYLORD			PRINTED IN U.S.A.